FINDING JUDGE CRATER

Finding Judge Crater

A Life and Phenomenal Disappearance
in Jazz Age New York

Stephen J. Riegel

Syracuse Univeristy Press

∞ The paper used in this publication meets the minimum requirements
of the American National Standard for Information Sciences—Permanence
of Paper for Printed Library Materials, ANSI Z39.48-1992.

For a listing of books published and distributed by Syracuse University
Press, visit https://press.syr.edu.

ISBN: 978-0-8156-3719-6 (hardcover)
978-0-8156-1134-9 (paperback)
978-0-8156-5538-1 (e-book)

Library of Congress Cataloging in Publication Data
Names: Riegel, Stephen J., author.
Title: Finding Judge Crater : a life and phenomenal disappearance
in jazz age New York / Stephen J. Riegel.
Description: First edition. | Syracuse, New York : Syracuse University Press,
2022. | Includes bibliographical references and index. | Summary: "Riegel's work
discusses the unsolved 1930 disappearance of Supreme Court Justice and prominent political player Joseph Crater and sifts through the many theories surrounding
his disappearance, as well as previously untapped sources"—Provided by publisher.
Identifiers: LCCN 2021026195 (print) | LCCN 2021026196 (ebook) |
ISBN 9780815637196 (hardcover) | ISBN 9780815611349 (paperback) |
ISBN 9780815655381 (ebook)
Subjects: LCSH: Crater, Joseph Force, 1889– | Judges—New York (State)—
New York—Biography. | Missing persons—New York (State)—New York—
Case studies.
Classification: LCC KF373.C68 R54 2022 (print) |
LCC KF373.C68 (ebook) | DDC 347.747/0234 [B]—dc23
LC record available at https://lccn.loc.gov/2021026195
LC ebook record available at https://lccn.loc.gov/2021026196

Manufactured in the United States of America

To Anne, with love and gratitude

CONTENTS

SEARCHING FOR JUDGE CRATER

ILLUSTRATIONS

(following page 122)

ACKNOWLEDGMENTS

This book would not have come to fruition without the help of many dedicated librarians and archivists. To name just a few (and my apologies for leaving anyone out): I thank Kenneth Cobb and his assistants at the New York City Municipal Archives for steering me to court and municipal records, which greatly clarified the complex Libby's Hotel proceedings. I thank the librarians at the Rare Book and Manuscript Library of the Columbia University Library for assisting my research in the Edwin Patrick Kilroe Papers, an amazing collection of correspondence, campaign materials, newspaper clippings, books, and manuscripts relating to Tammany Hall from its inception through the 1950s, compiled by its long-time secretary and archivist. Thanks also to Mark Swartz and Maryann Chach of The Shubert Archive who helped me with materials on the Shubert brothers and their shows in the 1920s which Crater regularly attended, as well as on his friend William Klein, the Shuberts' chief counsel and the last person to see him before he disappeared. Mark arranged for publication of my article about Klein and Crater in the archive's periodical, *The Passing Show*, in 2015, and provided permission to reprint images from the archive in this book. Librarians at the Easton (PA) Public Library were helpful in directing me to sources of information about Crater's childhood there.

I want to thank the New York City Police Department for making the remaining internal files in Crater's case available by request under the Freedom of Information Law (FOIL). These files, never before used in a nonfiction account of the case, were essential for accurately portraying the lengthy manhunt and clearing up discrepancies in contemporary news reports of the case, as well as for understanding the later developments in the case in the 1950s, which are presented in chapter 11. Members of the FOIL unit of the NYPD were gracious in providing time for me to review the case file and making me copies of much of it. The Federal Bureau of Investigation also made available copies of its files on the Crater case. I'm also grateful that I had the opportunity to interview the late Judge Simon Rifkind in 1993, who initially reported to the NYPD that Crater was missing and shared his impressions of his good friend and legal colleague, his beliefs about what happened to him, and why the search was unsuccessful.

I owe the deepest debt of gratitude, however, to members of my family who were unfailingly encouraging over the long trek to get this book published while I was engaged in my law practice. I want to thank my parents, Claire and Herbert Riegel, for their continual support. My son Douglas was born when I started this project, and twenty-five years later, he read through my manuscript and provided helpful comments and suggestions that much improved the book. My greatest debt is to my wife, Anne Simon, to whom the book is dedicated and who put up with my obsession with it for far too long. This book simply would not be here today without her endless love, support, understanding, and patience.

FINDING JUDGE CRATER

Introduction

IN THE HEART OF Broadway on a summer night in 1930, a tall, distinguished, but odd-looking man was bidding goodbye to his dinner companions, a lawyer friend and a chorus girl, outside a chophouse on West Forty-Fifth Street in midtown Manhattan. Despite the sweltering heat, he was dressed to the nines in the flamboyant attire of the Roaring Twenties—a flashy double-breasted suit with a bowtie, gray spats, a high-choker collar to hide his long, skinny neck, and a Panama hat rakishly cocked on his disproportionately small head. He had come to his favorite part of the city—the lights, crowds, and frenetic energy of its primary entertainment venue around Times Square. But as friends he had run into that night would later tell investigators, it was not clear what he was actually doing there, and he seemed depressed and quiet, not his usual bantering self.

Forty-one years old, Justice Joseph Force Crater had skillfully navigated and quickly achieved prominence in diverse circles of the Jazz Age metropolis. Since coming to Manhattan as a law school student twenty years before, he had established himself as a brilliant and well-respected lawyer, no small accomplishment in the nation's preeminent and august bar. Along the way, he had leveraged the help of influential people, none more so than US Senator Robert F. Wagner, for whom he had clerked when Wagner was a judge and then rented space in the senator's law firm office. That spring, with Wagner's help, Governor Franklin D. Roosevelt had appointed him, to numerous accolades, to fill a temporary vacancy on the prestigious New York trial court in Manhattan, fulfilling his greatest professional ambition.

The alacrity with which Joe Crater had made his mark in the nation's premier city would later be commented upon. As one article put it, he had successfully "cultivated impartially the great luminaries of the bench and bar and the political hacks, who were equally necessary to his ambition...[but] nobody had ever done it before so rapidly."[1] He was equally at home in the scintillating nightlife of Broadway and other areas of town. An avid theater goer and habitué of the city's risqué night clubs, he often cavorted there in the company of chorus girls and his mistress, when not enjoying them with his wife or friends as he was this night. Cutting a figure in the city's nightlife and his other milieus, Joe, it would be reported, was "known intimately to hundreds of persons throughout the city."[2] All of which, together with man's striking physical appearance, made what was now about to happen unfathomable.

A little after 9 p.m. on August 6, 1930, Crater hailed a taxicab, got in, and headed west down West Forty-Fifth Street into oblivion. It was the last time he would ever be positively seen, alive or dead. In the intervening ninety-one years, with the possible exception of clues discovered twenty-five years later, no one has come forward with a tip based on personal knowledge of what happened to the missing man or why. A special grand jury that was empaneled to find out what happened to him conveyed in its report the sense of shock caused by the disappearance of such a prominent person: "The public was astonished by an article...to the effect that Joseph Force Crater, a Justice of the Supreme Court, had disappeared and that his family, friends and associates had been uninformed as to his whereabouts for a period of several weeks....The case was made more remarkable because the justice in question was a man in the prime of life, in good health, serving under the appointment of the Governor, and considered...a probable nominee...for the office of Justice of the Supreme Court" that fall, which would guarantee his election.[3]

While inopportunely starting almost a month after Crater was last seen, the search for him would fall to the Missing Persons Bureau of the New York City Police Department (NYPD). By that time, the NYPD, having recovered from a series of corruption and vice scandals in the previous decades, was transforming into a more professional, nonpolitical, and competent law enforcement agency, which boded well for finding the missing man. The Missing Persons Bureau, even then, succeeded in finding those reported as missing in the overwhelming number of cases. Yet despite decades of actively pursuing the very high-profile case, the police department would close it as "unsolved" in 1979 (with a brief reopening in 2005), making the Crater case perhaps the greatest failure of the NYPD in its storied history.

The job of finding Crater was complicated by the very protean, theatrical character of the man, which, as will be shown, was quite characteristic of life and society in Manhattan in the Jazz Age. Even with "the contradictions which surround all real identities," the nascent *New Yorker* magazine would sardonically observe two months after his disappearance, the "identity of Crater...established him as a man of four rather sharply divided personalities":

> He was (1) a jurist of very recent appointment; a machine politician whose direction of a Tammany club gained him recognition and a public job. He was (2) the possessor of a quite distinguished legal mind, and at New York University, where he taught diligently three nights a week, he was regarded as a brilliant and devoted follower of Blackstone. He was (3) a paterfamilias whose chief diversion was thought to be the reading of good books. And he was (4) a fellow of the night clubs, good old Joe to a handful of pretty showgirls.[4]

His multifarious lives would cause investigators to look into many possible scenarios and suspects, further obscuring what had happened to him.

Crater's disappearance would spawn arguably the greatest manhunt for a missing person in the nation's history up to that time, unprecedented in its cost, length and scope. The search for the missing man, which eventually would extend over every part of the country and some parts of the world, would be facilitated by its sensationalized coverage in the growing national media network of newspapers, magazines, and radio. Tens of thousands of copies of Crater's iconic missing persons circular would be distributed and posted in public offices and places over the years, causing a deluge of reports from the public of having spotted him in an often comical variety of poses and situations. The case attained such public prominence and recognition that it became part of America's popular culture, its shows and films, its jokes, and its lingo. During the hard times of the 1930s, the Crater mystery became something of a national craze and distraction, with stories about it proliferating on the anniversary of his disappearance and in the popular detective magazines of the time. The city's offer of a large monetary reward for information leading to his location in the early years of the Great Depression especially motivated people across the country to be the first to find him.

As its title suggests, this book will try to find, to the extent that it is feasible now in this very cold case, what happened to Joe Crater and why. Because of his multifaceted life in the city, a legion of explanations for his disappearance has emerged over the years, which can be divided into two categories, voluntary or involuntary ones. The involuntary explanations have included

that he was a random victim of a robbery gone awry, he was killed in a blackmail plot hatched by one of his girlfriends, he was bumped off because of his
knowledge of political or legal misdeeds, or he simply suffered amnesia and
forgot his identity. Some of the voluntary explanations for his disappearance
are that he fled his life and identity to escape political or legal scandal, he ran
away with one of his paramours, or he killed himself. Tellingly, the only recent
efforts to resolve the case have been creatively advanced in fictional accounts.[5]

This book therefore aims to present a well-substantiated hypothesis of
why, how, and at whose behest Joseph Crater disappeared. It will compre-
hensively analyze all the evidence developed in the case over the decades in
order to evaluate which of the many explanations of his vanishing best fit the
evidence. A third way of looking at the case, which has not been explored previously, will be considered—whether there was more than one explanation
for his disappearance; in other words, whether he vanished due to a conflu-
ence of actions he voluntarily took and ones he involuntarily suffered at the
hands of others.

This book makes original and extensive use of an essential source: the extant NYPD files in the case.[6] Much diminished from the multiple file cabinets full of records, evidence, and the public's tips maintained at police headquarters in the heyday of the Crater case, there remains only a banker's box
of documents, including many of the NYPD's internal investigatory forms
that the detectives created. Unlike the contemporary newspaper and magazine articles about the case which often contained inaccuracies, the police
records were confidential, professional, and reliable accounts of the search
for the missing man that include the questioning and interviews of witnesses, the tips and clues pursued or not, and assessments of the evidence they
obtained.

Trying to ascertain what happened to Crater, however, requires finding
him in another sense, that is, in his historical time and place—the lost world
of Manhattan in the Jazz Age, whose rendering is another objective of this
book. Although he vanished almost a year after the Great Depression began
with the stock market collapse in the fall of 1929, he was a man who rose
to prominence in, thoroughly embodied, and was ultimately undone by the
city of the Roaring Twenties. As also will be explored, Crater's disappearance coincided with seismic changes in New York City's politics, business
dealings, legal practice, nightlife, and entertainment, which accompanied its
transformation into the modern metropolis. The city's changes would hap-

pen so quickly that the missing man, if he had returned in a few years, as many expected him to do, would hardly have recognized it.

Much attention necessarily will be devoted to the long-reigning New York City Democratic political machine, Tammany Hall, which exercised a seemingly impregnable control over the metropolis during the Roaring Twenties. By the summer that he vanished, Mayor Jimmy Walker, the Jazz Age personified but a machine-made man, presided over an administration almost entirely composed of Tammany's district leaders and loyalists, making the municipal government especially ripe for grafting opportunities in the prosperous times of the 1920s. Crater's intricate involvement with the machine and its political leaders was fundamental to his ascension into the city's upper echelons of power, and he played diverse roles for it as a lawyer, as a crony of a district leader, as a judge, and as a grafter.

Contemporaneous political and legal events occurring in the city at the time of his disappearance in the summer of 1930 also have not been sufficiently considered in assessing what happened to him. That year had seen an eruption of Tammany corruption scandals of various types—the sale of city pier leases, corrupt bidding on city contracts, bribes to obtain favorable government actions, and the machine's complicity in organized crime. That summer, new allegations were surfacing over its influence on the appointment of city judges, implicating people close to the missing man. Manhattan District Attorney Thomas Crain, who would be put in charge of the grand jury looking into the disappearance, was an honorary Tammany "sachem" or wise elder. All of which naturally raised questions about whether Crain and the Walker administration really were motivated to find the missing judge, who had ties to, and likely incriminating information about, the machine's leaders and lawyers. As an anonymous limerick quipped early in the search, "O, the mystery's great but 'twill be far greater, If they make a mistake, and FIND Judge Crater!"[7] The Tammany scandals in the summer that he vanished, in turn, would raise serious problems for Governor Roosevelt's bid for reelection that fall, which was a crucial step required for his anticipated run for the presidency in 1932. The bitter gubernatorial campaign that fall would showcase the political machine's corruption, an uncomfortable issue for Roosevelt, and it would require his canniest instincts to win the election, with a national audience watching, on a platform he could use in his run for the White House.

The search for Joseph Crater therefore cannot be separated from an understanding of Manhattan in the 1920s, the lost metropolis in which he lived and attained prominence, and the contemporaneous events that affected and perturbed him at the time he disappeared. And when after many years, when the NYPD did acquire information that provided the best opportunity to solve the case, the detectives assigned to it would incorrectly discredit and reject the information. They would do so, however, not because of any political or personal motives not to find the missing man, but rather from simple ignorance about Crater's life and times.

The search will start with his awakening in the bedroom of his new apartment near Union Square in Manhattan, and making his way in confounding fashion on the last known day of his life, with his ultimate destination that night maddeningly elusive.

Judge Crater Vanishes

CHAPTER ONE

When Last Seen...

I

On the morning of August 6, 1930, Joseph Force Crater awoke alone in his luxurious apartment in a new high-rise building located at the foot of Fifth Avenue in Manhattan. The building, according to an advertisement, was situated in the "quaint Washington Square section," where, surrounded "on all sides by street or church property, it affords sunlight and outlook rare, indeed, in New York." He and his wife Stella had moved the previous fall into the spacious five-room, two-bath cooperative apartment at 40 Fifth Avenue, complete with amenities such as "mechanical refrigeration," a fireplace, and a maid's room.[1] Upon his appointment to the bench that spring, he had hired a cook and a maid for the apartment as well as a chauffeur to drive his Cadillac sedans, signs of his affluence despite the stock market crash the previous fall.

New York City was in the midst of an extreme heat spell since Crater had returned from his summer cabin in Maine three days before. There had been a record-setting temperature of 93 degrees the previous day, and no break was expected this day. The newspapers were replete with lists of people killed by the heat, as well as stories of drownings of those seeking relief at the local beaches.[2] The courts were closed for summer recess, but the judge first traveled downtown to his judicial chambers to catch up on some work.

Crater shortly arrived at the newly constructed New York County Courthouse on Centre Street in lower Manhattan, which still, ninety years later, functions as Manhattan's busiest courthouse. A hexagonal-shaped building of six stories patterned after the Roman Colosseum, the granite-clad courthouse had cost an exorbitant amount to build. The project faced sundry allegations of embezzlement and fraud, which were a hallmark of the municipal government run by the city's Democratic political machine.[3] Its majestic front entrance facing an open square was placed atop a series of broad cascading granite steps and surmounted by a portico supported by thick columns, on top of which, engraved in stone, was the following inscription: "The True Administration of Justice Is the Firmest Pillar of Good Government." Inside, classical white marble hallways led to a three-story, columned rotunda where elevators rose to the courtrooms and the justices' private chambers on the top floors. With the court in recess, the courthouse was largely vacant. Crater took the elevator up to his chambers, where he met his law secretary (or law clerk) Frederick Johnson and his deputy clerk Joseph Mara, whom he had asked to assist him that morning in some unspecified task.

That April, Governor Franklin D. Roosevelt, looking ahead to his upcoming gubernatorial reelection bid that fall and the growing expectation that he would run for the presidency of the United States in 1932, had carefully chosen Crater from several suggested names to temporarily fill the seat of a retiring judge of the New York Supreme Court (which contrary to its name, is the lower trial court of the New York judicial system). Crater's selection, although something of a surprise, had been well received by the press and the bar associations in the city, while also placating to some degree Tammany Hall, whose electoral support would be crucial to Roosevelt's reelection bid that fall. The governor personally congratulated his appointee afterward in Albany, predicting that he would go on to an outstanding judicial career.[4]

Crater's first months on the bench seemed to confirm his potential. He had confidently presided over hearings and trials and had adeptly issued opinions and rulings on complex legal issues in cases before him. As the newest justice on the court, he would have the honor of presiding at the end of August over the opening session at the courthouse, which with many prominent lawyers in attendance, would provide a good opportunity to kick off his own campaign for election to a full fourteen-year term on the Supreme Court that fall.

His judicial attendants Johnson and Mara would later tell police that their boss appeared troubled by something at his chambers that morning. Crater spent most of the time behind a closed door in his private office and was heard taking papers from files and desk drawers. He also came out of his office at one point to ask Mara to cash at local banks two personal checks he had written in amounts totaling over $5,000, in large denominations, a very substantial sum at the time. When Mara returned to the chambers, Crater quickly pocketed the cash inside his suit jacket without comment and went back to work in his office. Both Mara and Johnson would later tell the police the judge was unusually taciturn and secretive, which was out of character for him.[5]

A little before noon, the judge came out of his chambers and asked Mara to carry out two legal briefcases and a few folders he had filled with papers, and to accompany him back to his apartment uptown. When Mara entered Crater's office, he could see that other papers from Crater's desk and files were stuffed in the trashcan, but he was unable to get a closer look at either the papers being disposed of or at those stuffed in the bags and folders he was carrying out. When Johnson closed up the chambers for the day, he also noticed that Crater's desk was empty, and many papers had been thrown out.[6]

Crater and Mara then came down from the chambers to the grand entrance of the courthouse. The judge directed his deputy, who was carrying the legal bags and folders, to descend the wide, deep flight of steps to the street and hail a taxicab. When he had done so, and a taxi had stopped, Crater emerged from among the large columns at the top of the stairs, and as Mara would later tell the police, hurried down the steps, furtively glancing in all directions "as if being afraid of something," before he hopped into the cab. During the ride home to his apartment, the judge "who was usually talkative, did not have a word to say."[7]

The two men soon arrived uptown in the midday heat at the Craters' apartment building on Fifth Avenue. Exiting the taxi, Crater asked his deputy to bring up to his apartment the legal bags and folders he was carrying from his chambers. Once inside, Mara was told to put everything down on a chair in the living room. As he was leaving, his boss repeated twice that he "was going up Westchester way" and that he would see him back at his chambers tomorrow. Mara assumed he meant he was headed to Westchester County, a sparsely populated area located north of the city with some access to beaches and water, to escape the broiling temperatures in the city. Perhaps for a swim, he thought.[8]

Leads connected to Westchester would be avidly pursued in the early days of the search for the missing man, but when none panned out, Crater's parting words to Mara would become lost in the vast accretion of clues and evidence in the case in subsequent years. Remarkably, it would be another twenty-five years before the NYPD would come across new evidence involving Westchester County that would suggest his final remarks to Mara on the afternoon of August 6, 1930, were more than idle banter.

2

Joe Crater found himself alone in Manhattan that day because a sudden change in his summer plans had happened three days before. He had intended to spend the first three weeks of August with his wife, Stella, at their summer "camp," a bungalow on the Great Lake, largest of a chain of lakes known as Belgrade Lakes in central Maine. An attractive, demure brunette, Stella Wheeler had come to the city from upstate New York and found employment as a bookkeeper and stenographer. Already estranged from her first husband, she began dating Joe while he was a law student at Columbia University. Once she obtained a divorce, they married quietly in a Manhattan parsonage in March 1917, with no family in attendance. Joe and Stella appeared a devoted and compatible couple in many respects, both enjoying the theater, music and dancing, playing bridge, get-togethers with friends, and their summers at Belgrade Lakes.[9]

In the years after her husband's disappearance, Stella would profess ignorance of her husband's life outside of the marriage. She explained in a magazine article in 1937 that she "became what might be termed a politician's wife," who felt "that by asking too many questions she will oblige him to break confidences." Because she "did not want to embarrass Joe, or make him break the rules of the game...I withdrew into the background and knew only as much as he felt he could tell me."[10] To her chagrin, Joe had not even invited her to his official swearing-in ceremony as a Supreme Court justice that spring.[11] Then there was her husband's rather flagrant philandering, keeping of a mistress for years, and consorting with chorus girls, all of which would embarrassingly surface in the press and investigations after his disappearance. Apparently these stories were too painful to her ever to confirm and for the rest of her life, she would dismiss them as unfairly demeaning her husband's reputation.

Joe had spent most of that summer vacationing with his wife at their cabin in Maine, except for a motor excursion they took from there to Canada, a popular destination at the time to avoid the Prohibition laws. He also did make some intermittent brief trips back to Manhattan to take care of work, fulfill some political obligations, and enjoy some of its entertainments, all without Stella. On one of these trips, Crater had attended and played a small but symbolic role in Tammany Hall's 141st Independence Day celebration, which had been observed with gala festivities each year since the founding of the organization as a patriotic society shortly after the end of the American Revolution.

The well-attended and largely ceremonial event was held in the auditorium of the new stately building of red brick and limestone overlooking Union Square Park, which Tammany had moved into the year before and was dubbed the new "Wigwam." Named after a legendary Indian chief, much of the vocabulary of the organization had been borrowed from supposedly Native American words, and often real Indians were used as props in the Independence Day celebrations. While Justice Crater's part in the ceremonies that day was minor—the reading of an old patriotic poem and his appearance on the same stage with its elder "sachems" or wise men and prominent politicians, his presence was a testament to his rapid ascension in the political machine. Newly reelected Mayor Jimmy Walker, one of Tammany's own, made a brief appearance, while US Senator Robert Wagner, who had played a key role as a mentor in Crater's legal and political career, gave a traditional "long speech" extolling the organization's patriotism and other virtues.[12]

As Stella later recounted in her memoirs, early on in their marriage, Joe had told her that in order to achieve his ambition of becoming a judge, he had to enter local politics and make connections. In New York City of the early twentieth century, that meant joining Tammany Hall, the much-maligned and long-reigning Democratic Party of Manhattan (which included the Bronx at that time). She remembered the exhaustive effort he spent making his way up in its politics—organizing the party's voter turnout during elections, making speeches at meetings and dinners, representing it in election disputes in the courts, and socializing with its leaders and hacks. His efforts and talent paid off when, in the late 1920s, he became president of a Tammany district club in Harlem, the Cayuga Democratic Club, and was one of the elite lawyers selected to the Tammany Law Committee, which represented the machine's interests.

When Crater had joined the machine in his early years as a lawyer in the city, the "Tiger" (as it had first been caricatured in Thomas Nast's political cartoons in the 1870s) was undergoing an image makeover of sorts. It proclaimed a transformation from the notoriously corrupt organization of the previous fifty years, which had been run by a series of greedy bosses, including William Tweed and Richard Croker, and been heavily engaged in bribery, gambling, prostitution, and other illicit enterprises. Under the prudent, capable leadership of Boss Charles Francis ("Charlie") Murphy, a self-made man and an Irish Catholic from the city slums like his predecessors, a "New Tammany" had begun to emerge. Murphy had attempted to realign it with the new progressive political agenda and popular socioeconomic welfare laws that were being enacted by the New York state government. With the rise of popular young politicians like Alfred ("Al") Smith and Robert Wagner, Tammany would retain political power by using the local and state governments to press the reform political agenda that favored the same groups of supporters and voters it always had attracted—immigrants, ethnic Americans, and working-class men and women.

But the New Tammany's leaders, including Boss Murphy, had no intention of abandoning their raison d'être—to generate money using the revamped machine control of the municipal government as its fulcrum in myriad and blatant ways. Rather, it would simply make the grafting more official and businesslike. Often mediated by lawyers, it dispensed government jobs, awarded sweetheart contracts with the city, granted lucrative licenses and regulatory approvals to businessmen, and wrung money from the judicial system. With the booming prosperity of the city in the 1920s, its soaring real estate developments, its burgeoning business and commerce, its expanding infrastructure and remunerative public contracts, its leaders would have almost limitless opportunities for engaging in what was known by the oxymoron, "honest graft." With his strong political and legal ties to the New Tammany, Crater was well placed to take advantage of these lucrative opportunities.

Furthermore, once Governor Roosevelt had appointed him to a temporary seat on the Supreme Court the previous spring, Joe's good standing in Tammany became crucial to the attainment of his ultimate ambition of a permanent place on the bench. Having the machine's endorsement and financial support in the upcoming fall campaign for election as a judge was tantamount to a guaranteed victory in a city of predominantly Democratic voters controlled by it. A full term as a Supreme Court justice lasted for fourteen years at an annual salary of $22,500, providing Joe and his wife with financial security in the face of the recent stock market crash and the ominous signs of the incipient depression during 1930. Given Crater's token appearance on the stage of Tammany Hall in the Independence Day festivities that summer, his standing with the machine seemed solid.

Another of Joe's visits to the city at the end of July featured an excursion to Atlantic City spent in the company of friends and some women escorts, during which one of his fingers was mashed in a car door, an injury that found its way into his physical description on his missing persons circular issued by the NYPD. On Friday, August 1, his chauffeur drove him back to his Belgrade Lakes cabin, which they arrived at the next morning. Talking with some friends at the lake later that day, Joe said he was planning on staying up there on vacation until he had to return to the city at the end of the month to preside over the ceremonies opening the Supreme Court's term at the 60 Centre Street courthouse.[13]

But while in the town of Belgrade Lakes with his wife and friends on Saturday night, Stella remembered in her memoirs that Joe "was gone several times for varied periods" when he could have made telephone calls (the Craters' cabin not having a telephone). As they later walked home to their cabin, he told her that he had to return to city the next day to "clear up a few things" and "to straighten out a few people," who were not identified. The next day, Sunday, August 3, he said goodbye to his wife and boarded an overnight train at the Belgrade Lakes train station, having promised his wife he would return to Maine to celebrate her birthday the following week.[14] So she was not initially too concerned about her husband's abrupt departure for the city that afternoon, presuming that he had to deal with some emergent legal matter or perhaps something concerning his nomination for a full-term as a Supreme Court justice the next month.

3

What exactly Crater was doing alone in his Fifth Avenue apartment on the afternoon of August 6, 1930, with the large amount of cash and the legal papers he had taken from his judicial chambers that morning, was unclear. When the detectives first searched his apartment a month later, they found the lawyers' bags which his deputy Mara had carried to the judge's apartment earlier that day, but the mysterious papers in them were nowhere to be seen. Also found during the search were some of his personal items bearing his name or initials, which he typically carried with him—his monogrammed calling card case, pocket watch, and pen—suggesting an intent to leave his identity behind when he left his apartment that night.[15]

Joe's attire that evening suggested a night out on the town in the Jazz Age, as would be described in the NYPD's circular: a brown sackcloth suit with pinstripes, an "[a]ffected colored shirt" and "probably bow tie"; and a "Panama or soft brown hat worn at a rakish angle."[16] He was headed to his favorite part of town, the "Great White Way" of Broadway. A big fan of the theatre and showgirl revues that were in their heyday during the 1920s, he was a frequent attendee of opening nights, sometimes in the company of Stella, and at other times with girlfriends and his show business friends. He also felt quite comfortable in those spaces, even after being appointed a judge that spring, keeping company with chorus girls late into the night at the notorious, often gangster-owned and gangster-frequented nightclubs around Broadway and in Harlem, and earning him the sobriquet "Good time Joe."

But as those who encountered him that night out on Broadway would attest, Crater's behavior and demeanor were once again noticeably out of sorts. Around 6 p.m., he appeared at the Arrow ticket agency on Broadway, and asked the proprietor, his friend Joseph Gransky, to have a ticket held that night for a musical named "Dancing Partners." But as Gransky knew and subsequently would tell police, he had accompanied him on the jaunt to Atlantic City ten days before, where they had seen a preview of the same musical. Without any mention of this, his friend promised to have a ticket held at the theater box office that night. His friend also mentioned he would be returning to Maine soon.[17]

Crater next was seen at a restaurant he often frequented, Haas' Chophouse, located on West Forty-Fifth Street between Eighth and Ninth Avenues, which like many establishments in the area purveyed alcohol as well as food. Once inside, Joe greeted his friend, the proprietor Bill Haas, and Haas thought there was something amiss with his regular customer.[18] Sitting near the front door of the chophouse was Joe's good friend William Klein, chief counsel for the Shubert brothers, whose Broadway theatrical empire was starting to feel the effects of the coming depression that would shortly drive it into bankruptcy. Klein was dining with Sally Ritz, a dancer in the Shuberts' annual edition of their *Artists and Models* revue, notorious for its nudity and salacious content, which he had seen earlier that summer in the company of his mistress of several years.

The judge appeared to reluctantly join the couple for dinner. Klein thought he was "very nervous and disturbed" for reasons he could not discern. The chorus girl also described him as "somewhat depressed" at dinner that night.[19] After a desultory dinner, a little after 9 p.m. the three walked out of the restaurant. Crater then hailed a taxicab coming across Forty-Fifth Street in a westerly direction (it being a one-way street). Having said their goodbyes, he got in the back of a cab that had pulled over and headed off in the direction of the North River (now named the Hudson River), which borders the west side of Manhattan. Klein and Ritz walked in the opposite direction back to the

Shubert offices on West Forty-Fourth Street. They would be the last people who would admit to seeing Joe Crater alive.[20]

But his taxi apparently was not headed to the Belasco Theater on West Forty-Fourth Street where a ticket was being held for him. In addition to its being about a half-hour past the typical starting time for musicals and his having seen the same show in rehearsal days before, the Belasco was two blocks to the east of Haas' Chophouse.[21] It would have been a quick walk for Joe, or if he wanted to take a cab there, the fastest way would have been to walk east to Eighth Avenue, hail a taxi there going south, and go east on West Forty-Fourth. The taxicab he got into, however, was headed west, away from the Belasco Theater and toward a less populated part of Manhattan, with warehouses, factories, railway yards, and the piers on the North River.

In any event, Crater never claimed his ticket to Dancing Partners that night nor were the police ever able to ascertain the identity of the driver of his taxicab despite repeated public appeals asking him to come forward. This would give rise to speculation that the taxi he had hailed and got into outside Haas' Chophouse was a rogue cab dispatched by someone to trail and abduct him. More likely, the driver of the taxi may simply have forgotten his passenger by the time news of his disappearance became public nearly a month afterward.

4

Up at Belgrade Lakes, Stella was expecting her husband's imminent return to celebrate her birthday, as he had promised when he had abruptly left for the city on August 3. On her birthday a week later, she received delivery of Joe's present from a local store, a bright red canoe, but there was no sign of him, causing her more anger than concern. As she stoically put it in her memoirs, "I had become accustomed to the demand which I knew politics were putting on Joe and in the cocoon of my heretofore calm existence had never been one to become confused or agitated too easily."[22]

When still not having heard from her husband by the middle of August, Stella called Simon Rifkind, one of Joe's legal colleagues, to find out where he was.[23] A law partner and legislative assistant of Senator Wagner, Rifkind knew the older man from his renting space in Wagner's law offices downtown before having recently received a temporary appointment to the bench. Through their work together on some cases in the office, the two had become friendly, and Rifkind had come to greatly admire and learn from Crater's legal skills. After Stella contacted him, Simon immediately went to his friend's judicial chambers at the courthouse and spoke with his law secretary, Frederick Johnson, who reassured him that his boss was fine and would be back soon, although in fact he hadn't seen him in chambers since the morning of August 6.[24] Based on his discussions with Johnson and others, Rifkind shortly wired Stella back, reassuring her that her husband was well, to which she responded with relief that she had been "beginning to wonder if he was still alive."[25]

Meanwhile, Stella additionally had dispatched their chauffeur, Fred Kahler, to drive back to Manhattan to see what he could learn. He spoke to Johnson who again was reassuring because as he later admitted, he did not want to raise any suspicions or unwelcome publicity regarding the judge, in case he had gone on a bender or was involved in other behavior unbefitting a judge. Before he came back to Belgrade Lakes, Kahler wired Stella that he "hadn't seen Mr. Crater but everybody says he has been around and is all right."[26]

When the Supreme Court opened on August 25 without the new presiding judge, one of Crater's judicial brethren placed a call to a telephone in the town at Belgrade Lakes and had Stella summoned from her cabin. He said that her husband had failed to appear at the opening of the term that day. Knowing that Joe would not willingly pass up the opportunity of presiding over the opening ceremonies, Stella, now fearing the worst, had Kahler drive her back to Manhattan on August 28 to join the frantic private search for her husband that had commenced.

But even with the news of Crater not appearing at the court ceremonies, Rifkind, and a few others cognizant that he was missing, chose not to report his disappearance to the police. He instead had contacted Leo Lowenthal, a veteran NYPD detective who worked as a bodyguard for Senator Wagner and knew Crater well. After interviewing William Klein and another of Joe's friends, Lowenthal visited the Craters' Fifth Avenue apartment and found that all of Crater's clothes were at his home, except for those he wore on the night of August 6. The detective also interviewed Joseph Mara, who had carried those bags to the judge's apartment that day, and he recalled that "upon leaving the Justice told him he would see him in the morning, as he (the Justice) was going up Westchester way."[27]

Stella stayed at the couple's Fifth Avenue apartment for a few days at the end of August. Conferring with Rifkind, Lowenthal, and Garry Hiers and his wife, the couple's closest friends, Stella was advised that the discreet search for her husband should be allowed to continue. Like Stella, they too were concerned that the immediate disclosure of his disappearance to the police and press might ruin his chances of being nominated for a full term on the Supreme Court the following month. According to her memoirs, she placed telephone calls to "everyone of whom I could think," including Jimmy Walker and Martin Healy, to learn anything about her husband. When interviewed in her apartment by Lowenthal on September 1, Stella told him she could not think any of reason for Joe's absence nor give any information that might be helpful.[28]

But it was clear that the news of a prominent judge vanishing from the midst of the city could not be kept a secret much longer. Rifkind and Lowenthal by then had decided it was time to report Crater's disappearance to the police. Stella followed their advice and was driven back to Maine, hoping to avoid the inevitable media frenzy sure to be unleashed when news that her husband was missing became public. She later described her drive back to the Belgrade Lakes cabin: "It was a grim, bleak trip, and I was torn and nagged by ceaseless doubts, worries and fears. By now I at long last was really beginning to believe that the worst had happened and that something really had gone wrong for Joe."[29] Stella would remain largely sequestered up in Maine with family members until after the start of the new year, refusing requests from the police and prosecutors that she come back to the city to tell what she knew about her husband's disappearance. For much of September, she would still claim to be too debilitated and overcome by fear to even talk with detectives or the press, and would communicate only through brief statements made by others or provide vague and insufficient answers to investigators' questions.

Finally, on the afternoon of September 3, 1930, almost a full month after Joseph Crater was last seen in Manhattan, Rifkind contacted Police Commissioner Edward Mulrooney to officially report that the judge was in fact missing and to request the police's assistance in locating him.[30] As a result of this request, Joe's legal colleague and friend would have the dubious honor of having his name appear under "Name of Complainant" at the top of all subsequent police records in the files along with Complaint No. 13595, which would fill up increasing space in file cabinets and boxes of the Missing Persons Bureau at police headquarters over the ensuing years.

A small, dynamic man with spectacles and a moustache, Rifkind had emigrated as a boy from Lithuania and had worked his way through college and law school in the city. Overcoming antisemitism within the New York bar and law firms, he had rapidly been made a partner in Senator Wagner's law offices. After his part in the Crater case, Rifkind would go on to an illustrious legal career, working as Wagner's aide in enacting New Deal legislation, serving as a federal district court judge, and founding a premier litigation department in one of the city's mega law firms that still bears his name: Paul, Weiss, Rifkind, Wharton & Garrison. A 1983 *New Yorker* profile considered him "perhaps the greatest all-around lawyer of his time."[31]

In an interview with the author in 1993, over sixty years after the disappearance of his friend, Rifkind still remembered Joe as "a first class lawyer" and a mentor. From the time he reported his friend missing right up through his interview right before he died, he would steadfastly maintain that Crater was the victim of a random street crime, rejecting "any suggestion that he was privy to anything inappropriate" because as he put it, "that was not Crater." As Rifkind similarly told a reporter years later, Crater was "a man of impeccable manners and propriety. If you live as closely with a man as I did with Crater and he has unsavory innards, you discover it."[32]

News of the startling disappearance of one the city's more well-known denizens first appeared in the September 3 morning edition of the *New York World*. By this time, the *World* had progressed from a sensational "penny press" into one of city's major newspapers, known for its independent politics and crusading exposés. The front-page article bore the headline: "Justice J. F. Crater Missing From His Home Since Aug. 6."[33] It was based upon undisclosed sources (perhaps Rifkind and other friends of the Craters) who were familiar with the private search for him over the past two weeks.

The portrayal of the missing judge in the article, as in most of the initial newspaper coverage, was respectful and solicitous. The lead paragraph identified Crater as a New York Supreme Court Justice, the "former law associate of United States Senator Robert F. Wagner," and someone "known intimately to hundreds of persons throughout the city." Crater's appointment to the bench by Governor Roosevelt that spring "was hailed as excellent" by the New York legal community, and "[h]is wide knowledge of the law has been generally admitted." Expressing perplexity over the disappearance of such a prominent figure, the article fell back on platitudes such as that Crater "always has been noted for his geniality and fellowship," and no one could think of any enemies he had who would want to harm him. According to "intimate friends," the Craters' "married life was ideal" and the "devotion of Justice and Mrs. Crater to each other has frequently been pointed out as exemplary."[34]

The *World* article consequently played up innocent, exculpatory explanations of the man's disappearance. His wife and friends' belief, it was said, was "that some one may have observed him carrying the cash [taken from his bank accounts that morning], and after following him to some isolated place, attacked him," or that he was involved in an accident "which impaired his memory." Crater's connections to Tammany Hall and the Cayuga Club in Harlem were noted, then downplayed as, the article stated, his recent serving as president of the club was "virtually perfunctory," and the "actual and active head of the organization" was its district leader, Martin Healy. Additionally, "[i]t was quickly ascertained that no charge, not even among the countless anonymous allegations written about the various members of the judiciary has been made against Justice Crater" in the ongoing investigations into judicial corruption in New York City.[35]

So it was that on September 4, 1930, the longest and most expansive search for a missing person in American history officially began. In addition to its being severely hampered by its belated commencement nearly a month after the man had last been seen, the search would be rendered all the more difficult by the very protean nature of the person to be found, a man possessed of multiple personae, a player of numerous roles in the drama of Jazz Age New York.

CHAPTER TWO

The Search Officially Begins

I

The high-profile and potentially fraught job of finding Joseph Crater fell to the NYPD. By 1930, the department was in the process of becoming the professional, nonpartisan, and diverse law enforcement agency that it is today. But its corrupt past and lingering bad reputation due to its close ties with Tammany Hall would raise questions from the start of its search about whether it wanted to find the missing judge.

Organized shortly after the Civil War by Tammany Boss William Tweed, the municipal police force had evolved in tandem with Manhattan's political machine. In the following decades, the police ranks as well as its leadership were increasingly comprised of men from immigrant Irish families, who at the same time were joining and ascending in Tammany. The position of a police officer, then requiring few special skills, operating within a hierarchial organization that placed a premium on loyalty, and often occupied by family members, friends, and fellow countrymen, was a natural fit for the Irish who immigrated to the city in the mid-nineteenth century. According to a history of the NYPD, "as the city government's leading Irish institution, the police department occupied a central place in the Irish ascendance."[1]

By the turn of the nineteenth century, with the notoriously corrupt Boss Richard Croker and his henchmen in power, the police department had been transformed into a grafting arm of the machine. One of the periodic commissions on police corruption had found "a well-regulated and comprehensive system, conducted apparently upon business principles" for generating payoffs. Police recruits were required to pay local Tammany leaders to get onto the force initially and then exponentially higher sums to higher-ups in order to get promoted. To obtain the necessary money to make these payoffs to the machine as well as to line their own pockets, patrolmen systematically extorted money from brothels, gambling houses, and saloons for protection from raids and arrests.[2] By controlling the police department, Tammany also could ensure that its infamous manipulation of elections in the city and its rampant voter fraud could proceed relatively unhindered. These sordid ties between Tammany and the police exploded into public view in the 1912 murder of mobster Herman Rosenthal, who was about to divulge his alliance with a Tammany district leader, for which a police lieutenant subsequently was tried, found guilty, and executed.

In the ensuing years, the department had been freed somewhat from Tammany's grasp and its protection of vice crimes. Boss Charlie Murphy, Croker's successor, had helped steer the machine away from involvement in prostitution, gambling, and the drug trade, and towards more seemly and honest grafting schemes. The intermittent election of reform mayors in the first two decades of the new century led to the appointment of independent police commissioners who in turn created internal units to combat corruption from within the department. Additionally, the introduction of civil service requirements for admission onto the police force and more professional training during this time ended the traditional payoff system.

But suspicions of Tammany's continuing influence within the top echelons of the NYPD still lingered during Mayor Jimmy Walker's administration in the late 1920s. One of his police commissioners had to resign after promising and failing to solve the 1928 murder of Arnold Rothstein, the national gambling kingpin and mastermind of the 1919 "Black Sox" baseball scandal, who was known to have extensive connections with Tammany district leaders, judges, and magistrates. Under another of Walker's commissioners, a high-ranking police officer named Lewis Valentine, who had the effrontery to conduct raids of Tammany district clubs under whose auspices gambling was frequently allowed, was quickly demoted without explanation and transferred to the quiet extremities of the city.

Mayor Walker's appointment of Edward Mulrooney as the new police commissioner in early 1930 seemed to be a break with precedent. Though an Irish American like many of his predecessors, he was only the second chief to come up through the police ranks. His long and highly decorated career had begun more than thirty years before as a recruit under Commissioner (and future President) Teddy Roosevelt who sought to reform the partisan department. He had a reputation for honesty and integrity even while being stationed in areas like the "Tenderloin" district of Manhattan, located in the West Twenties and Thirties, when it was notorious for its concentration of prostitution and gambling joints and the rampant police payoffs that were a cost of doing business in the early years of the new century. A tough-looking, gruff, and unpretentious man, Mulrooney was characterized in a *New Yorker* profile as courageous, courteous, "personally beyond reproach," and a "Cop's Cop."[3] And having previously served as chief of detective of the department, he had experience heading up investigations into headline-catching crimes. Still, he recently had remarked that the secrets of good detective work were "thoroughness, patience and luck—especially luck."[4]

By the time of Crater's disappearance, the police department also had modernized its technology, equipment, and facilities, though there were some obvious deficiencies that would hinder its search for a man who would shortly be spotted in all different parts of the nation. In the 1920s, reliable motor vehicles and motorcycles were finally replacing horses and bicycles as the chief modes of police transportation within the city, although the advent of radios in police cars would not come until later. To get their assignments, policemen typically would have to call in to their local stations on signal boxes located around the city.[5]

Because of the poor condition of roads outside of the city, detectives working the Crater case in its early days, who would be dispatched to Canada, upstate New York, Washington, DC, New Jersey, and Maine, would have to use trains to travel if available, which were themselves rather slow for a quickly developing investigation. Although Crater's missing person poster, which would shortly be distributed throughout the nation, directed anyone with information to place a call to the local telephone number of the police headquarters, most of the communications from people outside the city would be by regular mail or telegram. In turn, the department typically used wire telegrams to communicate with its officers and with other law enforcement agencies outside of the city. Following up emergent tips and clues outside the city could take days.

Comprising a separate unit within the NYPD, the Missing Persons Bureau was commanded by veteran Captain John Ayres, who had been in charge since its inception in 1918. The bureau had an amazingly successful record in its endeavors; in some 250,000 cases it handled since it opened, it had solved an impressive 98 percent.[6] At the time of Crater's disappearance, about seventy people were reported missing on average each day in New York City, the great majority of whom were quickly located. The most common reasons for disappearances in New York—in order of decreasing frequency—were reported to be financial troubles, domestic difficulties and extramarital affairs, commission of a crime, and amnesia or mental illness.[7] Most persons went missing of their own volition; few were found to be involuntary victims of a crime.[8]

In his 1932 book about the Missing Persons Bureau, Captain Ayres would describe the basic process for finding a missing person: by "recreat[ing] a lifelike picture of the missing person" by "digging into his life," "from the material secured, reconstructing him," and "be[ing] in a position to know how that particular person would act under certain given circumstances." In other words, "We must know all about his past, his present, and his possible future." If these questions could be accurately answered, he believed, there would normally be a good prospect of solving the disappearance. But as would be all too true in the Crater case, he observed that "the difficulty with which the police are constantly confronted is that informative and truthful replies to questions often cannot be secured, either because of lack of information, or because of the desire of those questioned to evade the truth either through fear of consequences, or to shield themselves or the missing man from unfavorable revelations."[9]

At the start of the search for the missing judge, Commissioner Mulrooney and Captain Ayres naturally expected that a man as well known in the city as Joseph Crater would be quickly located. A reporter for the *Herald-Tribune*, having been given the assignment of finding the missing man on the day the news of his disappearance broke, had to write his disappointed editor that night, "I am sorry not to be able to find Judge Crater for you today. Maybe tomorrow."[10] But the Crater case would prove to be anything but a typical search for a missing person.

2

The handful of NYPD detectives initially assigned to the Crater case, some of them veteran officers like Leo Lowenthal, frantically set about finding and interviewing those reported to have last seen the missing man and those thought to be closest to him. These people included William Klein, the

Shubert lawyer who had dined with him on the night of August 6; William Haas, the proprietor of the chophouse they had dined in; Crater's deputy clerk Mara and law secretary Johnson, both of whom had been with their boss at his judicial chambers that morning, and the former also accompanying him back to his apartment; Joseph Gransky, his friend at the Broadway ticket agency at which he stopped to request a theater ticket be held for him that last night; and Garrett Hiers, a personal friend of the Craters who had seen Joe little that summer.[11]

A detective also was dispatched to the address of 303 West 122nd Street in Harlem—Crater's address according to the local telephone book. There, the detective learned that while the Craters had moved to their Fifth Avenue apartment the year before, Joe, along with other members of the Cayuga Democratic Club, had continued to use his former address for purposes of voting in their local assembly district. The local police commander there reportedly did speak with some members of the Cayuga Club he knew, who said they couldn't provide any information about the missing man.[12]

On September 4, 1930, the first full day of the search, two of the detectives were asked to come to the courthouse downtown at 60 Centre Street to speak with Supreme Court justices McGeehan and Valente about the disappearance of their associate.[13] The judges confirmed that Crater had inexplicably not appeared to preside over the opening of the term on August 25 and was not with Stella when they called her at Belgrade Lakes. But Justice Valente also told them some information that did not appear in any press accounts. On August 1, just before he left with his chauffeur to drive to Maine to join Stella, Crater had called Valente and asked for a sizable loan of $3,000 in cash. He readily agreed to provide Crater with the loan without asking any further questions but thought the request quite unusual. Soon after the call, however, Valente fell ill and was confined to bed for the next days, and he did not hear anything further about his fellow justice borrowing the money.[14]

Also that day, a crowd of people, including reporters, had gathered at the docks on the west side of Manhattan in anticipation of the arrival of the oceanic liner *Bremen*. Onboard was Robert F. Wagner, the US senator from New York, returning from a trip to Germany to see the former hometown of his family, who could possibly shed some light on the whereabouts of the missing man. During the past decade, the lives of Bob Wagner and Joe Crater had closely intertwined, and Crater considered the older man his legal and political mentor as well as something of a father figure.

Wagner had first emerged as one of the political stars of the New Tammany, groomed by then Tammany boss Murphy in the 1910s. He had come to the Democratic machine, like many, from a poor immigrant family that settled in another of the ethnic neigborhoods of Manhattan, the largely German Yorkville section on its Upper East Side. After working his way through law school, Wagner paid his dues at the local Tammany clubhouse, and with its support, he won election first to the New York Assembly and then to the New York Senate of which he soon became the Majority Leader. Together with Al Smith as Speaker of the New York Assembly, Wagner had championed the enactment of landmark workers' protections, industrial safety, social welfare, and other progressive legislation in New York in the second decade of the twentieth century.

With Boss Murphy's backing, Wagner then had been elected a New York Supreme Court justice in Manhattan in 1918. Two years later, he had hired Joe Crater, a talented and ambitious young lawyer with Tammany ties, for the prestigious position of his law secretary, as law clerks of the court are still referred to today. During the following years, Joe impressed him with his brilliant legal mind and relied heavily on his skills and abilities. Crater in turn looked up to Wagner as a role model of sorts, a powerful and respected jurist while also a leading Tammany politician, who had been able to avoid the taint of the machine.

Although considered at various times as a candidate for governor of New York, mayor of New York City, and even boss of Tammany Hall after Charlie Murphy's death in 1924, Bob Wagner got the nomination he wanted and was elected as the junior US senator from New York in 1926. A magazine profile of him after the election predicted that "[h]e will bring to the upper house of Congress a high measure of intelligence, a sympathy for the masses that does not sour to demagoguery and a talent for hard work."[15] Crater, after turning down Wagner's offer to accompany him to Washington as his legislative aide, had opened his own law practice by renting office space in Senator Wagner's law offices, a suite in the Equitable Life Assurance Building at 120 Broadway, a massive, new skyscraper occupying a full city block in downtown Manhattan and containing the most office space of any building in the world in the 1920s.[16] Joe's lucrative practice included cases he worked on with other lawyers as well as assisting the senator and his two law partners, Francis Quillinan and Rifkind, with their cases.

Disembarking from the ocean liner on September 4, the squat, distinguished-looking and usually genial man was met by reporters who asked for his reaction to the news of his protégé's disappearance the day before. Apparently tipped off while on the ship about the press frenzy, Wagner was very reticent, commenting, "All I know of the case is that it is as much of a mystery to me as it is to you." He said he had last seen his friend on August 1, before departing on his trip to Germany, when Joe had stopped by his office to wish him bon voyage, and he had seemed "normal and as gracious as usual." Probably fearing that his protégé's disappearance had the taint of scandal, Wagner appeared to distance himself when talking to the reporters, emphasizing that Crater was not his partner in his law firm, as had been mistakenly reported, but merely rented office space there, while denying that he had played any role in Governor Roosevelt's appointment of Crater to the bench earlier that year (which likely was untrue). He then added somewhat cryptically, "Like most young lawyers he had of course sought to reach the Supreme Court bench. I thought he may have been a little bit in a hurry."[17]

That night, Wagner's niece visited him in his Upper East Side apartment. She found him alone and "boiling mad," whacking a golf ball around the living room with such big strokes that she "feared for the furniture," as he muttered "what a dirty game politics is." Wagner's biographer Robert Huthmacher would explain his behavior that night as representing "the response of one who, possessing 'imperturbable integrity' himself was sometimes inclined to judge rashly the conduct of others."[18]

3

As the press storm about her husband's disappearance inundated New York City, Stella remained ensconced in the Craters' rustic bungalow at Belgrade Lakes, showing no intention of returning to the city. Shortly joined in Maine by her mother and brother-in-law, she was reported to be in a state of utter shock and prostration over her husband's vanishing. On September 7, NYPD detective Edward Fitzgerald, one of the first officers assigned to the case, was dispatched to Belgrade Lakes to speak with her.

He was allowed in the cabin to question her as she lay in bed. When asked about the last time she had seen her husband, Stella's initial account left out some key details as she later would admit. She recounted that Joe and his chauffeur had driven from New York and arrived there on the morning of

Saturday, August 2. That night, Joe and Stella walked to the village with Joe's niece, who was at summer camp nearby, where they went bowling and saw a moving picture. On Sunday, she said Joe "stayed around the camp all day and he did not seem to be nervous nor sick." She last saw Joe that Sunday afternoon when their chauffeur was taking him to the Belgrade Lakes train station to board an overnight train back to the city. She additionally mentioned that Joe had come up for periods of time earlier that summer, and they had made short trips to Canada.[19] But she left out what else had happened on Saturday night in Belgrade Lakes Village, when Joe went off to make a phone call and afterward he had told her his plans had suddenly changed; he would be returning to the city the next day to deal with some urgent business.

Stella also turned over to Detective Fitzgerald what would prove to be significant pieces of evidence although their import apparently eluded the police at the time. She provided the checkbooks for the bank accounts on which her husband had written the two checks for large amounts in his judicial chambers on the morning of August 6 and that Mara had cashed. In one checkbook, written on the stub from which the check was torn, was an entry with that date for "Cash for $2150"; in the other, an entry for "Cash for $3000." While perhaps not knowing at that time about Stella's frantic visit to her Fifth Avenue apartment at the end of August, the detective oddly did not question Stella about how these checkbooks that were in her husband's possession in his judicial chambers on the last day he was seen had ended up in her possession in Maine a month later.[20]

Detective Fitzgerald also returned to the city with Stella's letter to Commissioner Mulrooney, officially requesting his assistance in locating her husband. Handwritten on incongruous "Camp Minne Wa-Wa, Belgrade Lakes, Maine" stationery with a photo of the Crater's wooden cupola overlooking the lake, Stella's letter stated,

> The strange disappearance of my husband, Joseph Force Crater, which I am at an utter loss to explain, forces me to request the Police Dept of New York to aid in the search, and I hereby request that you do anything in your power to solve this mysterious affair.
>
> Needless to say your Dept will have every cooperation from me and your Dept may call upon me at any time you feel I can be of assistence.
>
> Yours respectfully
>
> Mrs. Joseph F. Crater[21]

Fitzgerald's overall impression from his interview of Stella, candidly expressed in the NYPD's internal records, was that Stella was a "homebody" and was totally in the dark about her husband's political, legal, and business activities.[22]

During the following months, Stella would continue to maintain her ignorance of what happened to her husband and in fact, did not provide much cooperation and assistance to the police and investigators looking for him as she had promised. As will be seen, however, she knew much more than she let on at the time. In refusing to disclose what she knew until years later, Stella demonstrated an instinct for self-preservation and a savvy ability to navigate the perilous waters of the inquiries into Joe's disappearnance.

4

As Crater had last been seen alive in the company of a chorus girl and the chief lawyer for the Shubert brothers in the heart of Broadway, the police investigation and its coverage by the press initially focused on whether one of his girlfriends was responsible for his disappearance, either by enticing him to run away or by blackmailing him to avert disclosure of his extramarital liaisons. The latter possibility seemed especially plausible in light of his withdrawal of over $5,000 in cash the morning of August 6, combined with the likelihood that such a disclosure of his womanizing would have been very detrimental to his prospects for nomination and election to a full judicial term that fall. With the advent of sensationalist tabloid newspapers and magazines in New York and the sexualized, hedonistic, and anything goes culture of Broadway and its nightlife in the Roaring Twenties, this angle unsurprisingly would eclipse all others in the police department's investigation and the media coverage of the search in its initial days.

As the investigation commenced, Missing Persons Bureau Captain Ayres had dispatched detectives to talk to William Klein, one of the last people to see Crater on the night of August 6. In several interviews, Klein provided valuable insight into their uncomfortable dinner on that night and was very forthcoming with details of his missing friend's injudicious lifestyle.

A tall, spectacled, homely looking man, Klein was the powerful chief counsel and confidant to Sam, Lee, and J. J. Shubert, the brothers who by this time had established a theatrical empire that controlled Broadway as well as theater houses and circuits throughout the country. Joining the brothers when they had arrived in New York City at the turn of the century, Klein had become an indispensable lawyer on a multitude of legal and financial issues arising in the Shubert's theatrical business, such as contractual disputes with star entertainers, price-fixing of theatre tickets and monopolization in the industry, the sale and protection of intellectual property rights, and the admission or exclusion of customers and critics from their theaters. A biographer of the Shuberts has credited Klein with having "the distinction of becoming the chief architect of much of American theatrical law." Like the surviving brothers Lee and J. J., Klein had a penchant for Broadway chorus girls and dancers who were often with him as on the night in question.[23] By this time, Klein and Crater, with their elite legal practices and love of Broadway, were close friends and were involved in court cases together.

When asked about their unexpected meeting for dinner at Haas' Chophouse on August 6, Klein provided some important context. Two nights before that, he and his girlfriend Sally Ritz had dinner at that very same restaurant, when Joe also chanced to enter and joined them. The judge, who Klein described as being "in the best of spirits" that night, had told them then that he was planning to go back to his cabin in Maine the next day, August 5, and to stay up there for a few weeks.[24]

So, as Klein told the detectives, he was very surprised to see his friend come into Haas' restaurant again two nights later. He described Joe as acting "very nervous and disturbed" when he entered the restaurant then, and once he saw Klein and Ritz dining at a table there, he seemed reluctant to join them. Klein described Joe as looking "sheepish" when he did go to their table, probably, he surmised, because he hadn't yet left town, contrary to what he had told them two nights before. Klein recalled that his friend had only one cordial and acted uncharacteristically quiet at dinner.[25]

The detectives also interviewed Bill Haas, the proprietor of the chophouse, and he made similar observations about his frequent customer on the night of August 6. He said that Crater had come into the restaurant in a bad mood that night. Haas even remarked to the judge "that he did not seem to be in his usual good health," but he "passed it off by saying that his appearance might seem different due to the large collar he was wearing."[26]

Based on what both Klein and Haas had told them, the detectives ought to have been curious about what had happened to Crater in the interim between Klein's first dinner with him at Haas' restaurant on August 4 and their second dinner there two nights later. By the time of their second meeting together, his plan to return to Maine had fallen through, and the judge had seemed despondent and out of character, after being in good spirits when he dined with Klein two nights before. Yet the NYPD, and subsequently the New York district attorney's office, inexplicably failed to ask what if anything had transpired within that day or two to Crater or those close to him that could have caused such a marked effect on his plans and state of mind.

The investigators in fact had to look no further than the front pages of the city newspapers in those intervening days, and the events covered there that might have been of especial interest to the judge. Such a connection between those events and Crater's disappearance was being made in some of the earliest newspaper accounts of the case, including the *New York World*'s initial exposé, but was soon dropped.[27] Whether this oversight by the police department was inadvertent or intentional, a key avenue of inquiry into why Crater had vanished was ignored in the early days of the search for the missing man.

When detectives inquired into the missing man's affection for chorus girls, Willie Klein had much to tell. Several times that summer, he had seen Joe in the company of chorus girls from the *Artists and Models* show, in which Sally Ritz, Klein's girlfriend, was a dancer. He also remembered frequently seeing Crater at risqué nightclubs and out on the town with female companions other than his wife that summer.[28]

It shortly would be learned that Crater had attended *Artists and Models* earlier that summer in the company of Connie Marcus, his partially subsidized mistress for the past several years. Marcus would tell the police that she was rather shocked by his apparent familiarity with some of the largely naked girls on stage whom he referred to by their first names.[29] The show, produced by J. J. Shubert, was one of the annual "revues" popular on Broadway in the 1920s, like the Ziegfeld Follies, whose main attractions, besides some star performers, were the young, leggy, scantily clad chorus girls and dancers on stage. According to the Shuberts' biographer, it was this show overseen by J. J. Shubert, a notorious skirt chaser himself, which had "earned [him] his reputation as flesh merchant."[30]

That summer's *Artists and Models* show, titled the "Paris-Riviera Edition of 1930," consisted of a number of skits, songs, and dances connected by a thin romantic plot, accompanied by over forty chorus girls and dancers. Scenes were set in the dressing room of a women's gymnasium and a boudoir, and credits thanked the Model Brassiere Company for the "scanties and brassieres."[31] Critics had roundly panned the show for its gratuitous nudity and sexual content. The theater critic of the *New Yorker*, the new highbrow magazine of the city's culture, was shocked by the nakedness of the girls in the show, commenting that "when ladies named Dimple Riede or Mary Clark or Jane Manners come on the stage in what practically amounts to nothing, one feels like saying: Ooop! Sorry! Wrong room." The reviewer claimed he was unable to describe some scenes and "still keep the magazine within the rigid limits of the postal laws" but thought the show would be popular because "people have got to have a revue of some sort in the hot weather, and this is the only one there is in town."[32]

Klein told the police he thought Crater had shown a particular interest in a chorus girl from *Artists and Models*, Elaine Orlove, whose stage name was "Elaine Dawn." He said Dawn was currently in a hospital in Manhattan, suffering from "gonorrhea rheumatism," and the Shuberts were footing her hospital expenses and her rent. Klein also mentioned that Dawn had a "pimp," who had been trying to collect money from the brothers; he thought the pimp could have also tried to blackmail Joe. (The terminology also suggests that Dawn was a prostitute as well as a chorus girl, probably not an unusual combination of professions at the time.) Klein and Crater also had been to a trendy nightclub in the area, the Club Abbey, a few times that summer, where Dawn had just started as a dancer. He had heard Crater had gone out alone with Dawn about a week before he disappeared. Crater "seemed to have taken more than a passing interest in her," he told police.[33]

Klein's information must have been taken seriously, for a detective was immediately dispatched to take a lengthy train trip to Toronto, Canada, where the cast of *Artists and Models* was now on tour. There, he interviewed the troupe, including J. J. Shubert, who said he knew the missing man very well but could think of no explanation for his sudden disappearance. Alice Wood, one of the showgirls also mentioned by Klein, reluctantly admitted she had been to a few parties with Crater the summer, and while he did take her home one night alone, she quickly added, "it was just a friendly 'good bye.'" The detective also interviewed Sally Ritz who also was in the cast about her two dinners with Klein and the judge at Haas' Chophouse. She recalled, just as Klein had told the police, that Crater seemed to have been in good spirits at their August 4 dinner but "seemed somewhat depressed" at their dinner two nights later at the same place, although she could not say why. Ritz, it turned out, recently had been Elaine Dawn's roommate, and she said that Crater had

gone out with Dawn many times and given her money to buy shoes and clothing as well as visited her recently at the Club Abbey.[34]

Meanwhile, back in Manhattan, Dawn, questioned by the police from her
hospital bed, confirmed that he had come to see her at the club on several
occasions that summer and would always sit with her between numbers, but
would leave alone. She had been introduced to him by Klein and some of
the girls in the show. She did recall that he was at the club on the night of
August 4, staying until about 3 a.m. and going home alone, and that was last
time she had seen him.[35] Presumably, his visit to the club followed his dinner
with Klein and Ritz that night, suggesting that as his companions had told
the police, he was relaxed and in good spirits that night, unlike his mood on
the night of August 6.

The salacious angle of the investigation into Crater's disappearance quickly
became fodder for the tabloid press. The pages of these newspapers were soon
festooned with vampy pictures of the chorus girls who were mentioned as the
judge's companions. The *Daily News*, one of New York's new photo-laden
tabloids, ran a story on September 5 about his "girls," alongside a picture of
Alice Wood in a seductive pose with the caption, "Sure—She Knew Him."
The article began: "That old police custom, 'cherchez la femme' was being
vigorously pursued, albeit rather tardily, yesterday, by police and investigators searching for the missing Supreme Court Justice Joseph Force Crater.
This investigation began when it was learned the jurist had a penchant for
beautiful girls from the nude shows of Broadway, and the nuder floor shows
of night clubs." Wood was interviewed and was quick to downplay her relationship with the missing man, stating, "I am not a New York girl, I am from
Virginia and I live [in Yonkers] with my mother." Ritz similarly was quoted,
"We were only friends. And not friends in the Broadway sense, either."[36] Such
sensationalist articles about Crater would festoon the tabloids in the early
days of the search.

Detectives learned more about the missing man's penchant for the fast
life and his promiscuity when they interviewed Joseph Gransky, the owner
of the ticket agency on Broadway. After initially telling them only about his
friend's request for a ticket to Dancing Partners on the night of August 6, days
later, he admitted that he and Crater had gone to Atlantic City on July 25 and
had "met two women who were already there" and another friend who had
a girl with him. They were introduced to a hostess at the Beaux Arts Café,

whom he thought Crater liked "very much." While there, they also had seen
a preview of the same show, which made Gransky think that his friend likely
had not attended the show now playing on Broadway the night he was last
seen.[37]

After travelling to Atlantic City, Philadelphia, and Washington, DC, in
search of the Atlantic City hostess Gransky had referred to, a detective on the
case finally found Marie Miller when he returned back to police headquarters. She had become aware through the newspaper coverage that the police
were looking for her and had come to Manhattan to answer any questions. All
she could provide, though, was an account of a continuous party in Atlantic
City during which she danced, drank, had dinner, and sat on the beach with
the judge at times, although she thought he seemed to be more interested in
another girl in the group with a Southern drawl and flapper bob, who was
"very extremely" dressed. The hostess thought Crater liked her "a bit" but had
not been in contact with him since.[38]

4

Days after the manhunt had begun, five thousand copies of Crater's missing
person circular were printed by the NYPD and were ready for distribution all
over the United States and eventually abroad.[39] Another version of it would
be distributed a few weeks later, which included the city's new offer of a hefty
reward of $5,000 for anyone "furnishing this Department with information
resulting in locating Joseph Force Crater," a sure impetus for false sightings in
the first years of the Depression.

At first glance, the iconic poster, with the words in all caps and boldface,
"MISSING SINCE AUGUST 6, 1930," under "POLICE DEPARTMENT" at the
top, exudes a certain aura of notoriety. This no doubt stems from its resemblance to "Wanted" posters for notorious criminals. The impression given,
though probably not intended by the police department, is that he was not
only missing but also suspect because of some nefarious conduct on his part.

The circular graphically portrays both the man and his times. The boldface
lettering has a modern, flamboyant, Art Deco style to it.[40] While the missing
man's physical description in the poster refers to his "mixed grey hair," his
hair in the photograph is dark, parted in the middle and slicked down, as his
description also states. His face is pictured and described as dark, "tanned,"

and wrinkle-free, firm of chin and jaw. His trademark high, starched, white choker collar adds to his suave, jaunty look.

The caption under the picture identifies him as the "Honorable Joseph Force Crater, Justice of the Supreme Court, State of New York," but the image shows more of a sharp, sporty, man-about-town than a dignified judicial mien. The poster's reference to the clothes Crater was wearing when last seen also point to the flamboyance of his appearance: he wore his hat "at a rakish angle," and his clothes were "made by Vroom," a fashionable tailor at the time, and included an "affected colored shirt" and "probably bow tie."[41]

Also, the photograph of Crater used on the circular, which likely was obtained by the police from one of their initial searches of the Crater's Fifth Avenue apartment, was surely taken years before his disappearance and bore only an attenuated resemblance to how he actually looked in the summer of 1930. Later photos of him, taken around the time he was appointed to the bench in April 1930, show a more corpulent and dissipated man: his hair is noticeably thinning with grey streaks through it, his lower eyelids are creased and pouched, his bloated cheeks sag below his chin and jaw, and his lips are set in a lecherous smirk. It was as if, by the end of the decade, Crater's countenance had absorbed and reflected the excesses and profligacy of his life in the fast lane during the Roaring Twenties. Perhaps this discrepancy between the earlier photograph of him in the poster and what he actually looked like when he disappeared helps explain the huge number of mistaken sightings of Crater over the subsequent years.

What would prove more useful to the NYPD and others searching for the missing man was the description on the poster of some of his other physical attributes: his "false teeth, upper and lower jaw," his six-foot height, and his small head atop a long, skinny neck, which was "unusual...for his height and weight." These provided at least some benchmarks that could be compared with the numerous unidentified corpses found in New York City and elsewhere, which bore some resemblance to the man in the poster. This was especially true for New York harbor, where bodies and parts of bodies frequently would surface and wash ashore in the rivers and bays ringing the city. The NYPD later would write to Stella in Maine, gingerly asking whether her husband's penis was circumcised, another attribute that could be used in ruling out a cadaver. Stella, whether out of a sense of modesty or ignorance, referred the police to Joe's physician for that information.[42]

Although Crater's circular was addressed to "Police Authorities [who are] to Post this Circular for the Information of Police Officers and File a Copy of it for Future Reference," over the years, tens of thousands more copies of the missing person poster would be circulated and posted in all types of public places—train stations, post offices, courthouses, passenger ships, ports, hotels, consulates all over the globe. Fueled by Crater's omnipresent poster distributed far and wide, the public's fascination with the case would escalate for obvious reasons: here was a figure of prominence and rectitude, a judge from America's metropolis, who had dallied in Tammany Hall's dirty politics as well as consorted with chorus girls in wild nightclubs, and now had simply vanished for no apparent reason. For years to come, especially around the anniversary of Crater's disappearance, newspapers, magazines, and newsreels would carry the story with his picture and description, and reports of his sighting would flow in. In the hard times of the 1930s, his case would spawn a cultural craze, a national competition to find the missing man (especially when the monetary reward was in effect), and his name become a source of popular humor.

5

Within a week of the news that Joseph Crater in fact had vanished, the police investigation was foundering. Detectives already had been dispatched to Maine, Canada, upstate New York, Atlantic City, Washington, DC, Westchester County, and all over the city in pursuit of clues and tips from the public, none of which had panned out. They had spoken to his wife, his closest friends, his legal colleagues and judicial brethren, his Broadway friends and chorus girls, and the people who had seen him in the final days. The few public pronouncements by Commissioner Mulrooney and other police officials expressed confidence that Crater was alive and had voluntarily absented himself. After all, there were the large sums of money withdrawn from his bank accounts and the papers cleared out of his judicial chambers in the morning of August 6, as well as other clues suggesting that he had intentionally planned his escape. As one officer commented, "It's easier to find a dead person than a live one."[43]

Crater's colleagues and friends, however, in their comments to reporters during the early days of the investigation, conveyed a very different impression of the missing man and why he had disappeared. Simon Rifkind opined that because "[h]e was in love with his work and qualified for it, I am sure that if he was alive he would have appeared in court on August 25, at the scheduled time" of the opening of the court term. Rifkind also was quick to declare that his friend's disappearance had nothing to do with developing news about investigations into judicial corruption. Justice Valente, who had spoken with the police on the first day of the investigation, told reporters, "I'm sure he is dead....I believe, like many of his friends, that he flashed a large roll of bills and was taken for a ride."[44] For his family, colleagues and friends, Joe Crater having been an involuntary victim of a robbery or other crime had the salutary effect of relieving him of responsibility for his disappearance and his other disreputable activities that were coming to light. Another unattractive theory to his family and friends was that Joe had been despondent and committed suicide, which they downplayed by stating that he was not the type to kill himself.[45]

Tammany Hall also immediately sought to distance itself from any connection to the vanishing of its prominently affiliated lawyer and judge. "Justice Crater's unimpeachable public and private life and his creditable achievement on the bench allows no room for suspicion of any motives for his disappearance," the *New York Democrat*, Tammany Hall's newspaper, asserted, for "[his] re-nomination and re-election [to the Supreme Court] was assured." It warned against any rush to judgment about any wrongdoing by him, including escalating stories of his Broadway womanizing, for "[e]ven hard-shelled ghouls might find subsequent embarrassment if it be proven that an innocent public official for the past month has been dead or a victim of amnesia."[46]

It was the *New York World*, the independent, anti-Tammany newspaper having first broken the news of Crater's disappearance, that first called for additional investigations of what happened to him. Its editorial on September 10, exclaimed in disbelief, "The effect of closing the inquiry into [Crater's] disappearance, except for such information as may conceivably be turned up by a kindly fate, would be disastrous. A justice of the Supreme Court simply cannot be permitted to drop out of sight without an adequate effort being made to explain his disappearance." It proposed that the district attorney's office empanel a grand jury to look into the matter. For unlike the police, the district attorney "would have ample power to...subpoena bank books, he could subpoena records, he could subpoena witnesses. He could compel witnesses with knowledge to come before the grand jury and answer all questions posed to them."[47]

Thus was borne the special grand jury inquest entitled, "In the Matter of the Investigation into the Disappearance of Joseph Force Crater," under the jurisdiction of the Court of General Sessions of the County of New York, the city's main criminal court. On Monday, September 15, such a grand jury, led by District Attorney Thomas Crain, would start hearing testimony at the Criminal Courthouse, a few blocks from the Supreme Court building where Justice Crater had briefly presided in his courtroom. It was quite an unusual grand jury proceeding because it was uncertain that a crime had been committed, let alone a suspect who had committed a crime, the normal prerequisites for empanelling a grand jury.

Becoming Joseph Crater

CHAPTER THREE

On the Great Stage of Manhattan

I

Little is known of Joseph Crater's early years before he arrived in the metropolis in 1910, at age twenty-one, to matriculate at Columbia University Law School. As one article mentioned after his disappearance, "His life before he came to New York with a burning ambition and able brain is a mystery to many who knew him."[1] But as much as he may have been attracted to the allure of Manhattan, he also was driven away from the parochial, conservative, and overly moralistic world of his family and youth.

Joseph Force Crater Jr. was born on January 5, 1889, the first of four children of Frank Crater and Lilia Montague Crater of Easton, Pennsylvania. Situated on the Delaware River and the smaller rivers that flowed through the Lehigh Valley into it, Easton had developed by the time of his birth into a market center for the local region. His family, of Protestant and German ethnicity like most of the town of approximately 15,000, had quickly achieved some prominence there.

His grandfather, Joseph "Pa" Crater, after whom he was named, had started a wholesale produce company when he came to Easton in 1868. He quickly made a reputation as "a wholesale dealer in Butter, Eggs, Potatoes, Apples, Lard, and Foreign & Domestic Fruits," and his "large trade...extend[ed] throughout the Lehigh Valley, through Pennsylvania, New Jersey and New York." The business included a big warehouse and store in the center of town, with farms in the surrounding areas to supply the produce. When Pa Crater's four sons joined, the firm became known as "J.F. Crater & Sons," one of the town's more prominent businesses.[2]

By the turn of the century, Pa Crater was a "leading citizen of Easton" who had served on the city council, and was a director of a local bank and power company and head of various societies. He was a "strong ally" of the Democratic Party and frequent delegate at its conventions, perhaps explaining his grandson's political affiliation with the party starting in college. The patriarch was reported to be worth a half a million dollars at the turn of the century, quite a large sum for the time and locale. His sons, including Joe's father Frank, all built their houses close to his stately residence in the center of town. Given the paternalistic structure of the family, Frank's first-born son presumably would also enter Pa Crater's business.[3]

Showing early on a sharp intelligence and precociousness, Joe became his parents' favorite child, of whom much was expected. But this did not exempt him, as a boy and young man, from grueling work in the family business, picking fruit and vegetables at the company's farms and unloading and moving heavy crates of produce at the warehouse. The stultifying physical work did broaden and enlarge his shoulders and chest but accentuated his long, skinny neck.[4] Joe must have realized early on that the family produce business was not for him.

Physically fit and imposing at six feet tall, the young man's intelligence, flashy dress, and social poise made an impression on his school mates, teachers, and neighbors in Easton. He attained the highest final grade in his class of fifty-six in high school in 1906 and was awarded a free scholarship to Lafayette College in town. He and two other classmates graduated specializing in the "Classical" curriculum, likely signifying that he intended to go on to higher education. His entry for his class in Easton High School's yearbook, *The Rechauffe*, showed him busy in extracurricular and political activities. He was a member of the Mandolin Club, associate editor of the yearbook, a member of the "Senior Cabinet," and president of his sophomore and junior classes.[5]

Ironically, in hindsight, that year's "Report of the Superintendent of Public Instruction" in Pennsylvania proudly commented that "[w]ith the view of instilling right principles of character and conduct, a systematic course of instruction in morals was introduced" in the Easton schools. It explained, "In this era of graft, greed and corruption with their train of demoralizing influences victimizing the integrity of the community, there is an urgent demand for an effort to fortify our youth against these and other insidious and pernicious influences."[6] But any moral education Joe received in Easton, Pennsylvania, would prove quite inadequate in the metropolis he would make his home.

Joe's reputation in high school appeared to be more that of a popular, outgoing, and smart-alecky guy than a studious and smart one. A friend of his in high school and college, Dr. John West, later described him as "a sparkler—the type who would attract attention anywhere. Tall, medium-complexioned, dark hair and eyes, a natty dresser, positive, witty, with plenty of poise—the kind who could warm up to anybody—fit in anywhere."[7] The yearbook's comment about him suggested his focus was not on academics: "This young man is widely known for his extraordinarily large vocabulary. Most of his time in school, that is the Senior term, was spent in working out schemes of bluffing our faculty. Crater has become known as the 'Cheap Sport of 1906' as evidenced by his abundant supply of gaudy neckwear." His picture shows a debonair young man, flaunting a bowtie. But what was very evident from the start was Crater's attraction to, and obsession with, the opposite sex. An additional comment in his high school yearbook seems rather unusual for the Victorian times, stating, "Joe entered High School with the idea of studying for the ministry, but this is only a glimmer of the past. 'Woman' has become his permanent study. He claims to have passed the infants and is now studying the 'Elders' of that sex."[8]

Joe's pursuit of his interests and predilections continued in his four years at Lafayette College right in his hometown. Not seeming to make much of a scholastic mark there, he continued with his mandolin playing, joined the Democratic Club, and was a member of the Sigma Chi fraternity. His major at Lafayette was again a generic "Classical," but there were signs of his budding legal frame of mind, including a yearbook citation as an underclassman that "[h]e could distinguish and divide a hair 'twixt' south and southwest side."[9]

His graduation photograph in his college yearbook showed him with a serious expression, already wearing a high, stiff choker collar to hide his scrawny neck that he would permanently adopt, and his hair parted in the middle and slicked down on top. Much of the comment next to his picture focused on his social pretensions, calling him "one big good fellow," and his penchant for the opposite sex and jaunty appearance, referring to his "eagle eye and gay tie," his "finely-plastered hair," and his "authoritative work on 'Marriage and Neckties.'" His yearbook entry made short shrift of his other abilities, saying he was "some musician" in the Mandolin Club, and his having "at least, made it through sheer merit." A relative in Easton later recalled of his time there that "he liked night life and 'lived big.'"[10]

But there was a darker side to his coming of age in Easton which many in the town were well aware of. By the time he graduated Lafayette College, his sexual promiscuity was becoming compulsive. After his disappearance, the editor of the Easton newspaper would tell a NYPD detective sent to interview him that the young man was "a rotter, a debaucher, selfish, egotistical cad who had a venereal disease and transmitted it to the ruination of many girls of the City. To deflower seemed a fixation."[11] When asked on the thirtieth anniversary of his disappearance, a woman who had married into the Crater family and knew Joe as a young man would say, "He could talk on any subject. Teachers respected his brainpower. I could say a lot more but I'd rather not."[12]

Uninterested in the family's produce business and developing an unsavory reputation in the town, Joe set his sights on leaving Easton for good. After graduation from Lafayette College in 1910 and against his family's wishes, Crater applied and was accepted to the law school of Columbia University in Manhattan. His mother was said to have given him the proverbial warnings about New York City, that it was a "wicked city" and "den of iniquity," but to no avail.[13]

Crater's new life in the metropolis effectively ended his connections to Easton and his youth spent there. He henceforth would never use the "Jr." in his name, perhaps seeking psychological distance from his prominent Easton namesake. He thereafter rarely returned to his hometown and would become estranged from his parents, Frank and Lilia, who moved to Florida after the he and his brothers ran Pa Crater's produce company into bankruptcy in the 1920s. Joe's youngest brother, Montague, then living in North Dakota, would write a rather plaintive letter to Joe, which would be found and opened by investigators after its addressee had vanished: "How are you anyway, never hear from you and don't know what you are doing so all that is left me to do is assume....Joe, it sure makes me feel proud to think you are a Judge for I know you have been working hard for a long time for it."[14]

2

Just sixty miles east from Easton, Pennsylvania, lay the mecca of Gotham, a world unto itself and free of the many strictures and limitations of his hometown. Like many young and ambitious people flocking there from the nation's countryside and towns, Joe Crater came with few resources or connections to live in the preeminent city of America, its capital of business and finance, the legal profession, culture, and consumption. Using his talents and abilities along with an unusual facility to traverse the diverse worlds of municipal politics, legal practice, theater and nightlife over the next twenty years, Crater would remake himself on a larger stage.

By the time Joe Crater arrived in Manhattan, the population of the newly consolidated boroughs of New York City numbered approximately 4.8 million people, more than twice as many as second-place Chicago, with about half that number concentrated in Manhattan.[15] Spread over more than three hundred square miles, the metropolis contained the most spectacular buildings, the largest infrastructure, the most celebrated public works, and most extensive transportation system in the nation. Manhattan's skyline had begun its epic rise and expansion; in New York County alone in 1910, new construction of buildings totaled more than one-fifth of the construction in all the cities in the nation that year.[16] Its great port then took in about three-quarters of the country's arriving immigrants as well as about two-thirds of its commercial imports.[17] With the rise of Wall Street and the location of corporate headquarters there, the city had become the new center of the nation's financial, business, and legal worlds by the turn of the century. Not only the nation's first city quantitatively in the early twentieth century, the metropolis had come to dominate almost all facets of the nation's mindset and culture. "Its magazines go everywhere, standardizing ideas," a British visitor observed. "Its slang invades the remotest recesses, standardizing speech; its melodies are in every home, standardizing entertainment; the very thought of Broadway, the Main Street of all America, thrills millions who are scattered far and wide."[18] From the backwaters of a Pennsylvania town, Crater had landed in the heart of the bustling, rich, diverse, dynamic, and most celebrated metropolis of the nation, and increasingly, of the world.

When Joe matriculated in the fall of 1910, the new Columbia University campus, recently relocated from downtown, consisted of a few new Classical-style buildings set in an undeveloped area on the western edge of Harlem overlooking the North River. The university's law school, one of the nation's oldest, was in the process of enhancing its reputation as a premiere institution. That year, the law school had appointed a new dean, Harlan Fiske Stone, whose illustrious career would later include being appointed US attorney general and then to the Supreme Court, eventually becoming its chief justice. Also that year, a new building to house the law school had been opened, Kent

Hall (still standing but not as the home of the law school), which included a law library that "not only [is] admirably adapted for its purpose, but has great architectural dignity," and lecture rooms having a capacity of up to 250 students.[19]

At the time of Crater's admission, the law school had about four hundred students and fifteen faculty members in total.[20] A committee report that year referred to recent beneficial changes to the law school curriculum through "new methods of instruction, a better educated student body as a result of the elevation of the standard of admissions to the Law School, a large increased faculty, a broader curriculum, the extension of courses to three years, the development of research work in public and private law, and the monthly publication of the Columbia Law Review."[21]

The "new method" of instruction, which Columbia and other elite law schools were then embracing, would greatly influence Joe's legal career. Introduced by a Harvard Law School professor, Christopher Columbus Langdell, and known as the "case method" of legal education, it focused on analyzing judicial decisions and other precedents and attempting to deduce legal principles and rules from them that could be applied to new cases and issues that arose, instead of the rote memorization of the substance of the law as previously taught. Law professors also would engage students in class in Socratic-style dialogues about case decisions and the principles to be adduced from them. As one legal historian has described the method, "For Langdell, law was not an art but a science which by careful study, as if through a microscope, would reveal its classifications and principles."[22]

This new theory of legal education and its practice was greatly facilitated by the increasing availability of legal reference materials: more opinions from cases in different courts were being consolidated in case "reporters"; more statutes and rules of municipal, state, and federal governments were being compiled; and more legal commentaries and treatises explaining the law and cases were being written. All of these resources were published in greater numbers and distributed to law libraries and lawyers' offices throughout the country. As a prominent New York lawyer remarked around this time, "On the whole, the effect of the large number of adjudged cases contained in the [case] reports has virtually transformed the profession from a class of lawyers able to practice without law books to a class almost entirely dependent on the adjudged cases."[23]

But despite his intellectual abilities later evident in his legal career, Crater surprisingly did not make much of a mark academically at the law school. He did not attain any academic accolades such as selection to the Law Review, nor did he achieve any honors upon his graduation with a Bachelor of Law degree in 1913. Perhaps the distractions of Gotham were beginning to be too great for him. His lackadaisical academic record was similar to that of another recent graduate of Columbia law school, Franklin Delano Roosevelt, who by that time already had given up a legal career for politics. The two men's lives, however, would critically intersect in 1930, when Roosevelt, as New York governor, would appoint Crater a Supreme Court justice, the consequences of which would in turn imperil Roosevelt's ascent to the presidency.

Passing the New York bar examination after graduation, Crater's prospects as a lawyer in the city remained discouraging, with his lack of contacts, mentors, relatives, or other connections there. He was entering the nation's preeminent legal community, renowned for its talents, wealth, and the sophistication of its practice. The expansion of the legal industry there was an outgrowth of Manhattan's concentration of the country's financial, corporate, retail, trade, and manufacturing businesses. Furthermore, the new mammoth corporations, holding companies, banks, and trusts headquartered in lower Manhattan, needed counsel for their creation, operation, and expansion, and to navigate in the increasingly complex waters of the business and political worlds.

New Wall Street law firms, many of them still extant today with some name permutations, were formed to service their Wall Street clients in their stock offerings, acquisitions, commercial transactions, and litigation. The very purpose of these new business lawyers and firms advising the big corporations and financial institutions, was "to keep his client out of trouble, and, most of all, out of court," where attorneys traditionally had practiced.[24] But new opportunities for courtroom lawyers, now known as litigators, also arose from lawsuits involving violations of the proliferating laws and regulations governing the city, including those for workers' unemployment and safety, zoning, civil service, and vehicular traffic. When Crater graduated law school, it was estimated that the New York City bar numbered over fifteen thousand attorneys—plenty of competition for a young out-of-towner.[25]

Joe Crater quickly took to a relatively new area of legal practice, an outgrowth of the new legal teaching methods and the increasing importance of legal publications and law libraries. Referred to as appellate practice, its practitioners, then as now, appeared in the appeals courts, seeking review of and affirmance or reversal of legal rulings or determinations made by a judge in a lower or trial court. It required a more cerebral bent and a combination of strong research, analytic, writing, and oral argument skills. The mainstay of this practice, at which Crater especially excelled, was researching and writing legal memorandums or "briefs," which present for the appellate court an argumentative analysis of the legal issues on behalf of the client, replete with references to past judicial precedents and other authorities to support the client's position. An effective appellate attorney necessarily possessed a broad knowledge of many areas of substantive law and a good memory for pertinent precedents that could be analogized and rapidly marshaled into an effective argument.

While handling some appeals brought by criminal defendants early in his career, Joe's growing legal practice was comprised mainly of civil and commercial litigation matters in which he represented insurance companies, businesses, employers, wealthy individuals, investors, and even his alma mater, Columbia University—clients who readily paid his increasing legal fees. The variety of cases published in the legal reporters where he appeared as appellate counsel suggest the breadth of areas of his practice, including commercial law, negligence and personal injury law, employment law, landlord-tenant law, matrimonial law, contract law, trusts and estates, labor law, trademark law, and proceedings before administrative agencies.

In addition to writing briefs, an appellate lawyer, then as now, was (and is) responsible for orally arguing the appeal before the appellate court comprised of a panel of judges. Each counsel, allotted a limited time to argue, tries to highlight the most salient issues and arguments in the appeal as well as to answer any questions about their arguments posed by the judges. By all accounts, Joe Crater was not an outstanding oral advocate and not very quick on his feet when responding to questions. He typically appeared at these arguments dressed in a formal morning coat and said as little as necessary, relying instead on the strong appellate briefs he had submitted beforehand.

Crater soon had attracted attention in the city's legal community as a prolific and able writer of appellate briefs. Simon Rifkind, who later worked with Joe on legal matters in Senator Wagner's office, considered the older man his mentor in this regard. He still recalled sixty years later, "I was a very young admittee to the bar at the time....He taught me how to write...an appellate brief, and he could do it faster than anyone I'd ever seen, then or since."[26] Everyone agreed that Crater had a superb and facile legal mind. "He was a dynamic sort of man—full of nervous energy—his brain seemed to be working continuously," one longtime friend would later remark.[27] His fixation on his legal work was such that he purportedly gave up driving his automobile after almost running off the road in Maine while contemplating a legal matter. He would soon impart his legal wisdom to law students as a popular professor at local law schools, including those of Fordham University and New York University.

3

As a young lawyer trying to establish himself in the illustrious New York bar, Joe Crater quickly grasped the importance of becoming active in municipal politics, which would also be crucial to his achieving his ambition of becoming a judge later on. After a few years of living in Manhattan, he had to have been cognizant of the omniscient power and control that Tammany Hall, the Democratic political machine of New York County, exerted over all aspects of the city's government and business. This included its influence in the legal profession, where Tammany-connected lawyers were favored with lucrative court-appointed positions and representation of clients before governmental boards and agencies controlled by it, while some of the elite lawyers of the city bar were prominently associated as legal advisors to the machine's leaders. Joe "realized that politics was rotten," his wife would later recall, "but the excitement of the campaigns, the intrigue, the opportunity to make a lot of money and build up security overcame his natural feelings."[28]

Crater's entry point into Tammany Hall was at a peripheral local clubhouse not far from the Columbia University campus and near where he was residing after law school. He joined the Cayuga Democratic Club of the Nineteenth Assembly District, which encompassed the middle of Harlem, extending roughly north from West 118th Street to 136th Street, and west from Madison Avenue to around Eighth Avenue. As Crater undoubtedly realized from residing there, it was a section of Manhattan undergoing a wrenching transition.

At the turn of the century, Harlem had been an affluent white neighborhood known for its stately brownstone homes on tree-lined streets. Comprised largely of German and Jewish residents, the area had its own businesses, stores, churches, synagogues, and theaters and was considered a suburb of the city downtown. New public transportation connections between Harlem and midtown and downtown Manhattan resulted in a boom of construction of brownstones, apartment buildings, and tenement buildings in the upper part of the island. In the first years of the new century, as real estate prices began to fall because of overbuilding, African Americans living in downtown Manhattan and those migrating from the Southern states, along with immigrants from Caribbean islands, began to move to cheaper, plentiful housing above 135th Street. New real estate companies started by black entrepreneurs, such as the Afro-American Realty Company, hastened the process, buying apartment buildings and brownstones in the area from their white owners and renting them to people of their own race in overcrowded, overpriced, and subdivided apartments and rooms, which in turn caused an increasing exodus of white and ethnic residents.[29]

By the time Crater joined the Cayuga Club in the second decade of the century, African Americans and other minorities had begun moving from northern Harlem into smaller, cheaper residences in the West 120s and 130s streets, leading to further white flight. For example, the change in percentage of black people residing in the Nineteenth Assembly District went from almost nothing in 1910 to almost 35 percent ten years later. Over the 1920s, nearly 170,000 African American residents would replace about 118,000 white residents in Harlem, contributing to the increasing overcrowding and poverty of the area.[30]

The changing racial demographics of Harlem during this time also had a marked effect on its politics. At the turn of the century, most blacks who were still able to vote in the nation maintained an allegiance to the Republican Party of the "Great Emancipator," Abraham Lincoln, and were hostile to the Democratic Party as the party of secession and the Jim Crow South. Still, the Tammany Democratic machine had begun to make some efforts to attract black votes in Manhattan. Boss Richard Croker, wanting to preserve the white, largely Irish, leadership of Tammany Hall, had set up an auxiliary party organization known as the United Colored Democracy (UCD).

Composed of parallel but racially separate local clubs, the UCD was directed by an African American Tammany boss, who by the time Crater entered Tammany politics was Ferdinand Morton. As a historian of black politics in the city described the arrangement, "The [UCD] which, on paper, controlled all political and patronage matters that concerned the city's blacks was, in fact, a powerless segregated institution whose primary tasks were winning votes for Tammany and isolating blacks from positions of real political

influence."[31] Additionally, while growing numbers of black people were moving into central and southern Harlem, Tammany had gerrymandered Harlem's assembly districts in 1917, "so that no one black segment could outvote
the white territory to which it had been attached." In 1920, the Nineteenth
Assembly District was composed of approximately 65 percent white residents,
including those of German, Irish, and Jewish lineage. By 1930, the year Crater
disappeared, the district included 70 percent African American residents.[32]

A rigid racial segregation still pervaded the Cayuga Democratic Club
throughout the 1920s. J. Raymond Jones, who was a young community leader
from the Caribbean islands and much later would become Tammany's first
black boss, recalled an incident during that decade when he was working as a
Democratic election inspector in black neighborhoods in the assembly district. Seeking to deliver as instructed registration books of its voters to the
Cayuga Club then located "in a limestone house in one of the better neighborhoods of Harlem," Jones was refused admittance by the doorkeeper and
told, "Never mind what the instructions say....This club is not for coloreds.
Chicken Bank's [Restaurant] is the club for coloreds."[33]

Despite its electoral appeals for the black community's support, Tammany
maintained an uneasy relationship with it in the latter years of the 1920s. In
each of his mayoral victories, Jimmy Walker obtained less than half of the
black vote, far less that his predecessor John Hylan who was not affiliated
with the machine.[34] Walker's imposition of a 3 a.m. curfew on the city's nightclubs in early 1927, a crackdown on gambling in Harlem, and diminishing
patronage opportunities from his administration further alienated African
American voters.[35] That same year, Oscar Waters, an ex–district leader of
the UCD, reportedly stated how "the interests of the negro Democrats have
been absolutely ignored by Tammany Hall," adding facetiously, "We might as
well be back down South for all the consideration we are receiving from the
Tammany organization." Waters also blamed Tammany for "every negro club
in Harlem ha[ving] been raided by the police even where card playing was
confined to the members."[36]

As a result of the racial segregation and electoral gerrymandering in Harlem during the 1920s, the Cayuga Club remained an exclusively white bastion
while Crater was active in it. Like the assembly district in general, its membership was composed largely of Irish American members, with some of German and Jewish ethnicity. In keeping with the continuing Irish domination
of the political machine, the boss of the Tammany club whom Joe would be-

come closely associated with also was of that ethnicity.[37] Still, the Cayuga Club, where the young lawyer would get his political legs, increasingly came to resemble a colonial outpost of the Irish American–led Tammany dominion downtown, a last bastion of white men's control over a racially changing Harlem.[38]

Shortly after joining the Cayuga Club, Joe Crater was made a Democratic election district captain. Captains were selected by the Tammany district leader to run the party's operations in a small area known as an "election district," which at the time typically encompassed one or two city blocks, housing about five hundred voters. The election captain functioned, in the words of a contemporary, as "the nuclei of the club-organization, the personal representatives of the [district leader] boss in the neighborhoods and his emissaries."[39] As an election captain, Crater had responsibility for maintaining the party loyalty of the residents in his district, and ensuring they got to the polls and voted the Tammany ticket on election day. But as a lawyer, he had more to offer his club than a typical captain. Stella recalled her husband working "assiduously during election periods," making unending speeches at meetings, luncheons and dinners, and volunteer[ing] his services for any matter concerning elections which arose in the courts." The Craters also entertained a "motley assortment of neighborhood politicos and Tammany Hall hangers-on" obviously not to her liking.[40]

Once he had settled into the Cayuga Club, Crater made the acquaintance of a young, up-and-coming member, Martin J. Healy. Photographs of Healy at the time of Crater's disappearance show a tough-looking man, unsmiling and sometimes with a glowering visage, looking every bit the hard-nosed, street-smart Irish Catholic Tammany ward heeler that he was. Healy seemed to have little in common, personally or professionally, with Joe Crater, the well-educated and ostensibly respectable professional and native-born Protestant from a Pennsylvania town. Yet, improbably, the two men would become close associates, effective collaborators, and friends.

4

As stories of the missing judge's intimacies with chorus girls and mistresses quickly came to light in September 1930, the elite of the New York legal community expressed some surprise at his unprofessional and injudicious lifestyle. "I am shocked and mystified," commented Presiding Justice Victor Dowling of the Appellate Division, who swore Crater in as a judge, "He was a highly qualified lawyer and jurist and I regarded him as a scholar and almost an ascetic. What I have been told about his being a frequenter of night clubs and the subject of a proposed breach of promise suit is entirely at variance with my estimate of his character."[41] But Joseph Crater's obsession with and immersion in Manhattan's world of entertainment and nightlife in the Jazz Age were quite in keeping with the culture and spirit of the times, and his comfortable occupancy of such disparate worlds was not uncommon.

While Crater was a devoted fan of the traditional theater, often attending opening nights of musicals and plays with his wife or friends, there were other attractions drawing him and crowds of others to this section of town in the evenings. By this time, Broadway at night had become a physical fantasia as "on every wall, above every cornice, in every nook and cranny, blossom and dance the electric advertising signs," creating "this massed effect of tremendous jazz interpreted in light."[42] In a very materialistic age, Broadway was the epicenter of entertainment and consumption in the city, frenetically busy with celebrants throughout the night and deep into the morning, packed with heterodox crowds of people, feverishly seeking fun and spending large amounts to obtain it.

Conspicuous consumption was a big part of Broadway's appeal in the Roaring Twenties. Lewis Mumford, a prominent sociologist and literary critic, wrote in 1923:

> Broadway is...the great compensatory device of the American city. The dazzle of white lights, the colour of electric signs, the alabaster architecture of the moving-picture palaces, the aesthetic appeals of the show windows—these stand for elements that are left out of the drab perspectives of the industrial city. People who do not know how to spend their time must take what satisfaction they can in spending their money.[43]

A French author, in his travelogue of the city that was published the year of Crater's disappearance, similarly conveyed the sensual impact of Broadway, stating "The electric lamp is no longer a lighting device, it is a machine for fascinating, a machine for obliterating. Electricity bedizens this weary throng, determined not to go home, determined to spend its money, determined to blind itself with false daylight." Ford Maddox Ford, a British novelist visiting New York City, more succinctly observed, "It is the City of the Good Time—and the Good Time there is so sacred that you may be excused anything you do in searching for it."[44]

The Roaring Twenties also were the Golden Age of Broadway theater. In 1927, there were some sixty theater houses, many of them recently opened, in which 268 plays were presented, including classics like "Show Boat," "Strange Interlude," and "Porgy and Bess."[45] The reason for the extraordinary popularity of theater, however, went beyond the numbers of shows playing or the prosperity of the times. There was something inherently theatrical and dramatic in the mentality of the times. Cultural historian Ann Douglas has described the people of 1920s Manhattan as "the most theatrical generation in American annals," people who "wanted, sometimes desperately, to find out not so much who they were as who they could appear to be, those who needed the gaze of others to come alive, exhibitionists and attention addicts." Attendees of theaters, whether live performances or films, could project or envision their own lives as part of the fantasy depicted. As a British visitor to Broadway explained in 1927: "The theaters have disgorged their gazers and listeners, and those have crossed the footlights and have all become actors themselves....New Yorkers know how to act their parts, but they are greatly helped by the stage and setting."[46]

Crater's fascination with shows in theaters and clubs likely grew out of similar impulses. He was compulsively drawn to watch the stars and fantasies created on stage, where he could have imagined himself, the center of attention. The exceptional amount of nudity and sexually risqué references in 1920s shows such as the *Artists and Models* surely satisfied his prurient interests. Perhaps he especially enjoyed being viewed himself in those venues, a prominent lawyer and later a judge, who was comfortable with throwing aside the trappings of status and stature and to immerse himself in the nightlife. He also seemed intent upon breaking the barriers between the audience and the players on the stage, when for example, he pointed out to his companions that he was familiar with the chorus girls on stage.

Perhaps no contemporary of Crater's embodied this theatrical and epicurean spirit of the decade better than the city's own mayor who was first elected to that office in 1926, the iconic James (known only as "Jimmy") Walker, one of the first successful performer-politicians in American history. A small, boyishly good-looking man with a charismatic smile and sparkly wit and humor, his dress (or costuming) was flashy and often changed a few times each day. Jimmy led the circus and festivities that were Manhattan in the latter part of the Jazz Age, sometimes from city hall but more often from Broadway, the sporting scene, and the nightclubs. Although short on governing accomplishments and long on style, Walker would remain the most popular and beloved mayor of the city, for years after his resignation in the face of corruption charges in 1932.[47]

Walker was a remarkable amalgam of the realms of entertainment and politics. Having actually began his career as a Broadway songwriter with a few hits to his credit (which would become standards during his mayoralty), he reluctantly went to law school and like his father, went into Tammany politics. In his rapid ascent as a New York state senator and its majority leader and then as a two-term mayor, he was at his best as a public speaker and figure with an actor's grace and composure. A 1925 *New Yorker* profile observed that "[e]ach performance is as good as his last; he never disappoints an audience" and "[t]here is the quality of the actor in [him]." While mayor, he made surprise onstage appearances in Broadway shows and "was almost certainly the first American public official to appear in a Hollywood feature film."[48]

He claimed to have only read six books since law school, could only take in information when it was spoken to him, and had attention-deficit issues when it came to governing. Not getting out of bed before noon and spending an inordinate amount of time getting dressed for the day with the help of a butler, Jimmy only worked a few hours in the afternoon, yet because of his agile mind and snap decision-making, he was able to manage the city's complex affairs in a slap-dash fashion. The great prosperity and spree of building in the city in the Twenties, together with the ample property tax revenues generated, made its governance somewhat easier and more profitable for the grafters, whom as later would be revealed, included his oblivious self. When his mayoral salary was increased to a hefty $40,000 in the middle of his tenure, he quipped, "That's cheap! Think of what it would cost if I worked full time." And he proved to be a great booster of the New York City he loved, with his frequent ticker tape parades and receptions for celebrities and foreign figures on lower Broadway, as well as his numerous and extended vacation trips across the country and abroad. As one historian has described Walker's administration, "The people had chosen a musical-comedy mayor to head one of the greatest corporations in this world....If Walker neglected his responsibilities as Mayor, it was not an age of caring about civic responsibilities."[49]

But Walker made his greatest mark on the metropolis after dark. Dubbed the "Night Mayor," he could be found then driven around town in his elegant Duesenberg limousine with his beautiful chorine girlfriend Betty Compton, who was half his age (while his wife of many years lived separately), and attending the theater, boxing fights and other sporting events, nightclubs, and gambling joints. His nightly escapades would be eagerly reported in the newspapers, adding to his celebrity. On one occasion, Jimmy and Betty were gambling at a club in Long Island when it happened to be raided by the local police. The mayor quickly reacted, purportedly running into the kitchen, donning an apron, and posing as kitchen help, while his girlfriend was led away by the police.[50]

Jimmy and "Monk," his nickname for Betty, even had their own nightclub to be seen in. At the Mayor's request, an ornate, luxurious Art Deco restaurant and nightclub named the Casino was built in Central Park by a restauranteur friend with money raised from Tammany men and other questionable sources. Its main ballroom, stylishly decorated in silver, maroon, and gold with a black glass ceiling, featured top jazz bands that played dance music for the assembled revelers, most of whom had ties with Jimmy. Upstairs, out of the public eye, there was a private duplex where he would entertain and meet with friends, Tammany associates, and those who wished to transact city business. It was joked that the mayor spent more time at the Casino than at city hall.[51]

5

The nightclubs opening in Broadway and other areas of town had become the new venue for much of the voyeurism, conspicuous consumption, and exuberance of the Jazz Age. Featuring celebrity hosts and hostesses such as the eponymous "Texas" Guinan, top bands and orchestras, and barely dressed dancers and chorines, the clubs brought together a socially and economically diverse crowd, all clamoring for fun and hoopla, and often paying an exorbitant amount to do so. "The spectacular décor, the entertainment, and the exhilarating experience of breaking the law [during Prohibition] in a nightclub or cabaret attracted a mixture of people from all levels of society," as one historian has described the scene. "Whether midtown clerks, Fifth Avenue socialites, Irish politicians, street toughs, plumbers or housewives, patrons were transported by the sense of freedom and possibility brought about by dancing and drinking in an unregulated environment with unfamiliar people." At Connie's Inn, a popular Harlem nightclub that Crater attended, it was reported in 1929 that the assembled public figures in attendance on one night included journalist Mark Hellinger, actor Jack Pickford, heiress Gertrude Vanderbilt, gangster Dutch Schultz (believed to be an owner), and Harry K. Thaw, who gained celebrity as the man who killed architect Stanford White over a chorus girl. A reporter described the club as "merely Texas Guinan's with a colored orchestra" and "the guests...are mainly graduates of the Guinan school of spending."[52]

For Joe Crater (himself not a big drinker or a liberal spender) and other attendees, the nightclubs offered a place of entertainment and merriment, a chance to be part of (as well as seen by) a glamorous and high-profile crowd, and to gain social cache and even notoriety. A chorus girl remembered him saying rather proudly to her at a club in the summer of 1930, "You know, I'm married and a judge, and a lot of people might see me here and talk about it."[53] Like so many others frequenting the clubs and hot spots of the new Manhattan nightlife, he wanted and needed to see and be seen.

By the end of the decade, racketeers and gangsters, having obtained a monopoly on the importing, distributing, and selling of liquor and beer in the city, had infiltrated the nightclub world. Many popular clubs were openly owned, financed, or protected by gangsters and bootleggers. After a murderous gunfight in a nightclub owned by Jack "Legs" Diamond in 1929, Police Commissioner Grover Whalen announced with some anxiety that "gangdom is in control of the night clubs" and warned "decent people to keep away from such places." But the actual presence of gangsters in a club seemed to add cache to it, leading a *New York Times* editorial at the time to criticize the "reputable citizens" who patronized such clubs: "Many find it 'thrilling' to see gangsters in dinner coats as fellow-guests. It doesn't bother them that their cover charges go into underworld pockets, so long as they are 'entertained' and have 'places to go.'"[54]

Crater had frequented one of the "hot" nightclubs, the Club Abbey, during the summer of 1930, and as recently as August 4, two days before he vanished. Owned in part by gangster Owney Madden, the Club Abbey was located in the Harding Hotel at Seventh Avenue and Fifty-Fourth Street, benefiting from the hotel's exemption from the city's curfews for nightclubs. It boasted "a 'cuff' or 'red ink' section for celebrated gangsters, representatives of the law, and a few Broadway columnists who don't feel they should be called upon to pay for their food, drink and entertainment." Comedian Jimmy Durante, who headlined shows there, wondered why the Club Abbey was the only spot doing a strong business during that summer, since its chorus girls "aren't any more nude than the chorines elsewhere." But the club would be shut down a few months later, after deadly gunplay broke out among some of the show-piece gangsters, including Schultz, the bootlegging and gambling kingpin.[55]

Like many of the city's white revelers in the Jazz Age, Joe Crater also ventured up to Harlem on occasion. Earlier in the 1920s, shows with black performers had gone from Harlem to Broadway, where they popularized the new dances and music, while books like Carl Van Vechten's *Nigger Heaven* had created the image of Harlem as a wild African American mecca. By the end of the decade, white celebrants "began making the trek north in large numbers, partly for the wider opportunities for alcohol and partly because of the aura of exotic release surrounding the area and blacks." Durante raved about the "primitive" Harlem night clubs, putting on "real hotsy-totsy" shows where "[t]hese coloured people have a feeling for dancing and singing" and "[t]hey can shake their feet like nobody's business." Or as James Weldon Johnson, one of the leaders of the Harlem Renaissance, more sarcastically saw it, "On occasions, I have been amazed and amused watching white people dancing to a Negro band in a Harlem cabaret;...striving to yield to the feel and experience of abandon; seeking to recapture a state of primitive joy in life and living;...in a word, doing their best to pass for colored."[56]

As the police would later learn, Crater went with his mistress in late July that summer to Connie's Inn, which Durante called "[t]he swankiest of all the Harlem places." He described the décor as tropical, including a "three-foot barrier around the dance floor, and the room is made up like a village, with miniature bungalows." While Connie's and other top Harlem clubs featured top black entertainers like Duke Ellington, Cab Calloway, and Fats Waller, only white audiences were allowed to patronize them. Drawing "racial lines" was necessary, the comedian added, "to prevent possible trouble," and "the chances of a war are less if there's no mixing."[57]

For Crater and his contemporaries, such immersion in exotic fun, acting, and crossing into other milieus came naturally. One journalist, trying to recapture the man and his times a decade later, wrote, "Broadway knew Joseph Force Crater and liked him for the Jekyll-and-Hyde it knew him to be. It isn't often you will find a man who can strip off the dignity of high places and descend without conscious effort to rub elbows with the guttersnipe of the Roaring Forties [of Manhattan]." Back then, "[t]here were few doorkeepers in front of the hot spots of mid-Manhattan who failed to recognize Judge Crater when he passed."[58]

Crater's immersion and comfortable presence in the theatrical and night-life circles of Jazz Age Manhattan, replete as it was with opportunities for blackmail because of his extramarital womanizing and the presence of criminal figures capable of disposing of someone, would provide constant grist for explaining why he disappeared. His being last seen in the heart of Broadway and parting from the Shuberts' lawyer William Klein and a chorus girl he had dined with naturally stoked such explanations.

CHAPTER FOUR

The New Tammany Hall

I

As Joe became a regular at the Cayuga Club in Harlem, fundamential changes were taking place downtown at the Wigwam of Tammany Hall on East Fourteenth Street. For the first fifty years of its reign in New York City, the political machine had been run by a succession of street-smart, working class, and venal bosses—William Tweed, Richard Croker, and the misnamed "Honest John" Kelly—who were jailed, fled the country and deposed, respectively. But after the turn of the century, a new leader had taken charge who sought to transform the machine from a corrupt political ring into an effective political organization, from a graft-generating enterprise enriching only its leaders to a progressive and popular one that used the government and its perogatives to benefit its supporters.

There was little in Charles Francis Murphy's early years to suggest he would become a different type of leader than his predecessors. From an Irish American immigrant family and with little formal education, he had risen in his local Tammany club in the "Gashouse District" in the East Twenties of Manhattan, helped by his being an outstanding baseball player on his local team, and he owned neighborhood saloons at which his club often congregated. Once he became district leader of the club, he leveraged his new power to rapidly enrich himself, being appointed by Tammany mayors to some lucrative municipal posts, such as dock commissioner, and getting sweetheart contracts from the municipal government for his businesses.[1]

A taciturn, owlish, and officious-looking man with the mien of a bookkeeper, Murphy was so reserved both in public and in private, that he earned the nickname "Silent Charlie." He got his moniker, according to one story, when a reporter questioned why he didn't appear to be singing the national anthem at one of its Independence Day festivities. In response, one of the attendees told him that perhaps Murphy remained silent because he didn't want to commit himself.[2] He did keep his own counsel, and rarely confided in others about his plans. Also unlike his predecessors, Murphy had a strong moral and religious streak and abhorred the immoral ways previous Tammany leaders had made money through prostitution, gambling, and other criminal activities. But he was a shrewd strategist, deliberate and cautious, and had an uncanny ability to read the political tea leaves, which had enabled him to beat out rivals to replace Boss Croker soon after the turn of the century, when he was run out of the city and spent his final years exiled in England.

Charlie Murphy's most inspired idea was to adapt Tammany Hall to the city's rapidly changing politics and demographics, and to attempt to modernize the old, rusty machine by realigning it with the Progressive reform movement sweeping New York in the second decade of the twentieth century.[3] Much of the Progressive agenda, such as reforms in working conditions and safety, government assistance to the disabled and poor, improved housing and health codes, and regulation of business in the public interest, was beneficial to Tammany's main constituents—the urban, immigrant, and ethnic working-class voters and their families. As Murphy once explained his support of a progressive-backed bill to a surprised reformer, "It is my observation that that bill made us many votes."[4] Franklin Roosevelt, a bitter foe early in his career, would praise him after his death, saying, "It is well to remember that he had helped to accomplish much in the way of progressive legislation and social welfare in our state."[5]

Murphy additionally helped launch and carefully guide the political careers of Bob Wagner and Al Smith, who would come to embody the so-called New Tammany he was aiming to create. Dubbed the "Tammany Twins" by the press, the two men from poor immigrant families had joined local clubs in Manhattan and were elected to the New York state legislature. Boss Murphy then had maneuvered to have Smith chosen as Speaker of the Assembly, the lower house of the legislature, in 1913, and Wagner as the Majority Leader of the Senate a few years before.

During the second decade of the new century, Smith and Wagner had overseen the enactment of a plethora of legislation for the benefit of Tammany's supporters and other constituents. Perhaps the high point of their legislative careers occurred when in the aftermath of the tragic Triangle Shirtwaist Company factory fire near Washington Square Park in 1911, Wagner became chairman and Smith vice chairman of the New York State Factory Investigating Commission. Holding well-publicized hearings and inspections of working conditions in factories across the state, they then pushed through the legislature a raft of pioneering laws regulating worker's hours and safety conditions and prohibiting child labor in New York, one of the first states in the country to do so. But the Twins' progressivism did have its limits. They also oversaw enactment of legislation that weakened the city's civil service system and preserved plenty of wasteful and unnecessary jobs in the municipal government to which the party faithful could be appointed.

Setting his sights on higher office, Al Smith, the self-schooled man from the Irish slums of the Lower East Side, ran for and was elected governor of New York in 1918, the first Roman Catholic and the first Irish American to hold that office. Murphy fully supported and assisted him in his race, and upon his protégé's election, he made a point of telling him that while he might ask for favors, "[i]f I ever ask you to do anything which you think would impair your record as a great governor, just tell me so and that will be the end of it."[6] The Tammany boss proved true to his word, and Smith lived up to his phenomenal political potential, serving three more gubernatorial terms during the 1920s. His success and popularity as governor in implementing the progressive agenda in New York, including laws regulating utilities and waterpower, providing benefits to the aged and the unemployed, and building housing, hospitals and public works, had raised his sights to the US presidency in 1924.

Boss Murphy's New Tammany also attempted to modernize the machine when it came to how it made its money. He abhorred vice and immorality in general and disapproved of the way its leaders profited under his predecessor Richard Croker, from interests in criminal endeavors like gambling, prostitution, and illegal saloons as well as from protection payments made to the police to allow such establishments to stay open. In the New Tammany, the gold standard in grafting was known as "honest graft."

To make sense of this peculiar and subtle change requires an understanding of then prevalent concepts of grafting that were colorfully explicated years before by a district leader with the hybrid name of George Washington Plunkitt. Plunkitt, of Irish immigrant stock and with little education, was in the habit of giving extemporaneous lectures about the political machine from his seat on a bootblack stand in the old courthouse, which a reporter had transcribed and published in 1905 with the subtitle, "A Series of Very Plain Talks on Very Practical Politics." A young Boss Murphy even penned a laudatory "Introduction" to the book.[7]

In one of Plunkitt's vernacular talks entitled "Honest and Dishonest Graft," he stated, "There's all the difference in the world between two." He admitted to making "a big fortune out of the game [of politics], and I'm gettin' richer every day, but I've not gone in for dishonest graft—blackmailin' gamblers, saloon-keepers, disorderly people,...levyin' blackmail on disorderly houses, or workin' in with gamblers and lawbreakers." Perhaps having in mind Boss Croker's rule, he asked, "[W]hy should the Tammany leaders go into such dirty businesses when there is so much honest graft lyin' around when they are in power?" He summed up his practicing of such graft with his mantra, "I seen my opportunities and I took 'em."[8]

Plunkitt gave several examples of honest grafting schemes, which typically functioned as follows: "[m]y party's in power in the city," and "I'm tipped off" to a government plan or action before it "makes its plan public," and his investment in property or materials that the government plan requires pays off. "Ain't it perfectly honest to...make a profit on my investment and foresight?" he rhetorically asked. "Of course it is. Well that's honest graft." What Plunkitt was condoning was insiders and allies being tipped off in advance with nonpublic, confidential information about government plans and using such information for their own private financial gain. Nothing was wrong with such schemes, in Plunkitt's mind, because "the Tammany heads of departments looked after their friends, within the law, and gave them what opportunities they could to make honest graft."[9]

Of course, such conduct as Plunkitt was encouraging would be blatantly illegal nowadays and would be prosecutable as crimes such as abusing insider information, acting on conflicts of interest, fixing awards of government contracts, or conspiring to defraud the public till. Indeed, Plunkitt analogized his schemes to "lookin ahead in Wall Street or in the coffee or cotton market," presumably with insider information, which has been an established crime for many years.[10] In the Tammany Hall of the 1920s, however, honest grafting was considered in political, legal, and business circles to be a legitimate and accepted way of making money as well as just reward and payback for leaders and allies of the party.

Throughout his twenty-year reign as boss, Murphy would practice what Plunkitt preached. While his grafting schemes sometimes failed, as will be discussed shortly, many others were quite remunerative. For example, he reaped huge profits from the award of state construction contracts to do the demolition and excavation work involved in building the original Pennsylvania railroad station on West Thirty-Third Street in Manhattan, through a company nominally owned by his brother but in which he had an undisclosed interest. When he died, the erstwhile city saloonkeeper had amassed an estate worth more than $2 million, including a fifty-acre summer home called "Good Ground" on Long Island, on which he had built a nine-hole golf course.[11]

2

In his first years practicing law in the city, Crater had assisted older attorneys with their cases and appeals, typically drafting legal briefs and other court papers. The official case reporters include five cases during that time where he is listed as the second attorney, including two appeals of criminal convictions to New York's highest court, the Court of Appeals.[12] His legal career received a huge boost, however, when he was selected to be Justice Robert Wagner's law secretary in 1920, a post he would remain in for six years until his election to the US Senate. It is not known whether he was recommended to Wagner through his legal connections or those of his Tammany district club but for the thirty-one-year-old, the job and relationship would prove crucial to his legal and political ambitions.

As the judge's law secretary, his job was to do much of Justice Wagner's legal thinking, writing, and even decision-making in the cases before him, all behind the scenes, and to be the liaison between the judge and the lawyers appearing in those cases. The job entailed extensive legal research, advising on resolutions of issues in cases, and drafting the legal decisions and orders for the judge, which by all accounts he did extremely well. Wagner quickly grasped his law secretary's exceptional abilities in this regard, and as his biographer would note, the justice would heavily rely upon the "brain power [of Crater], a brilliant young lawyer."[13]

In addition to working for a judge of sterling reputation who also was a prominent politician, the young lawyer would be situated at the courthouse downtown, where he had the opportunity to meet and make invaluable contacts with prominent lawyers there as well as other judges and law secretaries. Wagner, a star of the New Tammany, also had access to its politicians and top lawyers with whom Crater could ingratiate himself. Over the years, the two men would form a very close relationship, somewhat mentor-protégé and somewhat father-son, which explained his distraught and angry reaction (in private) to his acolyte vanishing in early September 1930.

Once elected to the Supreme Court with Tammany's support, Justice Wagner continued to aggressively promote the progressive agenda he had championed as a state legislator. His philosophy of judicial activism was quite different from the legal orthodoxies Crater had been taught in law school. Downplaying the significance of prior judicial decisions as having been "worn out by time and made useless by a more enlightened and human conception of social justice," he remarked in a speech, "[t]hat progressive sentiment of advanced civilization, which has compelled legislative action to correct and improve conditions which a proper regard for humanity would no longer tolerate, cannot be ignored by the courts."[14] Wagner's progressive bent was evident also in his rulings in some prominent cases to come before him. In one case he presided over, New York City landlords were challenging the new rent control laws enacted in the face of housing shortages after World War I, laws that have remain in effect. He ruled firmly that the legislature's authority to protect the general welfare of its citizens outweighed the landlords' property rights to maximize their profits, writing he "cannot subscribe to any doctrine that hinders or restrains our legislative power from enacting a clear and reasonable design to relieve the actual distress of thousands of tenants who would otherwise be made homeless."[15]

Foreshadowing his later role in championing the enactment of federal labor laws protecting unions during the New Deal, some of which would bear his name, Justice Wagner generally supported the unions' right to organize, strike, and enforce the terms of collective bargaining agreements. In one case before him, the garment workers' union was suing to prevent their employers from violating their collective bargaining agreement, a reversal of the usual lawsuits by employers to prohibit the union workers from violating the agreement. Wagner used the court's power to impose an injunction against the employers to abide by the agreement, ruling that the workers "are entitled to have exercised in their behalf the restraining power of the court, when their legal rights are obstructed, to the same extent as it had been exercised to protect the contractual rights of the employers."[16]

But shortly after his appointment as Bob Wagner's law secretary, Joe had an opportunity to observe firsthand Tammany's influence in the courts. Near the end of the First World War, Boss Murphy had invested in an American company that had a lucrative contract to supply the British government with a glucose product for British brewers to use in making beer. To ensure the success of his venture, he proceeded to employ his political connections to obtain approval from the US government to authorize the sale of glucose at a time when foodstuffs were being strictly rationed to the public. Growing concerned about the optics of the transaction, Murphy decided to pull out of the deal (but still wanted a share of the profits being made), commenting, it was reported, that he "can't afford to stay in this business—the head of Tammany Hall profiteering on foodstuffs, especially in war time."[17]

After the war, a county grand jury indicted Murphy and others involved in the deal for conspiring to defraud the US government of a large amount of wartime excess profits taxes that had not been paid on the profits they had received. The criminal case somehow wound up being assigned to none other than Justice Robert Wagner. Despite legal challenges that the criminal case was not properly before him, he retained jurisdiction and dismissed the indictment against Murphy for lack of "sufficient legal proof [of] a scheme to defraud the United States."[18] Tammany's ability to manipulate the state and local courts to protect its interests would become increasingly evident to the young lawyer as the decade progressed.

3

Having joined the Cayuga Club by the time of his appointment as Wagner's law secretary, Crater was introduced to a Tammany leader of a distinctly different bent than Smith or Murphy. Although possessed of a similar pedigree, Marty Healy, who would become the Democratic district leader of the Nineteenth Assembly District in 1925, operated in a world apart from New Tammany's leaders. His was an arena of nitty-gritty, corrupt ward politics as traditionally practiced, which by the end of the decade was particularly resistant to the spirit of change in the machine.

Martin J. Healy was born into a large family one generation removed from Ireland and grew up in an upstanding Irish neighborhood in what is now the western part of Greenwich Village. Like many of these new immigrants to a strange city, his father parleyed his personal and political connections in the Irish community into successful business enterprises and some municipal patronage jobs. As a young boy, Marty befriended a neighbor his age, Jimmy

Walker, and the two would remain close as they advanced to the higher echelons of Tammany politics.

At the turn of the century, Healy's family, which was part of the newly emerging middle class of "lace curtain Irish," moved uptown in Manhattan to the more affluent, then-suburb of West Harlem.[19] Trained as an accountant but involved in some business ventures of his own, Martin naturally gravitated to the local Tammany district club in Harlem, which would soon be known as the Cayuga Club, and the great opportunities it offered an ambitious young man for political and business advancement. Around the time Crater joined the club, Healy, with the machine's backing, had been elected as a New York state assemblyman from the new Nineteenth Assembly District for two terms at the end of World War I. In 1921, he went on to a more financially remunerative seat on the New York City Board of Alderman, the notoriously corrupt lower house of the city's legislature that had long been dominated by Tammany. In the days of Boss Tweed, the Board of Alderman was known as the "Forty Thieves" and had changed little in the intervening years, except for the number of thieves.[20]

One of the causes Healy did champion in his years as a legislator exemplifies the symbiotic mixture of public and private interests in the politics of the day. In the assembly, he had introduced a bill to prepare plans for a great bridge that would connect the three boroughs of Manhattan, Queens, and the Bronx, to be called the Triborough Bridge. Since one landing of the bridge would be in Manhattan at East 125th Street and would direct traffic into the heart of his district, the benefits of the increased commercial traffic flow to his constituents were evident, as were the opportunities to make money from contracts and construction work on that end of the bridge. He also contemporaneously set up on the side a real estate business and insurance company and served as a highly compensated salesman for a book company interested in increasing its sales to the Board of Education, the latter work in direct conflict with his duties as an alderman.[21]

In fact, at a public meeting in 1923, Alderman Healy was called out by Mayor John Hylan, a Brooklyn Democrat who was an uneasy ally of Tammany Hall, opposed his efforts to move forward on the development of the Triborough Bridge. The mayor warned, "If we make a bluff at going ahead with the bridge now we'll be perpetrating a fraud on the people....We'll open the gates for a gang of real estate speculators." What Hylan alluded to, and what Healy likely was contemplating doing was a classic Tammany graft scheme whereby political insiders would act on advance notice of government public works, such as a bridge, and cheaply buy properties that were to be used for the project from their oblivious owners and then later sell them to the city at a substantial profit. When Alderman Healy stood to speak on the bridge's merits, the mayor angrily retorted, "Don't think that because you are an Alderman you can get away with that stuff here."[22]

He then was appointed by his boyhood friend, Mayor Walker, to another patronage plum as a deputy commissioner of the city's Department of Plant and Structures. Overseeing the construction and operation of the city's tunnels, bridges, ferries, and related public works, the department was an obvious fulcrum of political graft because of its role in awarding lucrative construction contracts as well as providing confidential information about government building plans to partners and friends. Walker subsequently would promote him in 1928 to be first deputy commissioner of the department.[23]

But with Tammany Hall's backing in 1925, Healy attained the machine's most coveted and lucrative post besides boss — that of a Manhattan assembly district leader and head of the local Democratic club. The role of the Tammany district leader was that of the archetypal ward boss, as described in a contemporary magazine article:

> To the vast masses of the common people and most of the rest, the district leader is the chief point of contact with [Tammany], even with the government itself. Every night in the week, every week in the year, they can find him in the clubhouse during the entire evening, sometimes late into the night. In a little black book he enters his commissions—"contracts" he calls them. The next day he is busy about the courts, seeing clerks, district attorneys and judges, or better still, the leaders responsible for them. He sees Commissioner this or Chief Clerk that and arranges for peddler's and plumber's licenses, excuses from jury duty, transfers, reinstatements, the promotion of subordinates, valet permits, sewer connections, revision of assessments and passports.[24]

Soon after his elevation to district leader of the Nineteenth Assembly District, Healy was unctuously described in an article in the local business community magazine as an "earnest and loyal supporter of every civil movement for the progress and welfare of Harlem," and as "[s]turdy to the backbone, honorable in all business and social dealings, and with a quiet sense of humor." As for his leadership of his club, which "is continuing to thrive as a power for good in the community...[h]e is a true, able and dexterous political leader and is full of genial kindness and urbanity."[25]

But the ultimate bottom line for a Tammany club and its district leader was the mobilization of the vote for its candidates, whether fair or fraudulent, on election days. The Cayuga Club, its paper remarked after Healy became its leader, "has always given a good account of itself in past elections."[26]

4

By 1924, Al Smith, buoyed by his success as New York governor, had developed into a formidable national political figure. Dressed plainly with his trademark bowler hat and cigar clenched in his jaw, bantering in a baritone New York accent, he would prove to be a natural advocate for progressive causes and the urban working class, immigrants, and other disadvantaged groups. With Boss Murphy's support, he now sought the Democratic nomination for the US presidency, which no Irish American or Catholic, let alone both, had ever tried to obtain. They decided that the 1924 election would be especially propitious, because the Democratic convention was to be held at the old Madison Square Garden in Manhattan.

But Murphy's sudden death a few months before the convention deprived Smith of his political mentor and doomed his nomination hopes that summer, and would have dire repercussions for the New Tammany. His lavish funeral, with the requiem held at St. Patrick's Cathedral and sixty thousand mourners lining the streets on the way to his burial in Calvary Cemetery in Queens, attracted national attention befitting a head of state. Eulogies came from unexpected sources. For instance, Roosevelt, originally no friend of the political machine, recognized Murphy "as a genius who kept harmony [within Tammany], and at the same time recognized that the world moves on." But then State Senator Jimmy Walker had a blunter assessment, saying, "The brains of Tammany Hall lie in Calvary Cemetery."[27]

The concept of the New Tammany survived his death for a few years, at least in the press. Late in 1925, Walter Lippman, chief editor of the *World* and a major political pundit, gave a surprising speech extolling the reform accomplishments of the New Tammany: "The plain fact about Tammany told today is that the new generation of Tammany men are utterly unlike the conventional reform's pictures of professional politicians....If you meet a group of these men who are controlling the policies of Tammany you will find a very successful group of successful city men—successful lawyers, successful businessmen, and I might add constant but successful golf players." Even the *New Yorker*, in one of its first issues, voiced a rosy view of the future of the resurgent political machine, predicting in a 1926 article that "New York, during the next four years, probably will bask in the best administration given us for half a century" because "Tammany is putting its new honesty and its new ideals and its new self-respect on trial."[28] The New Tammany under Mayor Walker, however, would quickly put any such expectations to the test.

Lawyers, as well as other professionals, fit in well with the more sophisticated, businesslike image of the new machine. One contemporary book on the subject cheekily noted the change in the machine's grafters: "Once upon a time grafters had been only a step above safe-blowers in the social scale; under the beneficent influence of book learning and scholarship they found themselves stealing as politely as investment bankers and oil magnates, and with equal aplomb. The new methods were satisfying, the profits were greater, dignity was preserved, and the risk was negligible."[29] Also, as the city rapidly grew and transacted more business in the 1920s, it was awarding more contracts and leases, granting more zoning variances and development rights, requiring more insurance policies for businesses, and condemning more land for public works, all of which necessitated lawyers to do the deals, transactions, and litigation.

Moreover, attorneys had increasingly become instrumental in facilitating honest graft schemes. Al Smith, coming upon a law student studying during the Twenties, is said to have remarked, "There is a young man studying how to take a bribe and call it a fee."[30] A new cadre of "political lawyers," like Joseph Crater, emerged who "were men with definite Tammany backgrounds," were hired "for the influence they could swing," and often "served as discreet middlemen in the transfer of bribes" between clients and government and party officials.[31]

Tammany's selection of Murphy's successor was ostensibly in keeping with its new image. An ally and friend of Governor Smith, the new boss, George Washinton Olvany, clearly broke from his predecessors. He was the first college graduate to be its boss, a very successful lawyer and chairman of the prestigious Tammany Law Committee, and had recently served as a city judge. Because of his swarthy complexion, the joke was that he was the only boss who actually looked like an Indian. As another first for a Tammany boss (and in sharp contrast to his predecessor Silent Charlie), Olvany authored magazine articles and gave interviews with the press, publicizing the New Tammany at every turn. "If there is the slightest suspicion of grafting fastened upon any one in our organization, his resignation is demanded at once," he wrote in one of his articles, "I state with positive assurance that New York is the best governed city in the world."[32]

Boss Olvany then proceeded to take advantage of his opportunities with a vengeance. When asked if his leadership of Tammany might help his private law practice, he responded with a grin, "Well, it won't hurt it any."[33] As later learned, the Olvany law firm made bank deposits totaling about $1 million a year, in addition to deposits made to Olvany and his law partners' private accounts which could not be traced. Although he had pledged his firm would avoid litigation involving city matters, it turned out his firm frequently had appeared surreptitiously in such matters by appearing through other counsel of record, and then had the bulk of the fees paid to it mostly in cash. While boss, Olvany admitted to often having private meetings with the city's board members, but supposedly only in the role of "a good Samaritan," although he and his firm did have an uncanny success in obtaining agency determinations favorable to his clients.[34]

Talk of a New Tammany, as well as the extremely lucrative five-year reign of Olvany, largely ended in early 1929. While his unwillingness to share any of this graft with district leaders certainly made him unpopular within the machine, the event precipitating Olvany's downfall was the disastrous defeat of Al Smith, his key supporter, in the presidential election the previous fall. This greatly diminished Smith's power in Tammany Hall while strengthening the hand of Mayor Walker, whose adulterous lifestyle and nighttime carousing he had strongly disapproved of for some time. Consequently, a group of powerful district leaders, among them Martin Healy, with the support of Mayor Walker, deposed George Olvany in April 1929. Smith himself ended up with the largely honorary title of sachem, which he would continue to hold during the following decade, but any real influence he had with the Tiger was finished.

This change in Tammany leadership in 1929 was symptomatic of a greater devolution in its power structure. Around this time, one commentator summed up the years after Charlie Murphy's death as "the era of the domination of that political organization by the district leaders" and that "the power of the leader of Tammany to dictate nominations and appointment" was no longer "absolute" as it had been under Boss Murphy. Now "the Tammany district clubhouse instead of the new Wigwam at East Seventeenth Street and Union Square is the real center of Tammany's vote-getting activities and consequent control of the City Government."[35] And with this shift of power within the political machine by the end of the decade came an upsurge in "dishonest grafting," like gambling, prostitution, alcohol and drug trafficking, and some of its district leaders' increasing involvement and alliance with organized crime, which would become more prevalent in the 1930s.

After many prominent Tammany figures turned down the post, including Bob Wagner once again, John Curry was chosen as the new boss. An incompetent, older district leader from the West Side of Manhattan, Curry reaffirmed the machine's dishonest grafting ways in the days before Boss Murphy. As he simply put it when he became boss, "There is no old or new Tammany. There is and has been just one Tammany, one organization. Tammany has always been Tammany."[36]

5

In 1927, the Cayuga Club moved into a new clubhouse, a three-story brownstone building at 131 West 122nd Street between Lenox Avenue and Seventh Avenue, west of Mount Morris Park (now named Marcus Garvey Park). The stately, Romanesque Revival townhouse, with its rough-hewn limestone blocks and arched windows capped by beautiful stained glass on the first floor, had been built in 1890 when Harlem was a fashionable middle-class neighborhood.[37]

A contemporary observer's account of another Tammany clubhouse situated in a brownstone suggests what the Cayuga one might have been like on a typical night. On the first floor, a "reception room...is deserted save for the ubiquitous tiger over the mantelpiece." A long assembly room running the length of the building on the second floor is "filled with collapsible chairs" and a platform with a table, behind which a "large American flag is draped on the back wall as are portraits of Jefferson and other Democratic presidents." On the stairwell walls are "pictures of historic clambakes, outings and conventions,...with here and there an old hand-bill or a Currier and Ives print." On the third floor is the office of the district leader and his secretaries with "several roll-tops littered with papers, spittoons and waste buckets on the floors, more pictures, and an assembly district map on the wall." On the fourth and top floor is "a group of fat men, all with derby hats, florid faces and aldermanic paunches sitting about a long table, smoking, talking and laughing, and intermittently examining the pinochle cards which they hold in their thick but capable hands." Somewhere "near is a bar" from which steins of beer are brought to the room.[38]

The Cayuga Club, like other political clubhouses, was a frequent venue for social events. Political receptions and talks were held at the clubhouse, often followed by refreshments and dancing. In addition to the gambling, carousing and political dealings in the clubhouse, gourmondish beefsteak dinners with plenty of liquor were an attraction. The club often had its lavish annual balls, attended by hundreds of party luminaries, celebrities, local businessmen, and club members and their spouses, at the ballroom of the elegant Astor Hotel in Times Square.[39]

Joe regularly attended the club's social events and was a mainstay at the clubhouse, even after his appointment to the bench in April 1930. By all accounts, he was known for his geniality and good fellowship, slapping people on the back, always ready with a funny story to tell. He was a regular at the club's poker table, where he played in his characteristic shrewd yet cautious manner. It was reported he had a reputation of rarely bluffing his hand and only raising the bet when he had a sure winner.[40]

Within the club, Marty and Joe, despite the vast differences in their backgrounds and career paths, naturally gravitated to one another as each saw in the other something beneficial for his advancement. For Crater, his district leader's political connections with Tammany Hall had the potential to advance his ultimate objective of becoming a judge. And for Healy, a brilliant, respected lawyer with a wealth of knowledge as well contacts with the courts, judges ,and Tammany politicans was indispensible. People close to both men later would describe him as the "directing brains of Healy."[41]

A political lawyer like Crater was invaluable to the district leader and the Cayuga Club. Through his influence and connections with the judges, court clerks, and prosecutor's offices, he could assist members with legal difficulties, help obtain municipal employment for them, and defend those charged with crimes or obtain their release on bail. His knowledge of the arcane election laws was useful to bring or defend against judicial challenges on behalf of the political machine, arguing whether candidates had complied with all the technical requirements needed to get on the ballot, whether voters were properly registered, or whether voters were being interfered with at polls. His wife Stella recalled that a large part of the work her husband did for the Cayuga Club and Tammany Hall during this time was providing "his [legal] services for any matter concerning elections which arose in the courts."[42] In fact, Crater's legal abilities and reputation were such that he was soon admitted to the elite Tammany Law Committee, a group of lawyers who served as general counsel to the political machine in big matters and included prominent members of the city bar, such as Max Steuer and Samuel Untermeyer.

His legal knowledge and skills, however, also were of immense use in Healy's personal business ventures, which often involved grafting schemes employing his access to municipal departments and agencies. Marty made the most of his position. He and his brother had set up an insurance agency, Healy & Healy, conveniently located near city hall, which specialized in issuing surety bonds for city contractors, and reaped the lucrative commissions paid by Tammany-selected contractors. His Cayuga Club inner circle also incorporated the Cayuga Holding Company in 1926 "[t]o buy, sell, assign and transact real estate business in New York City." Crater would later be discovered to be a shareholder in one of these companies.[43] As a club officer as well as Healy's counselor and crony during these years, Joe presumably would have been in the know about, if not involved in, these various rackets and deals.

The strong ties between the two men are reflected in anonymous descriptions of them in the newspapers as "personal and political friends," "business and political associates," "close friends" and similar terms. A photograph taken the year before Joe's disappearance also suggests their bond. Martin Healy's parents had celebrated their fiftieth wedding anniversary on February 12, 1929, with a votive Mass held in a church in Harlem, followed by a reception for three hundred guests at the Astor Hotel in Times Square. In a formal picture taken of the Healy family and other guests attending the reception, Martin sits in the middle of the front row while two seats over from him sits Joe, not yet appointed to the bench, nattily dressed with a bowtie and looking like a guest of some distinction.[44]

When Healy's finances would come under closer scrutiny in the summer of 1930, one of his bank accounts was found to have multiple deposits totaling almost $100,000 each from 1927 to 1929, although he had paid no income taxes on them. During this time, he held a city job that paid only $7,500 a year and was the Cayuga Club's district leader, which had no official compensation. But he may not have been unique in this regard. It was estimated that a successful Tammany district leader at the time made over $100,000 a year from his "contracts," graft, and receipt of campaign contributions and expense money.[45]

The overlapping of Healy's business interests and his municipal office was exemplified in one court file found in the New York City Municipal Archives. Another of his companies, the Cayuga Realty Corporation, sued a real estate entity and others for a substantial commission allegedly owed on a real estate transaction in East Harlem, which never took place. In 1929, the defendant, who was looking to buy a multi-block section of land in the area to construct a huge stadium, was directed to discuss the government approvals necessary (for the purchase of the city's streets and air rights over the property) with Healy, in his capacity as first deputy of the city's Department of Plant and Structures. In return for the city's approval of the real estate transaction, an agreement was reached whereby his realty company would receive a hefty "broker's fee" of $40,000 once the properties were purchased. But at that point, Boss John Curry got wind of the proposed deal and directed the purchasers of the real estate properties to deal directly with him in order to get the city's approval. With the advent of the Depression, however, the city refused to approve the speculative real estate deal and the purchaser backed out of the transaction. That did not stop Healy's company, however, from bringing a lawsuit in 1932 against the defendant claiming that it was still entitled to its broker's fee of $40,000 because the deal fell through for no fault of his.[46]

The purported reach of the district leader's influence over Tammany-run agencies and boards was remarkably extensive. The grand jury investigating Healy and the Ewalds over office-buying allegations in September 1930 would find evidence of his involvement in myriad other bribery schemes: payments made to him for the granting of licenses by the Examining Board of Plumbers; payments made by a construction company to get the Board of Standards and Appeals to change its previous decision and grant a zoning "variation" for a piece of property; payment for the "fixing" of a building violation; and payments to the Cayuga Realty Company to have the Board of Standards and Appeals grant a zoning variance to allow the erection of a gas station.[47]

Because of Tammany district leaders' influence in the appointment of New

York City magistrates, they often could intercede on behalf of constituents, usually for a price, for favors in the administration of justice, ranging from fixing a parking ticket to the quashing of criminal charges. Healy and his associates in the Cayuga Club had reputations as "fixers" of court cases with special access to local judges. In a criminal case in Harlem in 1928, for example, the defendant's lawyer met with club member Felix Solomon, who promised that for a large sum, Healy could arrange it so that the judge would impose a light sentence for his client. But after paying the money to Solomon, the client pleaded guilty and was given a stiffer-than-expected sentence of imprisonment. In the subsequent proceeding debarring the defendant's lawyer for attempting to bribe a judge, the court took some solace in the fact that the bribe didn't work, stating, "Justice requires that attention be called to the fact that the claim of Solomon, that he could influence the Judge, was false."[48]

By the end of the decade, organized crime also had begun to infiltrate the fiefdoms of Tammany leaders in Harlem. Arthur Flegenheimer, better known as Dutch Schultz, was in the process of bloodily consolidating the local bootlegging trade and the numbers policy rackets in the area under his control.[49] A strong Tammany district leader could provide key services for the mobster, offering protection from local police interference with his criminal activities, as well as pull with local judges to have charges against gang members dropped. In turn, a mobster such as Schultz could provide for the district leader services such as muscle and intimidation of candidates and voters at the polls on election day and a share of the proceeds from his criminal endeavors. According to Schultz's biographer, some of his lieutenants held meetings regarding the numbers rackets in Healy's Cayuga Club shortly after Crater's disappearance.[50]

In the summer of 1929, rumors surfaced that some of the men at his club could be capable of darker deeds. A newly reappointed city magistrate, Andrew Macrery, age fifty-four, attended a meeting with a Tammany district leader in the Chanin Building in midtown Manhattan. Andrew Keating, who also held the post of Chief City Appraiser, was present with Macrery, as well as Herman Bitterman, a Cayuga Club member and Healy's business partner in earlier ventures. Macrery was rushed from the meeting to a doctor's office nearby, where he died shortly afterward. Word spread that the magistrate had been threatened and beaten at his meeting with Keating and Bitterman because he had not made the final payment to Keating on the $30,000 he owed for his reappointment to his magistrate's seat.[51] Though an autopsy examination concluded that Macrery's death was due to acute heart disease, rumors continued to linger. They would resurface the following summer when the shocking headlines appeared that Martin Healy had been paid $10,000 by another member of the Cayuga Club, George Ewald, while Ewald was being appointed a magistrate by Mayor Walker in 1927.[52] And attention would come to rest on another club member close to both men who just that spring had been appointed a Supreme Court justice.

6

On the eve of his landslide reelection in 1929, Mayor Walker had abandoned any pretense of running an honest, effective, and progressive municipal government. His true sentiments and intentions were best captured in his remarks in the newly erected headquarters overlooking Union Square park in the midst of his reelection campaign: "I am the candidate of Tammany Hall and if elected I will be a Tammany Hall Mayor. I never was a charlatan or a faker and I won't be one in politics."[53] Walker proved to be true to his word, following the machine's directions of whom to appoint in his administration, what his policies would be, and let it continue to wrest vast profits from municipal government in the still booming economy.

By the end of the decade, Tammany had assembled in the metropolis the perfect self-sustaining grafting machine, and it seemed like it could run forever. With the burgeoning economy of the 1920s, the flow of money into the city's coffers was unprecedented, meaning more money could be siphoned off by the machine. "Tammany's greatest asset has thus been the prosperity of the city," a reporter observed in the fall of 1928, "Its own prosperity has been merely the taking of its tithe of the city's....Property values have been increasing about a billion dollars a year."[54]

The higher levels of Mayor Walker's administration were not only controlled by, but were filled with, Tammany leaders. About 65 percent of his "cabinet" of commissioners of city departments and agencies was composed of its active officers, or members. Some ninety Democratic district leaders and their relatives were still on the city payroll when the mayor resigned in 1932, most in top administrative posts. The Tiger's domination of the legislative branch of municipal government was even greater, with 90 percent of the seats on the Board of Alderman won by Democrats in the last half of the 1920s. In addition to being machine-nominated and elected themselves, judges, magistrates, and county officials had a free hand in staffing their offices, which were exempted from civil service requirements, with its faithful.[55]

Municipal jobs still served the chief purpose of rewarding Tammany loyalists and workers, instead of functioning as an effective government. When Walker was elected mayor, it was estimated that one-sixth of Tammany voters had a city job, and the number likely increased from there. The number of municipal employees appointed from each Tammany district club was thought to range from two hundred to six hundred people. By the end of the Walker mayoralty, about half of city jobs were open to whomever the machine wanted to pick, whether the person had the skills and education for the position or not.[56] One historian of the city's politics during this period has stated, "So many city jobs required 'special skill and training,' the basis for exemption from civil service requirements, that New York should have boasted one of the most skilled staffs in the nation. Alas, these special skills had more to do with machine politics than municipal service." By the end of the Twenties, the municipal payroll was about half of its budget. And since the days of District Leader Plunkitt's talks, municipal workers who got their jobs through Tammany often kicked-back a percentage of their salaries to their benefactors.[57]

Consequently, almost every New York City executive official, department head, alderman, board member, judge, and government attorney was beholden and loyal to Tammany Hall in some way. Accordingly, anyone wanting to do business in or with the city was forced to compensate the machine and its leaders, whether by a bribe, campaign contribution, employment of its members, or in some other manner. Anyone seeking to obtain a license or governmental approval would have to apply to city agencies and boards or courts composed of Tammany, or Tammany-approved, members and staff, and would, if not making a direct payoff, hire for a large fee for a lawyer, agent, or other representative with solid Tammany connections, with the understanding that the fee would be split with others in the machine.

A prime example of Tammany Hall's co-option of municipal agencies during this period was the Board of Standards and Appeals. The board possessed the valuable and easily corrupted power of granting variances or exceptions to the city's real estate zoning laws and development plans. The viability of a proposed construction project was often dependent on whether a variance could be obtained from the board, whose members were appointed directly by Mayor Walker or by his commissioner. Those desirous of obtaining variances for their projects from the board learned quickly that the surest way to succeed was to buy the influence and representation of Tammany advocates. Prominent New York architect and developer Fred French admitted to paying a total of $75,000 in fees to a lawyer in order to obtain a zoning variance for the construction of his massive Tudor City project on East Forty-Second Street.[58]

Early in 1930, investigators made the surprising discovery that one of the ablest advocates who could be bought to represent developers before the Board of Standards and Appeals was "Doctor" William Doyle, whose only credentials were his prior work as a horse veterinarian with the New York City Fire Department together with solid connections in Tammany Hall. Having no background in law or real estate, he was paid over a million dollars in fees from 1922 to 1930 by builders, contractors, and landlords who sought variances from the board, and his record for obtaining what his clients wanted from the board was incredible. This money, typically in cash, would be split with Tammany lawyers, insiders, and other facilitators.[59]

The grafting machine devoured public improvement projects undertaken during the 1920s. The award of construction contracts was in the hands of the Tammany-dominated Board of Estimate, and it was not constrained by any requirements of public auctioning or competitive bidding. When members of that board or influential politicians were not given kickbacks for the award of contracts or outright bribed, they awarded contracts to politically connected firms, often those in which Tammany leaders held hidden interests or that had made generous campaign contributions to it. The implementation of large public works projects also in turn generated opportunities for lucrative professional fees, architect's fees, insurance brokerage fees, as well as legal fees, which also went to well-connected individuals who funneled money back to Tammany leaders.[60]

With so much money diverted to graft, payoffs, fees, and favoritism, most of the public improvements begun by Mayor Walker were never completed. Remnants of unfinished projects were scattered over the city landscape by the end of his administration. After $800 million was paid by the city to construct the Independent Subway System, little actual work had been done. The West Side Elevated Highway along the Hudson River from the tip of Manhattan to West Seventy-Second Street was completed but was not usable because it lacked any entrance or exit ramps. What Tammany-connected contractors did build was typically of poor quality. During the Walker administration, forty newly constructed schools had to be closed for major repairs within a year after opening. Construction of the Triborough Bridge, connecting the Bronx, Manhattan, and Queens, which Alderman Healy had earlier endorsed, had only progressed to the point of raising seventeen huge masonry piers standing more than one hundred feet high on Ward's Island in the East River, but no bridge had been built on them.[61]

Attracting less attention at the time was another of Mayor Walker's public works projects that had gone terribly awry. Its commendable purpose was to ease the dense congestion and dilapidated buildings on the Lower East Side of Manhattan and to construct model low-income housing in its place. The untold story of the rise and demise of the Libby's Hotel & Baths encapsulates so many aspects of the city during the Roaring Twenties—its real estate boom and ethnic boosterism, shady and unethical business practices, Tammany lawyers' influence with the Walker administration and the courts, and grafting from the city's treasury. Joe Crater, in one of the last legal matters he handled before ascending the bench in April 1930, would play an obscure but perhaps pivotal role in the complex legal maneuverings over the hotel.

CHAPTER FIVE

The Libby's Hotel Debacle
and the Newly Appointed Justice

I

In February 1934, newly elected Mayor Fiorello La Guardia would invoke the missing judge's name as he announced a major change in plans for the level strip of land that stretched for seven blocks in the heart of the teeming Lower East Side. By then, the "Chrystie-Forsyth Project" as it was known, which had been begun by Mayor Walker's administration, had run out of funds with the onset of the Depression and was being recommissioned by the new mayor as a city park and recreation area. "Page Crater," he remarked, as he blamed the failure of Walker's plans on "[a]ll the graft, crookedness, and corruption that figured in that [expletive]" project.[1]

La Guardia's piqued reference to the missing judge was an obscure one having to do with seemingly minor legal work he had performed before he had been appointed to the bench. In early 1929, he had officially served as "receiver," or temporary legal caretaker, of the Libby's Hotel & Baths, the newly built luxury hotel catering to Jewish clientele, which was among the numerous parcels of property in the area the city would shortly seek to condemn and acquire for its planned public works project. Crater's role as receiver in the proceeding would prove to be one of the most enduring but misunderstood explanations for his disappearance.

Libby's Hotel was the dream and achievement of Max Bernstein, who had emigrated as a child with his family fleeing from Russia and settled around 1900 on the Lower East Side of Manhattan. As a young man, living amidst the poverty, congestion, and dilapidated tenements of the neighborhood composed primarily of Jewish immigrants like his family, he had the quixotic vision of erecting a modern, luxury hotel for well-to-do Jewish visitors and patrons who were unwelcome at the better hotels of uptown Manhattan.[2] The prosperity and the booming building mania in New York in the Twenties gave Bernstein his opportunity. To finance the construction and outfitting of the new hotel, he appealed to his neighbors to invest in the future rejuvenation of the Lower East Side by buying small amounts of stock in his hotel company, which hundreds of peddlers, street vendors, scrubwomen, store owners, and other residents proceeded to do.[3]

In a decision that would prove more fraught with consequences, Bernstein obtained the other half of the financing for his hotel from a successful real estate investment company, the American Bond and Mortgage Company (ABMC), a Chicago-based firm that had ridden the wave of the national real estate boom. The firm's principal business was to provide mortgage financing on big real estate developments, but instead of using its own money like a bank, it sold "mortgage bonds" to the public, who would collectively own a piece of the mortgage on the development. While the ABMC had a national reputation, having by the end of the decade sold mortgage bonds to finance hotels and apartment buildings in New York, Washington, DC, Massachusetts, Florida, and elsewhere, it was privately owned and run by William J. Moore and his family from Chicago, crafty real estate speculators and operators who were playing under the very lax business ethics of the times.[4] When NYPD detectives on the Crater case would look into his involvement with Libby's Hotel, a source familiar with the ABMC would say that "any deal in which William J. Moore might be involved would undoubtedly be crooked."[5]

Completed in early 1926, the modern, twelve-story, unadorned, yellow-brick building at the corner of Chrystie and Delancey Streets towered over the aging and decrepit tenements and buildings on the Lower East Side. Costing over $3 million to erect and furnish, and one of the most expensive hotels in cost per square foot ever erected in the city to that time, Libby's Hotel was an extravagance considering its location. On May 17, 1926, the formal opening was celebrated with a large dinner party presided over by Max Bernstein. In attendance was the city commissioner of Public Welfare, as well as Jewish luminaries including the vice president of the United Jewish Appeal, the editor of the *Jewish Morning Journal*, and the president of the East Side Board of Trade. Dinner toasts hailed the hotel as the "redemption of the East Side" and a "milestone in the history of New York Jewry." Shortly after midnight, Bernstein unveiled a large portrait in the lobby of the hotel's namesake, his beloved mother who had died when he was a boy, and was showered with flowers and applause.[6]

An opening-week advertisement for the premier hotel appeared in the *Times* with the headline, "Max Bernstein Announces the Opening of the Largest Russian-Turkish Baths in the World." With accommodations for "over 1000 guests," the ad boasted of the "features...in the endless chain of accommodation and conveniences" in the hotel, including two restaurants, two barber shops, a theater ticket office, conference rooms, bootblack and hat-cleaning services, and a library.[7] But Libby's major attraction for visiting guests, as well as neighborhood customers, was its "Russian-Turkish baths," hot-water baths and saunas considered to be therapeutic and restorative. These traditional baths popular with Eastern European and Russian Jews, many of whom had become residents of the area, were now equipped with the "most complete and most modern appointments," such as "medical, electrical and physio-therapeutic baths...under the supervision of trained physicians and a select corps of experts." In keeping with the conspicuous consumption and excess of the times, it was advertised as the "only [hotel] in the World furnishing musical entertainment to bath guests," with a full orchestra playing in the bather's lounge in the basement. Once the hotel had opened, an article described the scene at the Libby's facilities: "East side merchants, garbed in togas made of towels, could enjoy songs and dancing while working off avoirdupois," and on one occasion, a magician went into a trance and was "lowered in a glass-covered coffin into the swimming pool, blissfully cataleptic for hours while the hotel guests splashed about him."[8]

The hotel additionally offered an array of Yiddish cultural activities for its guests as well as residents of the Lower East Side, a neighborhood (as many in the city) increasingly defined by ethnicity, nationality, and race during the 1920s. Every Sunday night, Yiddish radio programs were broadcast over a local station, including famous musicians, cantors, entertainers, and celebrities, as well as live Jewish weddings.[9] A popular travel guide to New York City referred to the new hotel as "the first orthodox Jewish hotel in America" situated in "the densest population in the city."[10] But despite all the publicity, by 1928, two years after its heralded opening, Libby's was having financial difficulties. Bernstein was not paying the hotel's creditors, and there were accusations that he had padded the payroll with relatives and friends holding phantom jobs. By the end of that year, Bernstein's company, the Libby's Hotel

Corporation, had failed to make timely payment to the ABMC due on some of its mortgage bonds.

Meanwhile, in one of his sporadic efforts at urban planning, Mayor Walker had proposed a major alteration in the landscape in the heart of the impoverished and rundown area in April 1928. The changes had been recommended by the Regional Plan Association, a private organization tasked with developing a plan for New York City and its surrounding areas. The Association, which characterized the Lower East Side as having been "for decades...an incorrigible slum," warned that without any planning "to accelerate the rehabilitation of the Lower East Side," the area "will continue for another generation...to be both a sore spot in the city's social economy and a wasted area in its [tax] assessment map."[11]

Under Walker's proposal, two adjacent streets that ran north and south between Houston Street and Canal Street, Chrystie Street and Forsyth Street were to be widened into major thoroughfares to relieve the congested traffic in the area. On the continuous seven-block-long strip of property that would remain between Chrystie and Forsyth, philanthropists would procure leases from the city and "erect model apartments" whose rooms "can be rented at an average not to exceed $10 a month."[12] One of the most valuable buildings and properties to be condemned by the city and ultimately demolished to make way for the renewal project was Libby's Hotel & Baths, which stood on the corner of Delancey Street at the end of the strip of land impacted.

The Walker administration initially had sought to reach agreements with the hundreds of individual property owners affected by the project, offering to pay an amount for each property based on its tax assessment value plus a small profit. The owners of Libby's Hotel refused the mayor's offer because their property's tax assessment value was well below its actual value including the immense construction costs of the hotel. So many affected property owners were rejecting the city's offer that the public works project couldn't go forward, so Walker announced in early November 1928 the abandonment of the entire Chrystie-Forsyth renovation project. In one of his rare public outbursts, he fumed, "By this action you have stamped yourselves as representatives of a neighborhood that does not want improvements."[13]

2

As the threat of the mayor's renovation project displacing the brand-new hotel receded, the hotel's prospects still seemed good. While small debts had accrued, the real estate market was still booming, and the hotel was generating about $50,000 a month in revenue, more than enough to satisfy the minor amounts owed on some of the mortgage bonds. In early February 1929, however, Charles C. Moore, one of the members of the Moore family controlling the ABMC, sued Bernstein's company and Libby's Hotel to foreclose upon its mortgage, which was secured by the mortgage bonds. Moore brought suit in his capacity as a trustee for all the holders of the mortgage bonds, which mainly consisted of public investors.

Moore's complaint filed in the Supreme Court at 60 Centre Street downtown was perplexing on its face. It alleged that Bernstein's company owed approximately $65,000 on a few mortgage bonds and sought the foreclosure of the entire mortgage of $1.5 million and the hotel's sale at auction.[14] In other words, even though a small interest amount was owing on a fraction of the total mortgage bonds, and nothing was yet owed on the great majority of them, the hotel would have to be sold to satisfy that small amount, while the remaining mortgage held by ABMC bondholders in the amount of over $1.4 million would remain on the property after its sale. The other troubling aspect of the lawsuit, although not discovered until later on, was that the mortgage bondholder who was owed money and who filed the foreclosure suit was none other than a Moore family shell company. Thus by bringing the foreclosure, Trustee Moore had violated his duty of acting in the interest of all bondholders and as Bernstein's lawyer would subsequently charge, "act[ed] wholly for the personal interests and gain of himself and the other said members of his family, who confederated and conspired with him in using his trusteeship for his and their personal gain by the oppression and betrayal of [Libby's Hotel], its creditors and shareholders."[15]

To bring and litigate the foreclosure lawsuit on their behalf, the Moores hired Martin Lippman, a successful real estate and trial attorney who was a partner in a prominent Manhattan law firm, McLaughlin & Stern (which exists in Manhattan to this day). Lippman also quickly sought to have the court appoint a receiver for the new foreclosure lawsuit whose role would be to take possession of and account for the income and proceeds generated by the hotel until the foreclosure occurred. For that position, Lippman proposed his well-connected colleague and friend, with whom he had worked on cases before. As Lippman was no doubt aware, Crater recently had remarkable success in being appointed to these lucrative receiverships by the justices of the Supreme Court, some of whom he knew from serving as Wagner's law secretary and from Tammany legal circles. After his application for appointment as the receiver of Libby's Hotel was routinely approved, Crater in turn chose another insider with clout, George Frankenthaler, to be the receiver's counsel. George was the brother of Justice Alfred Frankenthaler, who sat on the same court and was a fellow Tammany lawyer and Broadway aficionado, whom he knew well and would soon appear at a pivotal point in the foreclosure proceedings.

After meeting initial resistance when trying to secure possession of Libby's Hotel, Receiver Crater obtained a court order requiring the hotel owners to relinquish control. On February 23, 1929, Max Bernstein and hotel managers tried to obstruct the receiver's efforts by throwing all the guests out of the hotel, turning off all steam and hot water and preparing to shut the hotel. Crater then called in the police to restore order, who threw the manager out, let the hotel guests back in, and restored utilities to the building.[16] That night, he had attained possession of the hotel and its assets, most significantly, the monthly income generated by the hotel going forward.

Meanwhile, Martin Lippman had another politically connected lawyer appointed to be the "referee" in the foreclosure proceeding, another crucial position responsible for hearing and determining what amounts were due and owed under the mortgage bonds and for arranging and supervising the sale of the foreclosed property. Francis J. Quillinan was Al Smith's son-in-law, as well as a partner in Senator Wagner's law firm at 120 Broadway, where Crater had been renting space for his own law offices since 1927. On April 17, 1929, Referee Quillinan held a hearing there to take evidence on the amount owing on the defaulted Libby's mortgage bonds. Trustee Charles Moore gave testimony, as well as a representative for the owner of those bonds which was identified at that point as the American Mortgage Loan Company, another Moore company.[17]

Soon after this hearing, Quillinan issued his Referee's Report that calculated the total amount owing on the Moores' foreclosing mortgage bonds, including principal, interest, and other expenses, to be about $93,000. The Libby's owners not having appeared at the referee's hearing to oppose the foreclosure proceeding, the American Mortgage Loan Company obtained a Judgment of Foreclosure, entered on May 23, 1929, in which Bernstein's hotel company was ordered to pay the outstanding amounts due and owing on the mortgage bonds as determined in the report through the sale of the hotel "in one parcel at public auction" by Referee Quillinan.[18]

Coincidentally, new developments regarding the Walker administration's Chrystie-Forsyth street-widening plans were giving heightened significance to the timing of the hotel foreclosure proceedings. Despite the mayor's apparent abandonment of the project a few months before, he suddenly announced in early May 1929 that he was "very hopeful" that it could go forward. Walker now sought to expedite the administrative proceedings necessary for the city to condemn for its use, and acquire title to, the properties encompassed by the plan. Just three weeks after the Judgment of Foreclosure against the Libby's Hotel was obtained, the New York City Board of Estimate and Apportionment, chaired by the mayor, unanimously approved the formal changes to the city's map necessary for the implementation of the Chrystie-Forsyth project, and scheduled the city's final acquisition of title to all the properties affected for its meeting in two weeks. Chairman Walker reassured the audience that "[n]obody is going to profiteer on this."[19]

Just as the municipal condemnation plans rapidly progressed to their conclusion, Lippman, the Moores' counsel, rushed to schedule the sale of Libby's Hotel at auction as quickly as possible. Referee Quillinan published the requisite public notices in the newspapers, which were done so hastily that there were errors in the description of the legal boundaries of the property to be sold. The notices announced that an auction for the sale of the foreclosed property would be held on June 21, 1929, less than a week before the city would officially acquire title to the hotel and the other condemned properties at the next board meeting.[20]

By this time, Max Bernstein and his lawyers must have realized the import of the legal and political machinations unfolding before them. The owner of a condemned property had an alternative to accepting a settlement offer from the city; the owner could file a condemnation lawsuit in the Supreme Court to have a judge determine the value of the condemned property and order the city to pay that amount to the property owner. Also, the Supreme Court's general practice at the time was to make condemnation awards that were well in excess of the fair market value of the condemned property. As a special prosecutor's report on the city's condemnation process concluded the next year, "The existing method of valuing land acquired by condemnation by the city of New York is extravagant, wasteful, unfair to the city, frequently unfair to the private owner, and beneficial to nobody except favored and profiteering real estate and special interests, or a combination of both, with their supporting staffs of specialists, lawyers, and expert witnesses."[21]

Whoever actually owned the property at the time of the city's condemnation of it was central to Tammany's "condemnation racket," a staple of its grafting from the days of District Leader Plunkitt. In one of his talks from his bootblack stand at the old courthouse, he gave the following as an example of his coveted honest graft:

> My party's in power in the city, and it's goin' to undertake a lot of public improvements. Well, I'm tipped off, say that they're going to lay out a new park at a certain place....I go to that place and I buy up all the land I can in the neighborhood. Then the board or this or that makes its plan public, and there is a rush to get my land, which nobody cared particular for before. Ain't it perfectly honest to charge a good price and make a profit on my investment and foresight?[22]

In the intervening twenty-five years, the scheme and its process had become a bit more sophisticated, but Bernstein and his hotel company were in the same predicament as the owners in Plunkitt's example who unknowingly sold their property for minimal value rather than its greatly increased value once the city's plans became public. The key inside information here was whether and when Mayor Walker was going to revive the Chrystie-Forsyth plan, which he had publicly announced he was abandoning in late 1928. The Tammany-connected lawyers hired by Lippman, including Receiver Crater, likely would have been privy to such internal information about the Walker administration's plans in advance of his public announcement in May 1929 that the project would go forward again.

Consequently, the owner of Libby's Hotel at the time the Board of Estimate officially condemned the property on June 27 would be able to bring a condemnation lawsuit in Supreme Court and obtain the usually excessive award made by it. If the original hotel owners were able to somehow retain ownership of the hotel until it was finally condemned, the condemnation award from the city would likely be sufficient to pay off the remaining amount of the ABMC bonds on the property as well as other creditors and still provide them with a substantial profit for their endeavor.

So a day before the auction sale, Benjamin Bernstein, representing his brother Max and the other former hotel owners, applied to the Supreme Court for an emergency stay of the auction sale. He argued that rushing to hold the auction, as Lippman's clients were pushing for, would lead to a "fire sale" where the bids would not reflect the hotel's true worth. He further argued that "a delay can be of no harm to the plaintiffs [foreclosing bond-holders]" because the condemnation award to be determined for its property would be sufficient if paid to the former owners to pay off not only the Moores' bonds but the remaining amount of the ABMC mortgage bonds, thus obviating any foreclosure proceedings.[23] The following morning, Bernstein's application was denied without a decision.[24]

The auction of Libby's Hotel & Baths and its premises was held by Referee Quillinan later that day at a building near the Centre Street courthouse. Charles Moore and Lippman made the one and only bid of $75,000, subject to the remaining ABMC mortgage, which the auctioneer knocked down. Asked for the name of the bidder, Lippman replied after conferring with Moore, the "American Mortgage Loan Company," the same Moore company holding the mortgage bonds on which the foreclosure lawsuit was predicated. A "Memorandum of Sale" was signed after the auction by one "Anne Hetterick" on behalf of the American Mortgage Loan Company, stating that the company had purchased the property for $75,000, over and above the outstanding mortgage bonds in the amount of $1,420,000, plus interest.[25]

A few days later, the same Anne Hetterick executed a document assigning for an unstated value her new title and interest in the hotel to a "Mary J. Lyons" of Manhattan, who it would later be learned, was a secretary employed at Lippman's law firm. On June 27, the same day that the ownership of the hotel was assigned to Lyons, the Board of Estimate unanimously adopted a resolution finally approving the city's acquisition of title to the properties for the Chrystie-Forsyth project.

3

Referee Quillinan's final report of the auction sale of Libby's Hotel, which he filed shortly before the city officially acquired ownership of the property, offered Max Bernstein his final opportunity to thwart the Moores' scheme.

Benjamin Bernstein made a motion to the Supreme Court to reject and vacate the foreclosure and sale of the hotel as well as the subsequent assignment
of its title to Mary Lyons. The legal papers in support of the application bit-
terly charged that the "sale was conducted and the property purported to
have been disposed of under circumstances indicating the greatest oppression and inequity...and without the slightest justification or occasion for
such oppression and inequity by reason of any redress to which the [fore-
closing bondholders] were entitled." Recounting the lockstep chronology of
the hotel foreclosure proceedings and the city's condemnation plans for the
Chrystie-Forsyth project, the legal papers exposed the scheme engineered
by the Moore family, and executed by their counsel Lippman in court, to
gain ownership of Libby's Hotel right before it was to be condemned by the
city. Their papers also pointed out that the sole bidder at the auction was a
"subsidiary (I believe wholly owned) of the American Bond and Mortgage
Company," and that new owner Mary Lyons was "a dummy" for one or both
of the companies.[26]

The Bernsteins' motion papers did implicate Crater, though not by name,
as participating in the Moores' elaborate scheme. In Referee Quillinan's terms
of sale, read immediately before the auction had taken place, there was a reference that "the Receiver" had transferred approximately $45,000 in hotel
revenue to partially satisfy the amounts owed to the foreclosing bondholder.
Thus Crater, who had been procured by Trustee Charles Moore, was accused
of having "subsequently operated the property involved herein for the benefit of the [foreclosing] bondholders," and to the former owners' detriment.[27]
In other words, Crater had received and withheld income generated by the
hotel during his receivership sufficient to satisfy the amounts owing on the
foreclosing mortgage bonds, thereby requiring dismissal of the foreclosure
proceedings. Accordingly, it was argued, it was only equitable that the hotel's
original owners be reinstated as owners of Libby's Hotel as of June 27, the date
the city formally acquired title, so that they would be entitled to any judicial
condemnation award that was granted.

In August 1929, the former hotel owners' motion to vacate and annul Referee Quillinan's report of the foreclosure and sale of the hotel was briefed and
orally argued before none other than Justice Alfred Frankenthaler, Crater's
friend as well as brother of his personally selected counsel.[28] Justice Frankenthaler's terse written decision, issued in February 1930, confirmed the hotel
foreclosure and sale, adopting Lippman's legal arguments on all issues except

a minor one. Blinking reality, the judge found the city's possible condemnation of Libby's Hotel to have had "no relevance to the propriety and regularity of sale." Additionally, Quillinan's handling of the foreclosure auction had been in accordance with "well-established practices and usages prevailing at foreclosure sales," and Bernstein and the former hotel owners easily could have made a competing bid for the property at the auction sale to protect their interests but failed to do so. No mention was made of the accusation regarding Receiver Crater. "Moved as I am by the sympathetic consideration put forward by the [former owners]," Justice Frankenthaler concluded, "I can see no escape from the conclusion that the law requires that the motion to confirm be granted to the extent that the report of sale and the deed relate to the [hotel property]."[29]

Shortly after this decision was issued, Max Bernstein gave up on trying to regain his dream and tribute to his mother's memory. Perhaps legal fees and costs for mounting an appeal were too much with the stock market crash just months before; more likely, he saw the writing on the wall, illuminated by their adversaries' cunning legal maneuvering in litigating the foreclosure action in concert with the city's condemnation proceedings and their adept use of judicial and political pull to attain their ends. In March 1930, Max Bernstein, his hotel company and second mortgage bondholders on the property reached a final settlement with the hotel's erstwhile owner Mary Lyons whereby they would not pursue an appeal of Justice Frankenthaler's decision in return for Lyons paying them $130,000 from the city's eventual award.[30]

Days after this settlement, Martin Lippman's feat of legal legerdemain was completed when Mary Lyons quietly assigned the entirety of her interest in the future award for Libby's Hotel back to the Moores' ABMC.[31] Employing a wealth of legally and politically connected talent who would have had access to higher-ups in the Walker administration with knowledge of its plans, Charles Moore and his family had dispossessed Max Bernstein's hotel company and its shareholders, mainly peddlers, street vendors, and merchants of the Lower East Side, from the ownership of the hotel. The new owner of the hotel would be the recipients of an expected windfall award for the property to be paid by New York City, which despite the looming Depression, was still good for the money.

The trial of the city's lawsuit to determine the condemnation award the hotel's new owners would receive for Libby's Hotel commenced at the 60

Centre Street Courthouse (where Crater would soon be ascending to the bench) in April 1930 before Justice Philip McCook, a well-respected Republican jurist not favorably disposed to Tammany. But political and legal shenanigans continued to dominate the proceedings. In place of Lippman, the Moores retained a prominent lawyer specializing in condemnation proceedings to try the case, who used a cadre of well-paid expert witnesses to give inflated appraisal valuations of the hotel. At the trial before Justice McCook, the star expert witness called on behalf of the new owners of the hotel opined that its value was $3 million when the city acquired title to it in August 1929, more than twice its tax assessment value.

The city's attorneys, whose office had Tammany ties, failed to make a convincing case for a significantly lower valuation of the property, even though all they needed to show was that the hotel was a not a "suitable improvement" for its location. In assessing the value of the property, the city's appraisers ignored the fact that the brand new luxury hotel and baths on the Lower East Side, whose construction costs were exorbitant, had gone belly-up in just a few years at the height of the city's building boom in the late 1920s. McCook's initial condemnation award for the hotel came in slightly less than the ABMC's appraisers' valuations, at $2,850,000.[32] He did criticize the city's counsel for not presenting sufficient evidence of the hotel's true lower value and even granted a retrial on the issue of whether it was a suitable improvement for the neighborhood. When the city's lawyers again failed to make a case for a lower valuation at the second trial, the judge reaffirmed his previous award in the fall of 1930.

After paying from the city's award for Libby's Hotel, the remaining ABMC mortgage on the hotel in the amount of about $1.4 million (for the remaining mortgage bondholders), the settlement amount to Bernstein and his creditors, and other expenses, there would still be a gigantic profit of more than $1 million. But to whom did this windfall belong? The claimants would shortly include the ABMC, Lippman's secretary Lyons, and even Crater himself, in spectral fashion, after he had already disappeared. It also would later be discovered that the missing judge had continued to provide services for the ABMC in connection with the city's condemnation award, after his role as receiver in the hotel foreclosure had ended.

4

By the spring of 1930, Joe Crater's private law practice, opened in 1927 at Senator Wagner's law offices in the Equitable Building at 120 Broadway, was booming. His ties with the justices of the Supreme Court had landed him an inordinate number of lucrative appointments as a receiver and referee in cases besides the Libby's Hotel matter as well as to high profile judicial committees that oversaw practice in the courts. In fact, in just the first three months of 1930 before being appointed to the bench, he had been awarded a total of nine receiverships by the Supreme Court, County of New York, seven of which were by Justice Frankenthaler.[33]

He had also collaborated on cases with Senator Wagner and his partners Rifkind and Quillinan. These included some high-profile litigations and appeals, including the representation of unions in lawsuits to recognize their rights to collectively bargain with employers and to strike.[34] He also continued his own sophisticated practice representing companies and individuals in appellate litigation. During these years, Tammany Hall had appointed him to its prestigious Law Committee, where together with other prominent city lawyers, he represented the organization in election disputes, matters regarding patronage and civil service law, and other litigation central to the political machine's interests. Governor Al Smith had selected him to be a member of the Home Rule Commission, an agency whose purpose was to gain more autonomy for the municipal government from the state government in Albany.[35]

Crater also had exhibited his legal erudition for many years by lecturing at law schools several nights a week, including at Fordham and New York Universities. In the wake of his unfathomable disappearance, one of his recent students would remember him with glowing praise: "Although, in one minute, [Professor Crater] could explain clearly a theory of law which the average law professor, within my experience would take ten to express even vaguely, yet so engrossed both he himself and his class would become in the topic under discussion that the hourly bell...would go unheeded until the subject had been investigated from every conceivable angle."[36]

By the end of the decade, Crater's private practice was estimated to have grossed around $75,000 to $100,000, placing him in the elite of the city's bar. The stock market crash and economic turbulence in the fall of 1929 apparently did not worry him, as he had little of his money invested in stocks.

He had purchased earlier that year his new luxury cooperative apartment on lower Fifth Avenue for $13,500, and upon moving in, hired a chauffeur and a maid to befit his new lifestyle."[37]

But when an opportunity arose in early 1930 to achieve his overriding ambition to become a judge, Crater was ready. A temporary position as a Supreme Court justice in Manhattan became available when Justice Joseph Proskauer announced his retirement six months before his term expired that fall. By this time, he had made a prominent name for himself in the city's bar and in Tammany Hall, and now arranged for a number of powerful men to support his judicial ambitions. Senator Wagner, still having a very high opinion of his former law secretary, who was now working with his partners in his law offices, likely made a suggestion to his friend Governor Roosevelt that Joe would be a good choice, although he steadfastly denied doing so once the scandal of his protégé's disappearance erupted. Roosevelt also would receive letters of commendation for the relatively young lawyer from other judges, prominent lawyers, and Tammany (although he was not the machine's first choice). The governor placed his name in nomination before the New York Senate on April 8, 1930, to fill the vacancy on the Supreme Court bench. The New York Senate unanimously confirmed his nomination days later.[38]

Roosevelt's selection of Crater was highly praised, if unexpected, because some of the names recommended to him had stronger ties with Tammany or to Al Smith, who still was expected to have some political clout with the New York Democratic Party after his loss running for President in 1928. But he may have picked him for that very reason—in order to put distance between himself as a New York Democrat from the politically corrosive machine as well as from Smith, who might contest his bid for the Democratic presidential nomination in two years. Shortly after being nominated, Joe received an invitation from Roosevelt to join him for lunch at the Executive Mansion in Albany. Accompanied by Senator Wagner, and in a rare instance by his wife, Crater celebrated with the governor. In response to Crater's expression of gratitude for his appointment, the governor remarked, "You are the kind of man we want. You are an inspiration to your generation."[39]

Both the governor and the new justice received accolades for the appointment. A *Times* editorial extolled Roosevelt's savvy appointment to be not only "an adroit political solution of his difficulty...but also the appointment of a lawyer who, in the judgment of the members of his profession, is well qualified to be on the bench of the Supreme Court." Even the *New York Law Journal*, the apolitical newspaper of the city's legal profession, praised his "wise appointment...as a lawyer of capacity and broad culture, who has earned the regard of people of high standing who have come into close contact with him." It added that "[t]his designation undoubtedly marks the commencement of a long and valuable judicial career, begun under happy and comforting auspices."[40] The expressions of support for the new judge reveal how successfully he had cultivated the legal and political elites in furtherance of his own ambitions.

Joseph Force Crater was formally sworn in by Presiding Justice Dowling as a Supreme Court justice by the presiding justice of the new Appellate Division on April 17, 1930, in the ornate, wood-paneled, and stained glass-domed courtroom of the Appellate Division courthouse overlooking Madison Square Park where he had briefly worked as then-appellate judge Wagner's law secretary four years before. Among the guests attending the ceremony were Tammany Boss Curry and Justice Alfred Frankenthaler, who two months before had rejected the Libby's Hotel former owners' last-ditch effort to overturn its foreclosure sale. Simon Rifkind remembered years later that his colleague, upon learning of his appointment to the bench, "threw his arms around me and said, 'Si, I am the happiest man in the world.'" Stella described her husband as "walking on air."[41]

Crater's ascension to the bench also promised much financial security, as New York City and the nation entered the first full year of the financial cataclysm. If nominated by the city Democratic Party and elected to a full fourteen-year term as a justice that fall, which seemed likely, he would be paid the then munificent annual salary of $22,500 (shortly to be raised to $25,000). (By comparison, the salary for a US district court judge was only $10,000 at the time.) Joe seemed to also be expecting other nonjudicial sources of income once he ascended the bench, as when he opaquely told Stella that "if they will let me alone for five or six years we will have a lot of money."[42] Already having accumulated large savings before becoming a judge, he would have more than enough to continue to live quite comfortably in Manhattan, no matter the signs of the oncoming Depression apparent that year.

Beyond the pecuniary rewards, being a judge brought with it an aura of recognition, status, honor, and authority, which Crater surely exalted in. To quote a more prosaic job description of a treatise on New York City's government, judges "occupy places of great prestige, they are deferred to by their legal colleagues, by the social groups in which they move, and by the rest of officialdom....[T]he robes, the formalities, the authority of these men elevate them to something apart from ordinary human beings. Judges...are surrounded by an honorific aura that to many is both awesome and wonderful." District Leader Plunkitt naturally had put it more colorfully when he referred to the same judicial position twenty-five years before: "If you've got an achin' for style, sit down on it till you have made your pile and landed a Supreme Court Justiceship with a fourteen-year term at [then] $17,500 a year....Then you've got about all you can get out of politics."[43]

At the young age of forty-one, Joseph Crater had not only achieved his professional goal of becoming a judge in the nation's great metropolis but had catapulted to the highest echelons of its legal and political circles. With support from prominent lawyers, judges, and Tammany Hall, his election to the security of a full term as a Supreme Court justice that fall seemed assured. His future looked as secure and unassailable as it could be. But a mere four months later, he would be so irrevocably erased from this world that his future would be relegated to his past.

Exposing the Missing Judge

CHAPTER SIX

Dueling Grand Juries

I

In his first months on the Supreme Court bench at the 60 Centre Street courthouse, Justice Crater had tried cases and one of his decisions had been published in the official reporters.[1] Ecstatic at his appointment, he set about thoroughly enjoying the summer court recess. He spent most of it with his wife up at their summer cabin in Maine, taking a motor excursion to Canada in July. He had returned to the city alone a few times, ostensibly to catch up on his work and to attend Tammany's Independence Day celebration. While there, Crater also engaged in his peripatetic pursuit of pleasure, squiring his mistress around town, being seen with chorus girls in the city's more notorious nightclubs, and joining friends with women escorts on a bender in Atlantic City, New Jersey. On the night of August 1, he traveled back to his wife in Maine seemingly without a care in the world, planning on spending the next few weeks up there before presiding over the ceremonial opening of the Supreme Court term at the end of August.

Earlier that summer, however, a woman had come to the office of US Attorney Charles Tuttle, the top federal prosecutor in Manhattan. She complained of having invested in an apparently fraudulent mining company, not an unusual occurrence at the time. When Tuttle's assistants went to the mining company's office in the city and examined its books, they found the company to be hopelessly insolvent. Of more interest was that City Magistrate George Ewald, a Cayuga Club member, and District Leader Martin Healy were among the current directors of the company.[2] By late July, when combing through Ewald's and Healy's bank records, the federal prosecutors noticed large payments of money by Ewald and his wife to Healy around the same time that Mayor Walker had appointed Ewald a magistrate in May

1927. Within days of his appointment, it appeared, George Ewald's wife, Bertha, had withdrawn a total of $10,000 from her family's bank accounts, and through an intermediary, transferred these funds to Healy, who then deposited them in his personal bank account. Since Tammany district leaders were known to have great influence on Mayor Walker's appointments to city posts, it appeared that Healy, in return for the money paid him, had encouraged Walker to appoint Ewald as magistrate.[3]

These revelations, which followed a progression of scandals involving Tammany Hall and municipal officials over the previous year, quickly raised suspicions that the political machine was now in the business of selling judgeships in the local courts.[4] Yet when summoned by US Attorney Tuttle's office before a federal grand jury, Martin Healy refused to testify regarding the payments that Bertha Ewald had made to him, and then failed to return to the grand jury, leading to the issuance of a warrant of arrest for him on July 30. The next day, both Healy and Bertha Ewald appeared before a federal judge and each invoked their Fifth Amendment rights not to testify because it might incriminate them—in Healy's case, on the basis of his possible violation of income tax laws, while Bertha's counsel mentioned a potential violation of a state law against offering a gratuity to obtain the appointment of a public official. The judge found their refusal to testify based on their fears of self-incrimination to be legitimate and excused them from testifying.[5]

US Attorney Tuttle understood that if Healy and the Ewalds had violated the state law prohibiting the purchase of public office, such crimes were beyond his jurisdiction, which was only to enforce federal laws.[6] Consequently, on August 4, 1930, he sent a letter to the Manhattan District Attorney Thomas C. T. Crain, presenting the evidence his office had collected and the name of potential witnesses he had located regarding the Ewalds' suspicious payments to Healy. This news of the referral of the Healy-Ewald allegations to Crain appeared on the front pages of the city's newspapers the next day.[7] Crain did acknowledge the receipt of Tuttle's letter and promised a swift investigation into all the allegations and evidence referred to him, adding that he "will treat this matter exactly as I would any other case placed in my hands."[8]

Crain's statement, far from being reassuring, rekindled questions concerning his ability to conduct a fair and competent investigation of Tammany Hall, of which he was a prominent member. Thomas C. T. Crain was an oddity in the political machine, a member of the Protestant gentry who had risen into the higher ranks of the predominantly Catholic and ethnic Tammany machine. Born into a wealthy family descended from settlers who came over on the Mayflower and an heir to a real estate fortune, he had practiced law and became involved in Tammany's district club in the "silk stocking" assembly district on the Upper East Side of Manhattan. With Tammany's support, he was appointed to city administrative positions, and then elected first to the General Sessions Court (the city's criminal court) in 1907, and to the New York State Supreme Court in 1924. A well-respected jurist, he was made an honorary Tammany sachem.[9]

Then, in 1929, the machine unexpectedly drafted Justice Crain, aged sixty-nine, to run for the powerful post of district attorney for New York County, the top state criminal prosecutor in Manhattan, to which he was easily elected. But once in office, Crain began to display ineptitude as a prosecutor, especially in matters that seemed to implicate Tammany Hall. Upon taking office, he had promised to solve the 1928 murder of gambler Arnold Rothstein, who was suspected of having allies and protectors among the machine's leaders but never charged anyone with the crime. Because of Crain's botched prosecutions in the Rothstein case and others that followed, the following year Governor Roosevelt would appoint an esteemed lawyer and former judge, Samuel Seabury, to investigate District Attorney Crain's conduct. Seabury would ultimately recommend that Crain not be removed from office because while thoroughly incompetent, he was not corrupt, and incompetence was not an adequate justification from removing an elected official from office.

On August 6, the last day Joseph Crater would ever be seen, the *World* issued a skeptical editorial titled "A Test For Tammany." Questioning "not only how zealous is Mr. Crain but how active is the Tammany organization, beginning with [Tammany boss] Curry, in assisting the processes of law," the newspaper demanded that immediate action be taken against Healy if "Mayor Walker, Mr. Curry and Tammany Hall care about the honor of this administration."[10] That same day, Mayor Walker, aware of the mounting public outrage on top of a string of recent Tammany scandals, for the first time reprimanded a high administration official in his administration. He directed his commissioner of the Department of Plant and Structures to suspend Healy from his position as first deputy, without pay, pending the resolution of the new accusations involving him. "While such charges exist, no man can be an active public official in this administration," Mayor Walker announced, and "[i]f the charges against him are not disproved he will be completely removed."[11]

Walker's firm action against Healy, his good friend since childhood, must have been especially difficult for him. Tammany's newspaper, aware of the strong personal ties between the men, remarked, "When Mayor Walker directed the suspension of Commissioner Martin J. Healy he suffered what was probably the most distressing hours of a long career in public life. 'Marty' should have beat the Mayor to it, if lifelong friendships carry mutual obligations."[12] But despite the mounting pressure, Tammany itself took no action to remove Healy from his post as Democratic District Leader of the Nineteenth Assembly District which he would hold onto for the next five years.

A few days later, District Attorney Crain kept his promise and went before the new grand jury himself to present the charges. Under his gentle questioning before the grand jury, Bertha Ewald magically lost her fear of testifying in federal court about the $10,000 in payments between them three years before. Mrs. Ewald now was sure that she had beneficently given to Healy, whom she admitted she had never met at the time, an interest-free loan for his purchase of a Long Island summer house, and that she had just happened to use Healy's political aide, Thomas Tommaney, as an intermediary to give the payments to him. George Ewald further testified before the grand jury that though he was appointed a magistrate with District Leader Healy's blessing, he had no knowledge of his wife's charitable loan to Healy.

Healy, who was allowed the great advantage of being privately interviewed by Crain outside the grand jury and not under oath, confirmed that Mrs. Ewald, whom he likewise didn't know beforehand, had benevolently provided him with the loan so that he could purchase his summer house. And just by coincidence, George Ewald, whom he knew well from the Cayuga Club, had happened to approach him about that time and asked for his support for his appointment as a magistrate, which Healy agreed to provide. Healy additionally denied having any contact with Mayor Walker or Boss Olvany regarding Ewald's appointment.[13]

The district attorney next summoned Mayor Walker to the courtroom, who entered to the applause of the grand jurors themselves. He denied having consulted with Healy or any political figures about his appointment of Ewald. In fact, his selection of Ewald was based on his being of German nationality, in accordance with the then accepted practice of filling judicial posts with a person of the same nationality or ethnicity as the predecessor judge. Walker assured the grand jury that "if [Ewald] voluntarily contributed any money for that appointment he might just as well have thrown it in a sewer, for the good that it did him."[14]

After the witnesses had testified and the evidence presented, Crain's final charge to his grand jury was most unusual. Instead of seeking the indictment of Healy and the Ewalds based on the evidence presented (which a grand jury typically complies with since only the prosecution's evidence has been presented to it), Crain left it up to the "good judgment of the grand jury" as to how to proceed. The grand jury deliberated for less than thirty minutes and refused to indict anyone.[15]

The manipulation of the city's prosecutorial system by the district attorney, Healy, and Ewald in such an open and disdainful manner, sparked an immediate surge of civic outrage against the political machine from politicians, religious leaders, good government groups, prominent lawyers, and the city's newspapers. "The inevitable conclusion is that the investigation of a Tammany affair by a Tammany District Attorney is wholly ineffective," one newspaper editorial inveighed. In a letter to Governor Roosevelt, Rabbi Stephen Wise, a prominent Reform Judaism leader, warned, "The failure of the grand jury to act in the Ewald case, largely as a result of the methods pursued by the prosecution, is only another item of the breakdown of justice in the city of New York." He urged that the "as yet unchallenged threat of alliance between civic corruption and judicial conduct in New York demands that you act with the vigor and directness which the people expect of you at this time." Realizing the public condemnation of his conduct, Crain publicly admitted that the evidence presented to his grand jury actually "was sufficient to warrant the finding of an indictment" against Healy and the Ewalds and offered to try again before another grand jury.[16]

2

With his race for reelection to a second term less than three months away, Governor Franklin Roosevelt now faced a potential tipping point in his political career. He had just assumed the office a year and a half before and had spent much of that time separating himself, and more importantly his political persona, from the influence and legacy of his popular predecessor, Al Smith. Roosevelt knew that to have any hope of getting the Democratic nomination for the presidency in two years, he would have to not only win reelection to a second term as governor but to do so resoundingly. Further, realizing the growing anxiety and insecurity from the deepening economic catastrophe sweeping his state and the nation, he was convinced that his campaign had to address voters' economic and welfare concerns.

In the wake of Crain's bungling of the Healy-Ewald charges, the governor must have realized that the greatest obstacle to his reelection would be the Tammany Tiger and its spoor of corruption. With Tammany voters constituting about half of the Democratic electorate in New York State, he knew that antagonizing the machine likely would lose him enough votes to deprive him of the landslide victory he needed, or of reelection at all. On the other hand, being too closely associated with the machine also might provide fatal in the presidential election in 1932, as had recently been demonstrated by Smith's debacle in the 1928 election. Smith had been vilified in his campaign for his close association with Tammany as well as his Catholicism, especially in the South and Midwest portions of the nation where prejudice and hatred against political machines, Catholics, immigrants, and anything to do with New York was rampant. So in the coming months, Roosevelt would have to carefully maneuver between the shoals of being too antagonistic or too complicit with Tammany Hall.

Facing public calls in mid-August to take some action in response to District Attorney Crain's fiasco of a prosecution in the Healy-Ewald matter, Governor Roosevelt now attempted to thread the political needle. On August 19, 1930, he removed the Healy-Ewald prosecution from Crain and assigned it to New York State Attorney General Hamilton Ward, while designating Supreme Court Justice Philip McCook, who had presided over the Libby's Hotel condemnation trial earlier that year, to convene a special grand jury to consider charges being brought against Healy, the Ewalds and any others and to preside over the trial of any resulting indictments. Roosevelt's action entailed great political risk because Ward was a prominent Republican state politician, who himself was being mentioned as a gubernatorial candidate to oppose Roosevelt that fall, and Justice McCook was also an elected Republican antagonistic toward Tammany and Mayor Walker's administration.

But Roosevelt's putting the prosecution of the Healy-Ewald charges in Republicans' hands proved to be a quite astute and savvy move. While eliminating Tammany's ability to corrupt the investigation and distancing himself from the machine's increasingly toxic aura, he could still come to its defense, were the Republican prosecutors and judge to go too far in their investigations, and appear to be acting for only partisan motives. In the event the Republican prosecutor and judge failed to indict and convict Healy and the Ewalds, the governor couldn't be accused of protecting Tammany as District Attorney Crain had just appeared to do. The immediate reaction in the press was generally favorable to Roosevelt's measured response, although there was criticism in some of the newspapers that he had not gone far enough. Even Tammany Hall applauded the governor's actions, its newspaper calling his appointment of Attorney General Ward, "the one thing needed to remove the subject [of the Healy-Ewald investigation] from the field of partisan politics" and showing "that courage which [Roosevelt's] sponsors always claimed for him."[17]

By the end of August, Attorney General Ward announced the convening on September 15 of his special grand jury drawn from a "blue ribbon" panel of men, to investigate the allegations against Healy, the Ewalds, and Tommaney. When Ward's staff preliminarily issued subpoenas for witnesses to testify before the grand jury, one was sent to Joseph Crater, whose disappearance three weeks before had not yet been publicly disclosed. As one of the new prosecutors shortly remarked, "Crater had been president of the Cayuga Democratic Club for a long time. No doubt he would have been able to tell us how things were done up there and who did them."[18] The breaking news of Justice Crater's disappearance on September 3, amidst the uproar that Healy may have been bribed to obtain a judicial office for George Ewald, exponentially raised the stakes in both matters.

Crain's new assignment to lead a grand jury called to investigate Crater's disappearance, after being ignominiously removed from the Healy-Ewald investigation, cast obvious doubt about his motivation to find out what really happened to the missing judge who had strong ties to the machine. Crain publicly stated that he was grateful for the opportunity to redeem himself after his debacle the month before. But his situation was more realistically assessed in an anonymous limerick about the Crater case that would shortly be published in the *Daily News*:

> But in all this suff'ring, all this pain,
> Give a kind thought to Old Man Crain.
> He is forced to look, but he MUST NOT SEE,
> Or he might play h--- with Tammany;
> So a very busy man is he,

Like a cat on a roof of tin, you see....
O, the mystery's great but 'twill be far greater
If they make a mistake, and FIND Judge Crater![19]

3

Thus, beginning on September 15, 1930, there were two grand jury proceedings being held in Lower Manhattan courthouses a few blocks apart, which
on the surface appeared to be separate and distinct matters. In the Criminal
Courts building on Centre Street, there began an unusual proceeding before
another "blue-ribbon" grand jury, in which a district attorney was conducting
a criminal investigation into the disappearance of a prominent jurist when it
still was unclear if any crime had been committed at all or if so, by whom. In
the Supreme Court building farther south on Centre Street, where the missing judge briefly had his chambers, a prosecutor appointed by a Republican
attorney general began presenting criminal charges of judicial office-buying
against a Tammany Hall district leader and a city magistrate, both of whom
Crater knew well.

While accounts of the two grand juries' proceedings often appeared side
by side in the newspapers in the following weeks, little effort surprisingly
was made to connect the two, or to draw links between those being investigated. The *New Yorker* magazine soon expressed befuddlement at the "local
corruption situation" that has "become so complicated that it's hopeless....
Too many people are involved; it is impossible to separate the sheep from
the goats, the investigators from the investigatees." There followed a list of
twenty-five names involved in the two proceedings, of whom "[s]ome are
missing, some are accused, some are indignant."[20] Some articles considered
whether Crater had a role in the Healy-Ewald charges. There were reports,
subsequently confirmed, that Crater had presided as master of ceremonies
at a testimonial dinner held by the Cayuga Club for Ewald's induction as a
magistrate back in 1927.

Other newspaper articles, however, downplayed Crater's role and any
knowledge he may have possessed as Cayuga Club president and as Healy's
close associate. For instance, the *World* article breaking the news of his disappearance observed that the "presidency of a Tammany club is virtually perfunctory, the [district] leader always being the actual and active head of the
organization." And there were quick denials by the new Healy-Ewald prose-

cutors that Crater was a target of their investigation, or that Crater was ever suspected of buying his own Supreme Court seat as Ewald was alleged to have done.[21] But the question that surprisingly seemed to elude the prosecutors, the NYPD and the press, was whether the two proceedings were related in another way—whether Martin Healy and George Ewald or others in the Cayuga Club had any knowledge of or involvement in their club member's disappearance.

On September 18, as District Attorney Crain was calling his first witnesses before the Crater grand jury, the mistress-blackmail theory of the judge's disappearance gained new life when the *World* published a copy of an anonymous letter mailed from Chicago. Addressed to its city editor, the handwritten letter began, "This is a confidential communication—as much as I am inclined to withhold my name from the public until I will be convinced that the truth requires this sacrifice in my case." The author claimed to "know where Justice Crater is, so do others." The letter continued, "Mrs. Crater knows that the judge is in the West, that his departure from New York preceeded [sic] a tremendous domestic quarrel, which almost shook the roofs of their 5th Ave. apartment. She also knows that he had to get out the cash from the bank to satisfy the whims of a 'scanty' who threatened scandals."

The letter further identified certain people who knew "the whereabouts of Justice Crater," including a "Dr. Samuel Buchler, former Deputy Attorney General of New York State, who, I am informed, has been hired as attorney by the complainant to institute an action against the Judge" that "was closed in consideration of $5,000 paid by Justice Crater to Buchler's client." Among others, a brother of Lieutenant Governor Herbert Lehman, a "gentleman with the Initials of L.B.," and Senator Wagner were in the know. The letter writer was "more than certain that in less than one week" the mystery of Crater's disappearance would be solved.[22]

At first, the anonymous letter appeared to have been authored by a "crank" or a person seeking publicity, with whom the NYPD was becoming increasingly familiar.[23] In addition to the misspellings and awkward grammar in the letter, some of its information could have been gleaned from news reports about the case, such as that Crater had taken about $5,000 from the bank on the morning of August 6. Other information, however, was palpably false as the police knew, because Stella and Joe were not together to have a roof-raising argument in their Fifth Avenue apartment before he was last seen. Additionally, when the police spoke with some of the people mentioned in the letter as having knowledge about Crater's disappearance, they all denied it.

The letter was given more credence, however, when later that day, NYPD Detective Hugh Sheridan interviewed Dr. Buchler, a lawyer and rabbi who was active in Tammany Hall, at his office. Asked about the letter's reference to him, he readily admitted that on August 5, a woman named "Lorraine Fay," whom he described as a well-dressed, young, bleached blonde with a Jewish accent, had come to his office. She had wanted to institute "breach of promise" (to marry) proceedings against the judge, with whom she had been having assignations at different hotels in the city for several months. Buchler further stated he had asked her to come back the next day with the evidence she had to support such a lawsuit, but she never contacted him again. When asked why he had not alerted Crater, whom he knew through political connections, about this woman's threatening a court action against him, he replied that he did not want "to annoy him until he had received further evidence from this Fay woman." The police followed up on tips of the whereabouts of the mysterious Lorraine Fay in Pennsylvania and elsewhere but never located her.[24] That the meeting between Buchler and Lorraine Fay actually took place on August 5 also could not be independently confirmed.

But in light of subsequent events, Buchler's own credibility and motives must be questioned. A Tammany loyalist who had received low-level patronage posts in the city government, he would soon be convicted for defrauding clients by feigning his special pull with government officials to obtain dispensations, referred to then as now as being a "fixer," and be disbarred from practicing law.[25] But even if his story were true (and Crater's many liaisons with other women at the time of his disappearance made Lorraine Fay's accusations quite credible), the question remained of how the information about his meeting with Fay wound up with someone in Chicago to mail the letter to the *World*.

What was more evident was the effect of the public disclosure of the letter in the press. It caused attention to return to the original theory of the police and the press that Crater used the cash withdrawn from his bank accounts on the morning of August 6 to pay off a woman who was blackmailing him. As was reported soon afterward, "close observers" of the case "are of the impression that the letter to the *World* which resulted in the disclosure of the threatened breach of promise suit was merely a blind to detract attention from the political angle" of the Crater disappearance.[26] Someone with political connections to the missing man who wanted to divert the direction of the search presumably could have arranged for the sending of the letter from Chicago.

Police Commissioner Mulrooney himself still had not given up on his hunch that Crater had vanished because of his philandering. He was anxiously awaiting the return of Connie Marcus, a becoming, auburn-haired former cloak model, whom witnesses had identified as having been Crater's mistress for several years. It appeared that Marcus had fled the city for an unknown destination right after the news of Crater's disappearance broke, which made her seem even more complicit. Rumors began to circulate that she and the mysterious Lorraine Fay in Buchler's story were one and the same.

At last returning to her hotel on September 26, Marcus was whisked by detectives to police headquarters and interviewed at length by Commissioner Mulrooney himself. But she quickly established to the commissioner's satisfaction that she did not know anything about Joe's disappearance, and she was not Ms. Fay. She did admit to being his partially subsidized mistress for some seven years and that he generally came to visit at her apartment about once or twice a week and took her out on the town about a half-dozen times a year. While Marcus tactfully was not asked, it seemed apparent that in return for Joe providing part of her rent as well as occasional gifts and nights on the town, she provided him with sex and companionship. She did complain that he was tight-fisted with his financial support and was not a big spender on the dates.[27]

The last time she saw Joe was on the night of July 24. He had taken her to eat at "his place," Haas' restaurant on West Forty-Fifth Street. From there, they had gone to see the *Artists and Models* show, where she was surprised and annoyed to learn that he appeared to personally know many of the scantily clad girls in the show, pointing them out by first name. Afterward, they went to Connie's Inn and the Nut Club in Harlem, arriving back at her apartment early in the morning, where Crater stayed for another hour before leaving. From their conversation that night, she gathered the judge was pretty certain of, and "very much enthused and excited" about, Tammany's backing him for nomination and election to a full term on the Supreme Court bench that fall, and that the machine would provide the money for all his campaign expenses. Joe had told her when they last parted that he would be going shortly to Belgrade Lakes for the rest of the summer and would return to the city at the end of August.[28]

Marcus expressed obvious anger over what she had learned about her bene-factor cheating on her, his mistress. She said that while he was fond of her, she was kept in the dark about his carrying on with other women: "I didn't know what the whole thing was about to tell you the truth. Here's a man who was supposed to care for me and I didn't know of one thing or the other." When asked what she thought had happened to Joe, she couldn't offer any assis-tance. As far as she knew, he had no enemies and "was pretty well liked."[29] She described Crater as a "very brilliant" and "cold-minded" man whose "whole life and ambition was law." His current predicament she found "stupid" and completely incomprehensible. Success in his career was "the only thing he was trying to get in life," she said, and the "only thing that would hurt him would be a thing like this." Several questions were asked concerning Martin Healy, whom she heard Crater mention on occasion but did not know herself.[30] Commissioner Mulrooney found her credible and believed she had nothing to do with the judge's disappearance.

4

In the midst of the hoopla surrounding Marcus's return, District Attorney Crain did call Martin Healy and his younger brother William to testify briefly before his grand jury. The impetus for calling them was that investiga-tors in US attorney Tuttle's office had learned from telephone records for the Craters' Fifth Avenue apartment that at the end of August, Stella had called the Healys' Blue Point summerhouse, the same one supposedly bought with Bertha Ewald's interest-free loan in 1927. Stella apparently had made these calls when she had frantically come back to the city to help find her husband before the news of his disappearance had been made public. It now was re-ported that someone present in the apartment at that time observed Stella calling Healy's summer house and heard her hysterically asking the other per-son on the phone where her husband was and that if "he was hiding out any-where to protect [Healy], she wanted to know it and be in on it." Healy's lawyer confirmed that Stella had reached out to his client at that time, stating that "[n]othing could have been more natural, as Mr. Healy and the justice were close friends."[31]

Before the Healy brothers appeared before his grand jury, Crain first made them waive their immunity from prosecution for the testimony they would give the grand jury so that it could be used in the Healy-Ewald prosecution, if necessary. William Healy then testified that while at their summerhouse at the end of August, he had answered a phone call from Stella Crater in the middle of the night, and that she was "frantic," sounding, as he described it, "as if she had just learned that her husband was dead." He had assured her that "no member of the Healy family had any idea of her husband's whereabouts." A few hours later, Stella placed another call, which was answered by Healy's mother who said she knew nothing of the matter. Although not in on either phone call, Martin did testify about Stella's "half-hysterical" calls and stated it was the first he had heard that Crater was missing.[32] But Crain failed to ask other obvious questions of Martin Healy in his brief appearance before his grand jury—he asked nothing about Healy's very close relationship with the missing man, which his lawyer just had publicly confirmed; nothing about when Healy last had seen or talked with Joe around the time of his disappearance; and nothing about the business and political activities they were involved in at the Cayuga Club.

At the end of September, another grand jury witness stated what he had heard about the telephone call Crater had placed in Belgrade Lakes Village on the night of Saturday, August 2. Ludwig Traube, who had a cabin next door to the Craters' at Belgrade Lakes, recalled that he had run into Joe just after he had arrived from the city there earlier that day. The judge told him then that he would be staying up there for the next few weeks, and they made plans to get together during that time. When Traube went to the Craters' cabin the next night, however, Stella informed him that her husband had packed up a few hours before and "left for New York in response to a call concerning an important matter," but she did not say what that matter was.[33] Since the Craters' cabin had no telephone, the phone call that Stella mentioned to Traube likely was referring to the call or calls she later thought Joe might have made in Belgrade Lakes Village on Saturday night when he went off by himself a few times. While newspaper articles speculated about whom Crater had called in the village and what was discussed, Crain seemed to show little interest in the call that was compelling enough for the missing man to abruptly change his planned three-week vacation in Maine and rush back to the city.[34]

The Craters' "Puerto Rican maid," Amedia Christian, testified about a brief contact she had with the judge in the city right after he had returned to the Fifth Avenue apartment on the morning of August 4. She testified that she was in the apartment cleaning when the judge arrived there. He instructed her not to return to the apartment to clean until August 7 because "he intended to go back to Maine on the sixth."[35] This was consistent with William Klein's statements made to the police that when he dined with his friend and girlfriend at Billy Haas' Chophouse that evening, Crater told him that he would be returning to Belgrade Lakes by August 6 and intended to remain in the city for only two days.

In early October, there again were some points of convergence between the two grand jury investigations regarding Crater's financial affairs. Crain learned that shortly after his appointment to the bench that spring, he had requested his stockbroker friend to sell a large amount of stock for which he received approximately $16,000 in cash in large denominations. Around the same time, he had withdrawn almost $7,000 from his bank accounts, also in large denominations.[36] Investigators were unable to determine what the judge did with this exceptionally large amount of money, but rumors swirled that the money went to a certain political organization in connection with his nomination for a full term on the Supreme Court that fall.

Investigators' hopes were also raised when it was discovered that Crater had a safety deposit box in a company at his old law office building at 120 Broadway, where he was said to have kept stock and other valuable items. With Crain in attendance, along with representatives of his and Attorney General Ward's offices and federal prosecutors, Crater's deposit box was dramatically forced open, turned upside down and absolutely nothing fell out of it. As one reporter described the scene, "The revelation came as a distinct shock to [Crain] and other investigating officials who had expected that the box would yield a clew to Crater's sudden leave-taking, if it did not entirely solve the mystery."[37]

The district attorney continued to turn an exceptionally blind eye to the possibility that Martin Healy knew more about his close advisor and friend's disappearance. The *Times* observed at the end of September that Crain simply "refused to discuss the possibility that Justice Crater, who had been for years the legal mind among the Cayuga Club politicians had been called by them from Maine into consultation concerning the impending Ewald investigation and the position which they should take." Furthermore, it reported, Crain's "position...continued to be that he could not interest himself in anything concerning the Ewald case because it had been taken out of his hands by" Governor Roosevelt.[38] The district attorney appeared to effectively use the contemporaneous, separate proceedings in the Healy-Ewald criminal probe as a shield to preclude his grand jury from looking into any connections between Crater's last days in the city and the then-breaking news about the judicial office-buying charges.[39]

The following month, a reporter at the *New Yorker* attempted to take stock of the Crater search and the evidence that had been collected so far. The article was written in the sardonic style of the new, highbrow, modernist magazine. It described some of the false clues as to the vanished judge's whereabouts over the past five weeks: "the ransom letters written by cranks asked huge amounts of money" and "[f]rom all over the country came reports that the missing man had been seen: in barbershops, drugstores, walking along roads, in hotels" and "through the minds of imaginative people." While the article's references to facts in the case were sometimes inaccurate (for instance, it suggested Lorraine Fay and Connie Marcus were the same person), it did sum up well the current status of the search for Crater in the middle of October: "There began a slow and difficult reconstruction of the past, confused by the Case of the Dubious Magistrates [referring to the Healy-Ewald inquiry], moving into half a dozen alleys that were encouraging, then doubtful, then palpably wrong." It concluded with a literary flourish, suggesting that all of the prevalent theories of the case may have combined, Agatha Christie-like, to result in his disappearance: "One thinks at last of a legal-minded schoolroomish sort of fellow, pranking unfamiliarly through the devious ways of politics and of the fleshpots, fouling himself astonishingly in the tangled threads of both, and running at last into a corner where fleshpots and politics together meet on common ground for his destruction."[40]

5

In contrast with the plodding nature of the Crater grand jury, which had begun on the same day a few blocks away, Attorney General Ward's grand jury quickly accomplished its primary objective that had eluded District Attorney Crain the month before, and then some. With a prominant private trial lawyer, Hiram Todd, hired as the lead prosecutor, Ward's grand jury in its first week returned indictments against Martin Healy, Bertha and George Ewald, and Thomas Tommaney, without even calling the defendants to testify. The indictments charged them with the felony offense of buying public office, alleging that the Ewalds, with Tommaney as the intermediary, paid $10,000 to Healy in his capacity as "Democratic District Leader of the Nineteenth Assembly District" in return for influencing George Ewald's appointment as

Magistrate by Mayor Walker. The crime was punishable by two years of imprisonment and a $3,000 fine. At their arraignment, Bertha Ewald quipped, "I suppose we'll get the electric chair too." Her husband dismissed it as "just part of the circus."[41]

Not stopping with that indictment, however, the Healy-Ewald grand jury and its prosecutors began to investigate persons and entities associated with the Cayuga Club, with Justice McCook's encouragement. They sought the records of Healy's Cayuga Holding Company, a real estate business that was rumored to be "the repository of the special funds received by certain Democratic officials for fulfilling political contracts." Also subpoenaed to testify before the grand jury was Felix Solomon, another Cayuga Club member and Healy's partner in a corporation that was believed to be involved in honest grafting, including using "inside information on property sought by the city for public buildings...and purchasing on such inside information and holding for inflated valuations under condemnation proceedings." Solomon claimed that records of that company were missing.[42]

Now Roosevelt's and Tammany's fears of a runaway grand jury, led by Republican prosecutors and overseen by a sympathetic judge, investigating Democratic judicial officeholders began to materialize. In his opening instructions to the grand jury on September 15, McCook intentionally had broadened the scope of its investigatory authority well beyond the Healy-Ewald and related matters to include whether there "existed a system, course of conduct or understanding by force" according to which judges such as Ewald had to pay "a political party, party leader or public official" for appointment to the bench. These instructions blatantly exceeded Governor Roosevelt's initial directions to Attorney General Ward about the grand jury's scope, to now include investigation of a general "system" by which municipal judges and magistrates had to pay the Tammany machine to get their position.[43]

Acting in furtherance of Justice McCook's broad charges to the grand jury, lead prosecutor Todd then unexpectedly commenced calling the Tammany boss and various district leaders, one by one, to testify about the machine's role in the appointing of judges. Furthermore, all the Tammany leaders would be required by Todd to first waive any immunity from prosecution for anything they might say before the grand jury. Curry, the initial witness, set the script followed by the Tammany district leaders called thereafter. Angrily refusing to waive his immunity, Curry stormed out of the jury room, red-faced, telling reporters outside, "I came down here prepared to testify and I was insulted." His attorney characterized the subpoenas as "the event of a political campaign," and given that "the grand jury is supposed to investigate only the [Healy-]Ewald matter" and "[o]f that affair Mr. Curry knows nothing," his client had nothing to testify about. Over the next three days in late September, a parade of fifteen district leaders, most of whom also occupied high positions in the municipal and county governments, were called to the stand and likewise refused to waive their immunity.[44]

This stonewalling by Tammany leaders further added to the simmering public outrage against it. "The organization has put itself formally and spectacularly on record as determined to resist inquiry into the charge that it has been selling judicial offices," a *World* editorial intoned, "They have chosen to appear as men who have guilty knowledge to conceal." Another editorial in the *Times* raised the perennial suspicion about witnesses refusing to testify about what they know: "If they have nothing to hide, why do they decline to testify? If there are not larger areas of Tammany dishonesty, why are the leaders, from their chief down, forced to become obstacles...to the ascertainment of acts in a small area?"[45] Attorney General Ward and Justice McCook intended to force Governor Roosevelt to resolve the issue of Tammany's refusal to testify.

6

Meanwhile in Albany, the governor anxiously pondered the effect of the evolving grand jury proceedings on his crucial upcoming reelection campaign. Complicating matters for Roosevelt was his long, turbulent, and complex history with Tammany Hall and its most successful politician, Al Smith. It was primarily the political and personal relations of the two men who came from such different worlds—one from the impoverished Irish Catholic slums of the city and the other from the wealthy Protestant gentry in rural upstate New York—that would redefine the course of American politics in the twentieth century.[46]

Franklin D. Roosevelt had first attracted political attention in 1911 as a newly elected Democratic state senator from conservative Dutchess County, where his family's estate sat. He had immediately led a revolt against Boss Charlie Murphy's choice of a Buffalo politician named "Blue-Eyed Billy" Sheehan to be the Democratic candidate for US Senate from New York (senators being selected by state legislatures at the time). His novice attack against the machine's domination of the state government in Albany was rather farcical. Contemporary press accounts described the young man as "look[ing] like a boy," with the "finely chiseled face of a Roman patrician" and demonstrating the "silly conceits of a political prig," while Tammany's "Big Tim" Sullivan, a state legislator and district leader, thought him an "awful arrogant fellow." While Roosevelt's Democratic insurgency did lead to Sheehan's ultimate withdrawal from consideration as a candidate, it turned out to be a pyrrhic victory as Murphy's second choice for the position, also a Tammany loyalist, was easily confirmed.[47]

Murphy surely had no qualms about his decision in 1913 to move on to Washington, DC, and serve as assistant secretary of the navy in the Wilson administration for the rest of the decade. During his time away, his only attempt to get back into New York politics by seeking selection for a US Senate seat himself in 1914, was easily rebuffed by Murphy. The boss's further efforts supporting his nomination as vice president on the Democratic ticket in 1920, which was crushed in the Republican landslide, also served to keep the rising politician out of his way.[48]

But there also had been times when Roosevelt tried to mend fences with Tammany Hall, not only because he needed its support and votes to win New York State office but also because of Murphy's attempts at reforming it and his support for progressivism. At Tammany's invitation, Assistant Secretary Roosevelt even attended and gave one of the traditional "long talks" at its Independence Day festivities in 1917, just after the US had entered World War I. An article observed that "although a Democrat, [who] has been unsparing in his denunciation of Tammany," he was "warmly greeted" and his speech about the war effort well received. Afterward, he sat on the stage next to Murphy and they amiably chatted.[49]

In Al Smith's first run for governor in 1918, Roosevelt endorsed him largely because of his record as the leader of the progressive Democrats in the New York Assembly over the past decade and his significant legislative achievements there. During his four terms, Governor Smith would prove to be an exceptionally popular, pragmatic, and skillful conductor of the state government, who would transform it into a dynamo of progressive political, socioeconomic, and regulatory reform during the 1920s. His legislative and administrative accomplishments as governor included the enactment of measures benefitting the unemployed, disabled, and the poor; mandating safer working conditions for labor and recognizing labor unions; reorganizing and modernizing the state's government; providing cheaper and more regulated utilities and waterpower that benefitted consumers; improving public health facilities; and many others. As Frances Perkins, who served in Governor Smith's cabinet and inner circle, would say of him many years later, "He'd been the most important Governor we ever had, and done more than anybody thought could be done and had done it with such skill and such political effectiveness that people liked it. He made people like it."[50]

After his unsuccessful run for vice president in 1920, Roosevelt's rising political career was tragically cut short when he contracted polio. His inability to walk except with much assistance and effort seemed to spell the inevitable end of that career, except to a handful of people closest to him. But despite spending most of his time desperately struggling to perambulate in some fashion in the following years and founding his polio sanitarium in Warm Springs, Georgia, to assist himself and others, he still managed to stay in contact with Smith mainly through a mutually respectful correspondence about state politics. It was Al Smith, as well as Franklin's wife Eleanor and his advisor Louis Howe, who tried to keep him focused on politics. While witnessing Al's success in establishing in New York a more active and progressive government that appealed to working class, urban, immigrant, and ethnic groups, Franklin an increasingly capable politician began to perceive the coalitions of voters he would need if he returned to state or national politics.

Given the tremendous differences in the upbringing, social milieu, and personalities of Smith and Roosevelt, the personal ties between them were bound to be somewhat strained. Al from the start looked down on the younger man's abilities. His impression early on was that he was a rich man dabbling in politics, a dilettante who was out of touch with the people. After Roosevelt was sidelined with polio, Smith perceived him to be severely handicapped and physically unfit for public office. Although he liked Frank, he didn't feel comfortable with him socially or with his closest advisors. He once summed up his feelings to a friend that "Franklin just isn't the kind of man you can take into the pissroom and talk intimately with." Roosevelt, in turn, did not feel comfortable with the comradery, banter, drinking, and informality Al and those around him enjoyed. In one historian's words, He "had been brought up in an atmosphere that stressed the compulsive understatement....He could not, without denying his background, fail to disapprove of the kinds of people Al and his friends were."[51]

But Roosevelt's loyalty to and respect for Governor Smith provided him with a limited role in the latter's administration and campaigns, which helped keep him in the public eye. When Murphy unexpectedly died right before the Democratic National Convention at Madison Square Garden in the summer of 1924, Franklin stepped in to act as Al's campaign manager. He made an electrifying and memorable appearance at the convention when, physically unable to walk upright on his own, he courageously agreed to place Smith's name in nomination for the presidency. With heavy metal braces on his legs, a cane in his hand, and his weight borne on the arm of his son, he managed to awkwardly ambulate from his seat in the audience, climb the stairs to the stage, and move to the podium, all the time maintaining his charismatic smile while risking utter disaster. Clinging to the podium for support, he gave a rousing nomination speech for Smith (which was written by his aide and Roosevelt thought would be a flop), culminating with the christening of him as the "Happy Warrior" of the political battlefield based on a Wordsworth poem. He would end up losing the Democratic nomination that year, but the political moniker stuck.[52]

At Smith's request, Roosevelt once again nominated him for the presidency at the 1928 Democratic convention in Houston. In his nominating speech, Frank praised his mentor and friend in words that would mirror his own appeal and image just four years later, praising him as "a leader...who grasps and understands not only large affairs of business and government, but in an equal degree the aspirations and the needs of the individual, the farmer, the wage-earner—the great mass of average citizens who make up the backbone of our Nation."[53] And it was Smith, again with help from Eleanor, who cajoled and flattered a reluctant Roosevelt into running to succeed him as governor of New York, assuring him that he need only be a caretaker who could spend most of his time recuperating in Warm Springs. At the time, he told an aide that he thought the disabled man would only live a year longer.[54] Instead, Roosevelt, showing his grit and determination, exhaustingly campaigned all over the state for weeks, with many of his appearances and speeches made from the back of his automobile. His platform coopted Smith's progressive achievements as governor, such as government regulation of the economy, consumer protections, and providing for the health, safety, and welfare of its workers and citizens.

Al Smith lost the presidential race to President Herbert Hoover in 1928 by a large margin, including, embarrassingly, the state which he had headed as a popular governor for an unprecedented four terms. It was a disillusioning and effectively career-ending loss for Al Smith, the result of one of the most divisive, culturally fraught, and bigoted campaigns up to that time, in which he was pilloried as the puppet of Tammany Hall and the Pope. Although Smith appeared to take little consolation from it during the rest of his life, his defeat in 1928 marked the beginning of a new realignment of ethnically, religiously, and racially diverse voters largely from the cities into a new Democratic Party that would dominate national politics from 1932 through the 1960s.[55]

Smith's presidential debacle, according to a *New Republic* editorial, also "brought a great diminution of his power and prestige" within Tammany and "mark[ed] the end of the 'new Tammany,'" which it described as "to a large degree the invention of the Wigwam's astute press agents." Boss Olvany, Smith's ally, was forced out by Mayor Walker and the district leaders in 1929. With Walker's landslide reelection that year, he and his district leaders would control the machine, and Smith would effectively retire from active involvement in it, remaining as one of its honorary sachems.[56]

Despite Smith's defeat in 1928, Roosevelt unexpectedly had eked out a victory in the New York governor's race. Smith returned to offer his presumed protégé his advice on how to be governor and pressed him to take on his top advisors Robert Moses and Belle Moskowitz who together with Al, would really run the state government, leaving him as little more than a figurehead. To his surprise, Smith was firmly but politely rebuffed in these efforts by the man he thought incapacitated and incapable of governing.[57]

In her oral history taken many years later, Perkins, who served as senior political advisor to both men, analyzed the underlying psychological tensions between them. The reason Frank spurned Al's repeated offers to come up to Albany to help him, she thought, was that he had been damaged "in his own personality by this terrible misfortune that had overtaken him which put him on the level of dependent [his contracting polio]" and he felt threatened by these perceived attempts to control him. The new governor consequently gathered his own circle of advisors, most of whom (unlike Perkins herself) had no loyalties to Smith, so that he could "feel confidence in himself and [learn] to bear the burdens of his own decisions and not to have any doubt of his ability to make them." In his four years as governor, Roosevelt, in his "desire to outshine Al Smith," would "let the credit accrue to himself" even though he basically implemented the policies and programs that "had been started by Smith."[58]

With the national economy beginning its descent into depression during his first term as governor and President Hoover's inadequate efforts to revive it, Franklin Roosevelt grasped that a Democrat could successfully appeal to the country's electorate in 1932. But he first had to win a convincing reelection as governor that fall.

1. A full-length photo of Joe Crater in sporty attire around the time of his disappearance. (Courtesy of the New York Police Department.)

2. The initial version of Crater's missing person circular issued by the NYPD and distributed in tens of thousands of copies around the country and world. (Courtesy of the New York Police Department.)

DETECTIVE DIVISION
CIRCULAR No. 9
SEPTEMBER 8, 1930 | POLICE DEPARTMENT
CITY OF NEW YORK | BE SURE TO FILE THIS CIRCULAR FOR REFERENCE

Police Authorities are Requested to Post this Circular for the Information of Police Officers and File a Copy of it for Future Reference.

MISSING SINCE AUGUST 6, 1930

HONORABLE JOSEPH FORCE CRATER,
JUSTICE OF THE SUPREME COURT, STATE OF NEW YORK

DESCRIPTION—Born in the United States—Age, 41 years; height, 6 feet; weight, 185 pounds; mixed grey hair, originally dark-brown, thin at top, parted in middle "slicked" down; complexion, medium dark, considerably tanned; brown eyes; false teeth, upper and lower jaw, good physical and mental condition at time of disappearance. Tip of right index finger somewhat mutilated, due to having been recently crushed.
Wore brown sack coat and trousers, narrow green stripe, no vest; either a Panama or soft brown hat worn at rakish angle, size 6⅞, unusual size for his height and weight. Clothes made by Vroom. Affected colored shirts, size 14 collar, probably bow tie. Wore tortoise-shell glasses for reading. Yellow gold Masonic ring, somewhat worn; may be wearing a yellow gold, square-shaped wrist watch with leather strap.
COMMUNICATE with CHIEF INSPECTOR, POLICE DEPARTMENT, 18th Division, (Missing Persons Bureau), New York City. Telephone Spring 3100.

3. Tammany Hall Boss Charles F. Murphy leaving courthouse in 1923 after testifying in lawsuit involving his wartime profiteering. (Courtesy of the author.)

4. Tammany District Leader George Washington Plunkitt, the father of "honest graft." (© Archive PL/Alamy Stock Photo.)

5. Meeting of Tammany leaders and politicians during Mayor Jimmy Walker's administration in the late 1920s, including Boss George Olvany (first at left), Senator Robert Wagner (third from left), Walker (fourth from left), Governor Al Smith (fifth from left), and Surrogate James Foley (at right). (Courtesy of the author.)

6. A scene from one of the Shubert Brothers' salacious *Artists and Models* revues during the 1920s, which Crater attended shortly before his disappearance. (© The Shubert Archive.)

7. The building used as the clubhouse of the Cayuga Democratic Club in West Harlem at the time of Crater's disappearance. (Courtesy of New York Public Library.)

8. Max Bernstein's luxury Libby's Hotel & Baths on the Lower East Side of Manhattan. (Courtesy of Oldnycphotos.com.)

9. State Supreme Court Justice Crater after his appointment in April 1930. (© Shutterstock.com.)

10. Martin Healy, Tammany district leader of the Nineteenth Assembly District and boss of the Cayuga Club, in 1930. (Courtesy of the author.)

11. Mayor Walker meeting with Manhattan District Attorney Thomas Crain over the Healy-Ewald charges in August 1930, days after Crater disappeared. (Courtesy of the author.)

12. After losing the presidential election in 1928, Al Smith congratulating Franklin D. Roosevelt on being elected governor of New York. (Courtesy of Franklin D. Roosevelt Presidential Library & Museum, Hyde Park, NY.)

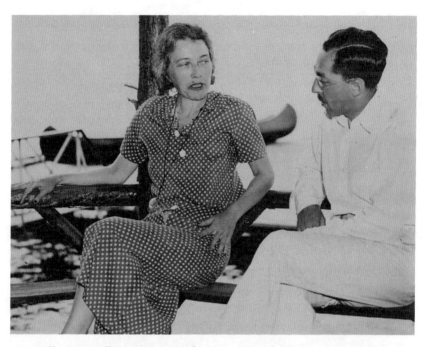

13. Stella Crater talking to Simon Rifkind in Maine after being interviewed by the *New York World-Telegram* in 1937. (Courtesy of the author.)

Governor Roosevelt's Quandary
and Tammany's Trials

I

In the autumn of 1930, President Herbert Hoover, as well as political leaders and commentators across the nation, would be watching the New York gubernatorial race, well aware of its repercussions for the presidential election in two years. If Franklin Roosevelt could be defeated in his bid for reelection or his margin of victory was slim, his momentum toward the White House could be slowed or stopped. Hoover's administration would try to intervene in the New York campaign, with unintended consequences.

On the other side, Governor Roosevelt realized that the growing calamity of the Depression together with the progressive socioeconomic agenda he had inherited from Smith boded well for his re-election. Yet standing in the way of the campaign he wanted to run for reelection, he understood there was a huge obstacle facing him as a Democrat that fall: the recent outbreak of Tammany corruption scandals and specifically, the imbroglio over the Healy-Ewald grand jury. Additionally, his widely praised appointment of Crater as a judge that spring would shortly turn into a major liability.

At the end of September 1930, US Attorney Charles Tuttle, having initiated investigations into the Healy-Ewald charges and other cases involving Tammany misdeeds, was quickly nominated by the Republican State Convention to run against Roosevelt. In many respects, Tuttle seemed to be the right man with the right message that fall. A devout Christian with choirboyish looks, he had become a prominent and successful business lawyer in Manhattan with a reputation that was beyond reproach. When he was appointed US Attorney for the Southern District of New York by President Calvin

Coolidge in 1927, his *New Yorker* profile was captioned a "Saint in Politics." With the recent brazen Tammany corruption in the city, and his record of prosecuting it, Tuttle had the moral authority, nonpartisan reputation, and crusading spirit to take on the aging political machine. Upon being nominated, Tuttle announced the main issue of his campaign: "Are we to have a Governor that is bigger than Tammany Hall or not?"[1]

At the Democratic State Convention held in Syracuse at the end of September 1930, Al Smith gave the key nominating speech for Roosevelt, returning the favor of the latter's nomination of him for the presidency two years before. Showing signs of the rift between the men which would grow increasingly wide in the coming decade, however, Smith's speech largely defended his own prior progressive leadership as governor. In his acceptance speech, in turn, Roosevelt stressed a theme of the necessity of an activist government that benefited a new constituency of voters, in contrast to the Republican leaders' failure, both on the federal and state levels, to effectively address the increasingly dire economic conditions. Noting his adversary's focus on "the 'issue' and not the 'issues' of the campaign," Roosevelt ridiculed Tuttle's "determination to go before the people and to ask them to select him as the head of one of the greatest and most complicated business and social organizations in the whole wide world" based only on the issue of Tammany Hall's corruption. He went on to enumerate all the reform measures enacted in New York over the years, and quipped that, according to the Republicans, "all the deep problems of our life...are no longer matters at issue; I have apparently converted the entire Republican majority to my views."[2]

Still, the Democratic convention could not ignore Tammany's new scandals involving the judiciary in the city, the most prominent of which was the Healy-Ewald charges. At Roosevelt's request, the keynote speaker, Senator Wagner, included a broad denunciation of the recent judicial office-buying accusations, stating "public office must be obtained only by honorable means." Wagner may have had his missing protégé in mind when he stated, "I know that I speak for the heart and conscience of the great rank and file of the Democratic Party in our State when I say that he who attains judicial or other public office by dishonest means should be driven therefrom, as also from the ranks of our party."[3] But the longtime Tammany loyalist refused to even mention the machine's name.

As the campaign began at the end of September, Roosevelt was facing an onslaught of Tammany defiance and obstruction of justice exhibited by Mayor Walker, Boss Curry, District Attorney Crain, and others that had been unfolding in public view in the last two months. As his biographer Kenneth Davis has written, the issue of Tammany corruption, "as he studied it for cues from on high, bred greater anxiety than he would ever publicly admit, the cues being far less clear and emphatic than he would have liked them to be." A *World* editorial warned that Roosevelt's attitude of "benevolent neutrality" toward the machine "may well prove to be one of the great political misjudgments of contemporary politics," and for him to win reelection "will take courage, wisdom and a brilliance in political leadership far beyond the ordinary."[4]

Even while the Democratic convention was being held in late September, the Healy-Ewald grand jury and Justice McCook continued to generate challenges for the governor. Roosevelt received a written request from the grand jury, sent with the approval of McCook, that they be permitted to broadly investigate, with additional funding from the governor, instances of "office-buying and misconduct by judges and other officials of this county and city."[5] In a vehement response, Roosevelt refused to grant the grand jury any broader ambit, criticizing its request as politically motivated and encouraged by the Republicans overseeing the investigation. He further asserted he did not have the right or power to interfere with the grand jury proceedings, "unless the charges presented [of other crimes] are specific and unless the local authorities have failed to act," neither of which had been shown. Nor, he added, did "[t]he fact that a Governor may be the target of those seeking political office at any price...alter the situation." But despite Roosevelt's refusal to approve a broadening of the grand jury investigation, Attorney General Ward announced his intention to commence a larger inquiry into a system of judicial office-buying in New York County, with funding to be provided by a private good government organization in the city, an arrangement that was permitted at the time.[6]

The governor then attempted to finesse the standoff between the grand jury and the recalcitrant Tammany boss and district leaders who recently had paraded before the grand jury and all refused to waive immunity. Not wanting to appear too defensive of Tammany and its leaders, yet also not desiring its leaders to be subjected to free-ranging examination by Ward's prosecutors, Roosevelt sent a letter to Mayor Walker, which was quickly made public. In it, he expressed his displeasure with the appearance of "government servants" refusing to waive immunity from prosecution for what they testified to as being "contrary to sound public policy." The mayor was instructed to tell only the Tammany district leaders who held municipal government posts, which did not include Curry, to return before the Healy-Ewald grand jury and to "freely answer all questions relating to their official acts."[7]

Mayor Walker quickly complied with the Roosevelt's request and called the nine Tammany district leaders who held municipal jobs to his office. He sternly gave them a deadline to return to Ward's grand jury and voluntarily testify about their "official acts or conduct," parroting Roosevelt's wording. But when several of these district leaders went back to the grand jury ready to testify about their "official acts," lead prosecutor Hiram Todd refused their new offers of testimony, contending it was a clever semantic trick by Governor Roosevelt and Tammany Hall—the "official acts" of city officeholders only included those they had done in their official capacity, but would not encompass any unofficial or improper acts taken in their capacities as district leaders. An editorial in the *Herald-Tribune*, the city's most prominent Republican newspaper, excoriated the governor's instructions to the grand jury and prosecutors. The paper opined that by "carefully limiting its authority" and permitting Tammany's leaders not to "testify as to any knowledge they may have of the way in which judges and other officials have been made," Roosevelt "has waited too long to satisfy the majority of voters."[8]

On the campaign trail, Tuttle continued to hammer Roosevelt for his refusal to stand up to the political machine, and his use of a legal "sleight of hand" to send the grand jury's "investigation into traffic in judgeships...up a blind alley." But his speeches now began to include Crater's disappearance as part of his indictment of Roosevelt and Tammany. On October 4, he made reference to recent news that a "Supreme Court judge, appointed by Governor Roosevelt, withdrew in cash from his various accounts shortly after his appointment in April 1930, $22,500, the amount of a year's salary of a Supreme Court judge," implying that Crater had purchased his seat. He added that this unnamed but easily identifiable judge "was last seen the day after the newspapers, on August 5, 1930, published my open letter to the District Attorney Crain containing the disclosure of the Ewald case."[9]

The Healy-Ewald grand jury quickly joined in Tuttle's questioning of Roosevelt's appointment of Crater to the bench that spring. Attorney General Ward, on behalf of his grand jury, sent a letter to Roosevelt, mentioning the large amount of cash the missing man had amassed at the time of his judicial appointment. The letter demanded that the governor disclose who had requested that he appoint Crater to the Supreme Court so that the grand jury could investigate whether those references received any money."[10]

Governor Roosevelt, whom Tuttle and the grand jury remarkably were now insinuating had been involved in Crater's possible purchase of his judicial seat, realized the precarious position he was being placed in. He quickly composed a letter to the grand jury aggressively defending his selection of Crater, stating he was "one of eight men officially recommended to me voluntarily by the Bar Association of the City of New York as well fitted for appointment to the Supreme Court and whose appointment it would heartily approve." Tammany Hall, the letter added, "had also suggested his name among several others," but he pointedly denied that the missing man's ties with Tammany had influenced his choice. He also had received letters of commendation after appointing Crater from impressive sources, including Victor J. Dowling, Presiding Justice of the Appellate Division; Charles Burlingham, the president of the City Bar Association; other sitting and former judges; and prominent city lawyers, who were unlikely to be recipients of bribes. When interviewed, however, Burlingham, an eminent figure in the city bar, revised his estimation of Crater in light of the disclosures of the past weeks, stating that while the missing man "had the reputation of a man of exceptional [legal] ability," he was "amazed to find that Mr. Crater had been living such a wretched, loose life."[11]

The governor's disclosures about his appointment of Crater, as well as of another lawyer to a temporary Supreme Court seat around the same time, tempered somewhat the Republican campaign attacks. No credible accusation could be made that he himself had received any money in return for his appointment of Crater and the other justice to the State Supreme Court. Nor could Tammany Hall exercise the same influence over him in the making of such temporary judicial appointments to the state courts, as it appeared to have done in Mayor Walker's appointment of city magistrates like George Ewald.

But the legal bar, good government groups, and much of the press continued to denounce Tammany's corruption. Together, they helped create a public reaction of moral outrage over the perceived collapse of government, justice, and public order in New York City. Rabbi Wise vividly condemned Walker's administration as a "Coney Island mardi gras managed by cheap and incompetent vulgarians." "What has the Mayor of New York done to uncover wrong or to enthrone right?" he continued. "Not one manly, valiant step on his part! Cheap gestures and cheaper words, clearly understood by his follow-ers."[12] The Republican effort to tar the governor by association with Tamma-ny's misdeeds appeared to be catching.

A month before Election Day, even the *Times*, which generally supported Roosevelt, expressed its concerns that Tammany corruption might upend his chances at reelection. One of its editorials began, "If Tammany Hall had set out to do its utmost to give Mr. Tuttle a campaign issue, and to make his election as Governor seem probable, it could hardly have chosen more effec-tive ways than those which it has adopted." It sensed Roosevelt's uncertainty, discomfort, and vulnerability on the issue of not doing enough to oppose the political machine, beginning "to wonder if the Franklin Roosevelt whom they knew of old had not lost something of his high-spirited and chivalrous bearing, and if his clear perceptions and moral poise had not been shaken a little by these unexpected reverberations of Tammany politics."[13]

Even if Roosevelt was not directly complicit in Tammany corruption in-volving the judiciary, the question remained whether he, in desperate need of Tammany's political support in his reelection bid, had by his inaction per-mitted its misfeasance to flourish. Or even worse, had he actively obstructed efforts, such as by the Healy-Ewald grand jury, to fully investigate that corrup-tion? Just days before the election, the *World* attacked him for only focusing on his administration's progressive agenda but not the overarching issue of judicial office-buying and Tammany corruption: "If it is Governor Roosevelt's purpose to accept Tammany as it is and through it to let the affairs of half the people of New York be administered, then our belief is that sooner or later the whole progressive program will suffer a severe setback....The progress under Roosevelt is dubious because it has been accompanied by the worst reaction in civic standards known to this generation."[14] At a time before polling of the electorate, whether the voters would similarly view the priority of the issues in the election was uncertain.

2

Tuttle and the Republicans' campaign pitch also played to a national audi-ence anticipating that Roosevelt's next election would be his run for the presi-dency in two years. As Tuttle remarked in one speech, "The object [of Roose-velt's campaign] is, of course, not to call attention to the Tammany Tiger but to try and put that away, keep the whole issue it represents as voiceless as possible, so that this issue of corruption, which is likely to attract, if it is dug into thoroughly, the attention of the entire nation, will not rise to plague him as he starts on his campaign for the Presidency." In the closing days of his campaign, he even mockingly compared Roosevelt's cautious behavior in this regard to that of his distant cousin Theodore who as New York City police commissioner had stood up to Tammany thirty years before: "I am reluctant to believe that a Tiger's eye can carry such hypnotism and that the pursuit of a Presidential bee can so readily deflect a Roosevelt from hunting big game." The *Times* even expressed Roosevelt's overriding fear that his closeness to the political machine would disqualify him as a national candidate because of how it had destroyed Al Smith's run for the presidency four years before: "Now, not only is [Roosevelt's] victory menaced, but the nature of his perplexity has served to renew feeling among national Democrats against nominating another candidate who has been in any way dependent upon the support of Tammany Hall."[15]

Eagerly following such attacks on Roosevelt, President Herbert Hoover in Washington, thinking he could deliver the fatal blow, had his administration intervene late in the gubernatorial campaign. Days before the election, a radio address by his secretary of state, Henry L. Stimson, a sometime New York resident, was broadcast from the nation's capital. Hoover hoped to narrow Roosevelt's victory margin or even better, to help defeat him, to bring a stop to the governor's momentum toward running against him in 1932.

Secretary Stimson began his address by stressing that the purity of the judiciary" is the "cornerstone of American civilization" and the "foundation upon which honest government...must depend," that it "dominates all other questions and has become the paramount issue before the State." He then launched into an attack on Roosevelt's handling of the widespread corruption scandals involving New York City judges, repeating many of Tuttle's accusations. For instance, the governor had unfairly limited the scope of investigation of the Healy-Ewald grand jury by not allowing it to look into whether there was a system of judicial office-buying in the city run by Tammany Hall. His direction to Tammany district leaders to testify only about their "official acts" as public officeholders was a "joker" because the real question of "whether [the judges] had purchased the judgeships which they now held" involved unofficial, illegal acts outside their public duties.

Stimson charged that Roosevelt additionally had left most investigations and prosecutions into judicial corruption in the hands of "Tammany office-holders," who were incompetent and useless, making special mention of District Attorney Crain. "By these actions which I have enumerated," Stimson concluded, "Franklin Roosevelt has shown his unfitness to deal with the great crisis now confronting New York State." It was reported that Roosevelt was furious in private at Stimson's use of the word "unfitness," which appeared in newspaper headlines the next day, considering it a cheap shot at his physical disabilities.[16]

On October 21, Tammany leaders tried to rally its supporters in a well-attended event led by Mayor Walker and Al Smith, held at its new headquarters facing Union Square Park in Manhattan. With his special flair for theatrical oration, Walker defended his city from Tuttle and the Republicans' efforts to defame and vilify it, declaring to great applause, "Because if there is one fair city on the American continent wherein decency controls, wherein honesty obtains, it is right in the city that I have the distinction and the pleasure and the honor of presiding over." A prominent Tammany lawyer came to the defense of the city's judges upon which aspersions had been cast, including Justice Crater, stating: "The processes of the law and the secrecy of the grand jury are being used by hostile prosecuting officials as a breeding house for lying, sensational rumors, manufactured for political consumption and to whip the press and the people into a frenzy over imaginary corruption...until our judges are literally ashamed to take their places on the bench."[17] Tammany, which had few equals in turning out the vote of its loyalists (and was often accused of irregularities in that regard) was solidly behind Roosevelt.

In the last days of the campaign, newspapers continued to opine that the governor's strategy of focusing almost exclusively on the progressive accomplishments of his and Smith's administration and the immediate material needs of the voters in the increasing throes of the Depression had misjudged the politics of the moment. A *Times* editorial ventured that "after all, [the voters] consider it far more important to have judges who do not buy their way to the bench, and that are in subservience to leaders, than it is to pay two or three cents less a kilowatt hour." The typically progressive *World* even refused to endorse Roosevelt because of his "inaction" in the Healy-Ewald investigation, "regretfully believ[ing]" this was due to "the fact that the Governor's loyalty was divided between the dictates of his own conscience and the dictates of political expediency."[18]

Charles Tuttle continued to hammer on his primary issue of Tammany corruption right up to Election Day. One of his last speeches was delivered at Cooper Union in the same auditorium, he pointed out, where Samuel Tilden and other New York leaders had met to overthrow Boss Tweed and his ring in 1871. Featured in Tuttle's litany of Tammany judicial corruption was the missing judge, who he again noted, a day after he had sent his letter to Crain referring the Healy-Ewald matter to him, "disappeared after having withdrawn in cash some $5,000 from his bank account" and whose "safety deposit vault has since been found empty. Tuttle ended the campaign, as he had begun it, with one overarching issue—"Shall we turn the city and State over to Tammany Hall as a conquered province, or shall we redeem the good name of government throughout our State, bring all the scoundrels to justice, and destroy public corruption before it reduces all government to the level of a racket?"[19]

On the night of November 1, the Democratic Party held its final rally at Carnegie Hall, where Roosevelt gave his fullest and final response to the Republican attacks and a defense of his campaign's focus on a progressive agenda. The concert hall was packed with five thousand supporters, while many state and local Democratic leaders, including Smith, Mayor Walker, and Boss Curry adorned the stage. In his lengthy address delivered in his warm, firm, and resonant voice which would make his "fireside chats" so effective as president, the governor began by reminding his audience how the Republicans had come to their single campaign issue of judicial corruption. Because of the state Republicans' "complete silence on all of those many questions which affect all of the people of this State" and their "falsification of the record and attacks instigated not by any desire for good government or for progressive legislation or administration" as the Democrats had championed, "their only hope was to distract the attention of the people of this State from these real issues."[20]

Roosevelt eagerly took on the Hoover administration and its lack of progress in battling the looming depression. One of the issues he mentioned that Republicans wanted to ignore was "the economic conditions under which the people of the State now find themselves...because that came too close home to the Federal Administration in Washington." Responding to Stimson's recent radio address, he sarcastically invoked the "spectacle" of the "Republican National Administration in Washington, suddenly solicitous for our welfare," and presuming to "have instructed us and lectured us on how we should have handled our local affairs in this great State." Looking forward to the election in two years, he stated, "We shall be grateful if you will return to your posts in Washington and...spend your time solving the problems which the whole nation is facing under your administration."

But Tuttle's and the Republican leaders' issue of supposed judicial misfeasance, Roosevelt asserted, was an unfair calumny against the entire city's judiciary which was done to "convince the people of this State and the people of this country that our judiciary is corrupt and judges are unworthy to hold their high offices." He then turned to his actions taken in response to the recent Tammany judicial scandals, most prominently, in the Healy-Ewald grand jury proceedings. He stated he had acted in good faith when on the eve of his campaign for reelection, he "sent into a Democratic county a Republican Attorney General and a Republican judge with an extraordinary grand jury." Ward's refusal to turn over to him any evidence obtained by his grand jury supporting charges of judicial office-buying other than in the Healy-Ewald matter, was "only further proof of what the people of this State have long suspected but now know—that the Attorney General is using his office in every way possible in attempting to pervert the function of the grand jury itself solely for the political benefit of Republican candidates."

Roosevelt ended his speech by stating that everyone "who believes in honest and decent government" resented the Republicans' campaign strategy, and he assured his listeners that he did "not yield place to any Republican candidate or editor in abhorrence of a corrupt judiciary." He asked "the electorate of the State of New York for their support...as a rebuke to those Republican national and state leaders who, substituting false charges and deliberate misrepresentations, have had the cowardice to ignore the great problems and issues before the whole State." With newfound conviction in his leadership and his accomplishments since his election as governor in 1928, he ended by stressing "the need, during the next two years, for a continuance of forward-looking, humane, and honest administration of the affairs our State. I ask this of the dwellers of this great metropolis, of the people of the other great cities, of the men and women of the villages and on the farms....Cheerfully and confidently I abide the result."[21]

By the end of the campaign, with New York and the country continuing its slide into a major depression, it had become increasingly evident that Roosevelt's reading of the voters' primary concerns was prescient. They wanted a progressive government to help provide for their material needs—for jobs, benefits and assistance, security, housing, and regulated prices for consumer necessities, while the Republicans' and a number of the city newspapers' focus on political and judicial corruption was a colorful distraction. Even Tammany could confidently predict in its last newspaper issue before the election the folly of Tuttle's campaign against it, stating, "In the last desperate attempt to save a once Grand Old Party from utter oblivion in this state, a candidate was chosen who has proved...a man of silence on such prominent and pertinent issues as public utility regulation and water power control, and a candidate with absolutely nothing to say on the outstanding problem today facing our government—unemployment."[22] Only the size of Roosevelt's margin of victory was in doubt, though that was crucial for his presidential aspirations.

The election results proved to be beyond Roosevelt's grandest expectations. He and his state ticket had swept to a landslide victory, receiving 725,000 more votes than Tuttle statewide. Not only had he racked up a 557,000-vote plurality in New York City, which surpassed Mayor Walker's total in his reelection race the year before by 60,000 votes, but he had also received an unprecedented surplus of 174,000 votes in the rest of New York State, historically safe Republican territory.[23] With his astute political instincts, Roosevelt had managed to surmount the great dilemma posed by his reelection campaign. He had succeeded in finessing Tammany's solid support in the city, while still appearing independent enough from the machine to attract conservative voters upstate and down, boding well for his national popularity in his upcoming run for the presidency in two years, which would be focused squarely on Hoover's inept handling of the Depression.[24]

In winning reelection, the governor also had assembled a new coalition of voters in New York State that would dominate American politics for years. Those supporting his progressive agenda included workers, immigrants, blacks and other minorities, urban residents, hyphenated Americans, farmers, the unemployed, women (due in part to his wife Eleanor), and senior voters. As the whole nation looked on in his reelection campaign, the governor had succeeded in running on a platform and attracting groups of voters he now was confident would win him the presidency in two years.

As was becoming increasingly apparent, the deepening national economic crisis and the growing unpopularity of President Hoover would give a strong edge to the Democratic candidate in 1932. While Smith would make a belated and doomed bid that year for the Democratic presidential nomination in order to stop Roosevelt, he had reached a disillusioning end to his path-breaking political career. Once elected, Franklin Roosevelt would largely implement the same policies through the federal government of social welfare benefits, labor union and employment protections, aid to struggling farmers and economic regulation of businesses as Al Smith had pioneered in New York. Years later, Roosevelt would graciously acknowledge to Francis Perkins, his secretary of labor throughout his presidency, saying that "[p]ractically all the things we've done in the Federal Government are like things Al Smith did as Governor of New York."[25]

A jaunty Mayor Walker misread the 1930 election results as a vindication of his administration and Tammany Hall. "The unmistakable answer of the people of New York to the vilifiers and detractors of our city, will, I hope, prove once and for all that the splendid people of the City of New York know that this is as clean and progressive a city as there ever has been on this American continent," he boasted. Boss Curry was also lauded for the Democratic victory, and his supporters predicted a long and successful reign like that of Charlie Murphy.[26] Neither man could possibly conceive that within three years, they would both be ignominiously deposed from power—Walker resigning in the middle of Governor Roosevelt's hearing of the charges against him for his personally corrupt finances and Curry thrown out by Tammany for his incompetence and lack of leadership.

3

As expected, District Attorney Crain waited until after Election Day to release the "Preliminary Report of the Grand Jury" investigating the disappearance of Joseph Force Crater, though the front cover of the document was dated a few days before the election. Crain no doubt realized that the inconclusiveness of the grand jury report would have been only more fodder for Tuttle and his campaign's theme of Tammany's cover-up of its corruption. The document itself, however, seemed to contradict its "preliminary" nature, for it was printed and issued with the caption of the proceeding of the Court of General Sessions of the County of New York on its front. While the names of the twenty-three grand jurors appeared at its end (which was unusual given the secrecy traditionally accorded to a grand jury proceeding), the report most likely was authored by Crain's office. The Crater grand jury would continue to sit for another two months, but the report appeared to be the final word on its investigation.

The Preliminary Report began with a statement of the obvious purpose of

the grand jury—to learn "the whereabouts of Justice Crater and the circumstances connected with his disappearance" and whether "such disappearance
was attributable to any criminal act within the County of New York." It did
concede at the start that Crater had no apparent reason to voluntarily disappear "because the justice in question was a man in the prime of life, in good
health, serving under an appointment by the [g]overnor, and considered in
the light of recognized political precedent a probable nominee by the dominant political party for the office of Justice of the Supreme Court to be voted
for at the election to be held on the 4th of November of this year."[27]

The self-proclaimed thorough efforts and great expense of the grand jury's
investigation were exhaustively catalogued: to date, the grand jury had sat
for eighteen days; ninety-five witnesses had been called in person and several
of them recalled; the grand jury and District Attorney Crain had interro-
gated "members of Crater's family, his relatives, his connections, his friends,
his acquaintances, his associates, his dentist, his doctors, his brokers, his servants, some of his debtors, some of his creditors, with hotel managers, club
officers, hospitals, sanitariums, the police, municipal officials, state officials
and federal officials"; the record of testimony ran 975 typewritten pages; six-
teen statements from persons not called before the grand jury were taken;
the judge's city residence and judicial chambers were visited; and subsidiary
inquiries were instituted by the police in Maine, Ohio, New Jersey, Pennsylvania, North Dakota, upstate New York, Westchester County, Havana, Cuba,
and Nova Scotia, Canada.[28]

The bulk of the report consisted of a chronology of Crater's physical
whereabouts as observed by others from July 21 until August 6, 1930. Its
chronology is striking in the very neutral recitation of the facts. It made no
effort to assess, weigh or emphasize some facts as being more probative of
what happened to the missing man than others. Nor was any effort made to
ascertain Crater's state of mind or emotions when his actions were described.
His only spoken words specifically mentioned in it are what he said to Mara
at his apartment on August 6, which were quoted in part—"Crater stated to
[Mara] that he proposed to go swimming 'up Westchester way.'"[29] No mention was made of other potentially crucial conversations involving him, such
as his phone call from Belgrade Lakes Village on the night of August 2, 1930,
nor Stella's phone calls to Healy's summer house at the end of that month
when she had first returned to their Manhattan apartment.

Typical of the report's neutral, observational, and nonanalytic rendition of the facts was its account of Crater's final night:

> At about half-past seven on the evening of August 6th, Crater stopped into 1539 Broadway, ticket agency of Grainsky, and endeavored to get his seat for that evening for the performance known as "Dancing Partners." Grainsky did not have a seat for Crater regarded as good enough but said that he would endeavor to get one and that Crater would find it under his name at the box office of the theatre. In the agency at the time was one Frank Bowers to whom Crater spoke. Crater left the agency and in a few minutes entered the restaurant of William Haas at 332 West 45th Street. It will be noted that this restaurant is only a short distance from the ticket agency referred to. Inside of this restaurant when Crater entered it was one William Klein, an attorney, who was seated at a table very close to the entrance door dining with one Sally Lou Ritzi....Crater was invited by Klein to dine and did so and left the restaurant with Klein and Miss Ritzi and parted from them on the sidewalk in front of the restaurant entering a taxicab going in a westerly direction, the street being a westbound street.[30]

Again, no mention was made of Crater's state of mind or affect in taking these actions, despite the fact that several people (Mara, Johnson, Klein, Haas) told the grand jury that on August 6, Crater seemed to be uncharacteristically subdued and distraught.[31]

While the Healy-Ewald office-buying charges and Crater's connections to both men were prominently featured in the press by the time the report was written, it simply made no reference to them. This is consistent with Crain's strenuous efforts to keep his Crater grand jury proceedings separate and apart from the contemporaneous Healy-Ewald proceedings. The report's only references to Martin Healy and the Cayuga Democratic Club in the chronology were, rather bizarrely, to a day more than two weeks before the judge disappeared.[32] It remarkably made no explicit mention of Tammany Hall, despite the missing man's strong affiliation with it in many roles, referring to it only once as the "dominant political party" whose nomination for a judicial seat Crater expected to get that fall.[33] Such omissions must again be attributed to the Crater grand jury being led by a staunch Tammany leader intent on protecting it.

Given its glaring omissions and flaws in analysis, the Preliminary Report's conclusion was foreordained: "The evidence is insufficient to warrant any expression of opinion as to whether Crater is alive or dead or as to whether he has absented himself voluntarily or is a sufferer from disease in the nature of amnesia or the victim of a crime." While the grand jury did recommend that all of the transcripts of the proceedings, referred to as the "minutes" of the grand jury, be made public, the presiding judge refused to do so, citing the traditional secrecy of grand jury proceedings.[34] The sealing of the grand jury minutes had the effect of depriving the investigators of any possible assistance that the public might have provided in response to the witnesses' testimony before it.[35]

4

Another serious challenge awaited Tammany Hall after the election: the trials of Martin Healy, George and Bertha Ewald, and Thomas Tommaney on charges of Ewald's buying of his appointment as a magistrate in 1927. Like the Preliminary Report, these prosecutions had been postponed until after the election to avoid their use for partisan purposes. Three trials arising from these charges took place during the next two months, with different defendants and different evidence presented, but all with the same result.

The first trial against only Healy and Tommaney was held before a blue-ribbon jury of men, commenced before Justice McCook on November 17. The prosecutors, led by Todd, called former Boss Olvany to testify about the general system of judicial appointments made by Mayor Walker and the role of Tammany district leader's recommendations in those appointments back in 1927. They also sought to undercut Healy's claim that Bertha Ewald's undocumented "loan" to him of $10,000, was for the purpose of buying his summerhouse in Long Island. Evidence was presented regarding Healy's bank accounts showing that at the time of Ewald's appointment, he had more than sufficient funds to purchase the house without the money provided by Mrs. Ewald.[36]

Using the prominent references by Republicans to the charges against them in the recent campaign, the defendants contended that the prosecution was merely a political "persecution" initiated by then US Attorney Charles Tuttle and the Republicans to create an issue he could run on in the gubernatorial race. Their attorneys also employed the classic criminal defense argument that Healy and Tommaney essentially were too smart to have committed such a dumb crime, contending that "[t]hese men with all their business experience" could not have committed so brazen and obvious a crime as the prosecution was alleging since they "left a trail a blind man could follow." For good measure, the defendants additionally called character witnesses, including Mayor Walker who testified that Healy never approached him regarding Ewald's appointment. Neither Healy nor Tommaney took the stand in their own defense.

In his instructions to the jury at the end of the trial, Justice McCook struck a moralistic tone: "Have we, in our admiration of the good fellow, our good-natured indifference to all but money-making, forgotten the righteousness that exalts a nation?...Woe to the nation, woe to the city in whose streets and theaters and over whose dinner tables the buying and selling of judgeships and justice can be and continue to be a jest." After twenty-two hours of deliberation, the jurors announced they were hopelessly deadlocked. Newspapers reported the jury to be seven to five for conviction.[37]

The second trial of the two men commenced in early December before a new blue-ribbon jury, with many of the same witnesses, evidence, arguments, and defenses presented. Prosecutor Todd, in his closing summation, called Healy and Tommaney "political racketeers, sitting at a table and coldly saying 'We'll get $10,000 out of this man.'...Is that the way you want your judges made?" There were reports that someone from District Attorney Crain's office had contacted one juror, the names of the jury having been listed in the newspapers, regarding his political affiliation. The jury again was deadlocked on the verdict.[38]

The final trial of the charges against only the Ewalds commenced in January 1931. The prosecution presented its strongest case, featuring two court attendants who testified that George Ewald had told them that he had purchased his magistrate's position for $10,000, and that the money had been paid to Healy. The Ewalds' counsel attacked the credibility and even the sanity of the prosecution witnesses, although two "alienists" observing one of the witnesses on the stand found him completely sane and credible. A witness also testified that George Ewald had approached him back in early August 1930 to obtain the list of grand jurors before whom Crain initially was presenting the Healy-Ewald allegations, so that he could exert some extrajudicial influence on them.[39]

Bertha Ewald was the only defendant in the trials to take the stand in her own defense, and she testified that not only did she not know who Martin Healy was when she made him the interest-free loan of $10,000 through

Tommaney, but she also claimed to be unaware that her husband was being considered for appointment as a magistrate at the time. This led to the prosecutor's remarks in his closing arguments which were directed at George Ewald, who did not testify at the trial, "[T]hat man is not a man, I say, who hides behind his wife's petticoats. That man in not a man who...sends his wife to that bank account to buy himself a job." The jury, after deliberating all night, was dismissed, once again, as inextricably divided the next day.[40]

In the new year, before a Democrat elected to replace Hamilton Ward as New York attorney general was to assume office later that month, the lead prosecutor, on behalf of Ward, agreed to the defendants' joint motion to dismiss the indictments against them. He announced he was satisfied that the three juries' "failure to agree fairly represents the collective conscience in cases of this character, which are thought by some to involve a quasi-political issue." A counsel for the defendants concurred, stating they "have been put to terrific expense and cannot continue their defense indefinitely." Accordingly, on January 22, 1931, Justice McCook reluctantly dismissed all pending charges against Healy, the Ewalds, and Tommaney and closed the special grand jury's investigation begun five months earlier. He would express surprise in his posthumously published memoirs "that none of the three trials resulted in a conviction, despite the very strong evidence for the prosecution." A few years after the trials, it was reported, at least one juror had been approached by a Tammany district leader during one trial and offered a city job, suggesting some of the jurors' votes may not have represented the "collective conscience" of the community.[41]

With the dismissal of the Healy-Ewald prosecution, Tammany Hall's leaders must have breathed a collective sigh of relief over the outcome of the first criminal prosecution of a high-ranking Tammany official and member of Mayor Walker's administration. From the start of his legal troubles in the summer of 1930, Martin Healy never had relinquished his post as Tammany district leader of the Nineteenth Assembly District, though the mayor would never restore his friend to his post in his administration. But the fact that the prosecutions in 1930 had gripped the attention of the press and public for the first time in years and highlighted the stranglehold of Tammany Hall over judicial appointments and Mayor Walker's administration ultimately would prove much more damaging than the inconclusive results of the Healy-Ewald trials.

Years before, a New York newspaper editor had remarked, "The three things that a Tammany leader most dreaded were, in ascending order of repulsiveness, the penitentiary, honest industry and biography." The Healy-Ewald matter, along with other investigations initiated by US Attorney Tuttle, had presented a compelling opening chapter of that biography. By the end of 1930, the good-government group City Affairs Committee, headed by Reverend John Haynes Holmes, issued a damning report card for the Walker administration, concluding, "[T]he citizens look back upon a year's record of political scandals and debaucheries worse than anything the city has known since the days of [Tammany Bosses] Tweed and Croker....The courts are obviously the playground of dishonest politicians and racketeers, with judges the willing or unwilling participants in the game....Every rock that has been lifted has shown the crawling and loathsome vermin beneath." Among the Tammany-related scandals noted by Holmes, in addition to the Healy-Ewald affair, were Crater's disappearance and the Libby's Hotel condemnation.[42]

Remarkably, in the following two years, the rest of the Tammany biography would largely be completed. Around the time of Crater's disappearance, Samuel Seabury, a prominent member of the city bar and former judge, would be appointed by a New York State court and then by the legislature to lead successive corruption inquiries into the Magistrates' Court, District Attorney Crain's Office, the NYPD, and ultimately Mayor Walker's administration itself. The charges proffered by Seabury against Walker involving personal financial malfeasance and bribery and seeking his removal from office would be heard at a trial presided over by Governor Roosevelt himself in Albany in the summer of 1932.

By then, Franklin Roosevelt had received his long-coveted nomination as the Democratic candidate for the presidency and was almost free of Tammany's machinations, which had posed such an imminent danger to him in the fall of 1930. Once more working in the glare of the national media before the start of his campaign for the presidency kicked off, he acquitted himself well as a jurist, officiating firmly and impartially over the Walker hearing while being fair to the still-popular mayor, who tried in vain to turn the proceedings into an entertaining spectacle. With the overwhelming evidence presented against him by Seabury and the consensus that Roosevelt would ultimately remove him from office, Walker decided to resign effective immediately at the end of the summer and sailed to Europe with his girlfriend Betty Compton.[43]

The next year, Fiorello La Guardia, running on a "fusion" ticket and campaigning against Tammany corruption and control of the city as well as for greater government intervention in fighting the Depression, would win the mayoralty on his second try. His first run in 1929 against Walker emphasizing Tammany corruption had been as unsuccessful as Tuttle's similarly themed campaign in 1930. With the assistance of now President Roosevelt in Washington and the new Democratic governor, Herbert Lehman, La Guardia would embark on a systematic effort to deprive Tammany of its power to control municipal jobs, business, and public moneys, without which it could not survive. By the end of his three terms as mayor, he would successfully extirpate the epic and seemingly indefatigable political machine from the city and state governments for good.

CHAPTER EIGHT

Joe's Phantom Bequest

I

District Attorney Crain discharged his grand jury in early January 1931, after it failed not only to find out what had happened to Joseph Crater but also in its other task of determining who was responsible for the recent shooting of racketeer Jack "Legs" Diamond in a nightclub. The grand jury issued no final report on the Crater matter but was harshly critical of Stella Crater for not coming back to assist in their efforts and believed that she knew more than she was telling. Days later, Stella and her husband's disappearance roared back into the news, raising new questions about what she knew and when she knew it.

Stella finally returned with her mother from her five-month exile in Maine, arriving at the Craters' Fifth Avenue apartment on January 18, 1931. The next day, NYPD Detective Martin Owens, who had been assigned to the case from the start, interviewed her at her apartment with her mother present, and nothing appeared out of the ordinary. Stella told the officer of her intention to stay in the city and to get some money from her husband's estate in order to pay her mounting unpaid bills and living expenses. She also mentioned her appointment to see Crain the following afternoon.[1] But the following day, Stella, sounding quite agitated, phoned the district attorney's office to report a startling discovery she had made. While unpacking that morning, she had found in her bedroom dresser drawer a bunch of her husband's personal papers together with a large sum of money. When detectives shortly afterward arrived at her building to question her, she would not let them up, claiming she was still in a state of shock.[2]

On January 21, Detectives Owens, Sheridan, and Lowenthal arrived at the Craters' apartment building. Stella, still suffering from prostration, requested that only Owens come up to the apartment. Present in addition to her mother, were her sister-in-law, a friend, and her new attorney. Stella, lying in bed, pointed to a drawer of her dresser in the bedroom in which she had made her discovery of Joe's papers and the money the day before. She did tell Owens that when she had last been in the apartment at the end of August before news of her husband's disappearance had broken, she believed that she had opened the same dresser drawer without seeing the new items, but then stated she wasn't sure whether she did open it or not.[3]

Sergeant Owens then asked that the other two detectives waiting downstairs be allowed to come up to view the dresser, which Stella agreed to. Unbeknownst to Stella, Detective Sheridan had been involved in a very thorough search of the Craters' apartment back in early September at the start of the police investigation into the disappearance. When he and Lowenthal had come up to join him in the bedroom, Owens pointed to the closed dresser drawer Stella had identified and asked Sheridan if he remembered what was in that drawer when he searched it more than four months before. Sheridan immediately recalled a few items, including a lady's hand fan, which he remembered using to cool himself with because it had been a hot day. Owens then dramatically opened the drawer revealing the fan and the other items he had just recalled. Sheridan then remarkably recited from memory what were in the other dresser drawers when he had searched them before, all of which were still there. An experienced and decorated detective, Sheridan certainly would not have overlooked a collection of her husband's papers and a large amount of cash when he first searched the dresser in September.[4]

Commissioner Mulrooney subsequently recalled that back in September detectives had "ransacked the Crater apartment, not once, but several times, searching all the articles of furniture and going to the lengths of shaking clothing and ruffling books in a hunt for concealed papers." Also, Milton Josephs, the foreman of the disbanded Crater grand jury, was contacted and told the police that he "remembers well" the search of the Crater apartment he and some other grand jurors made back on October 14. He recalled "searching every drawer" in Stella's dresser in the bedroom and he "did not see any money, papers or letter" in the drawer where Stella claimed to have discovered them the day before.[5]

Among the items and records Stella turned over to the police were an envelope containing $6,690 in cash, comprised of three $1,000 bills, four $500 bills, fifteen $100 bills, three $50 bills, and four $10 bills. The envelope also held Joe's 1925 will, leaving everything to Stella, a leather pouch with four life insurance policies totaling $30,000, five bankbooks and real estate records, including the cooperative lease for their apartment, a lease for a residence on West 122nd Street in Harlem (which Crater used for a voting address), and the deed for the Belgrade Lakes cabin. In another envelope marked "Joseph F. Crater, private" were some stocks of public companies, ten shares of Healy's Cayuga Holding Company, checks made out to her husband, and promissory notes and receipts for loans he had made to various individuals.[6]

But the document that drew the most attention from the investigators and in the subsequent press coverage was contained in a manila envelope with the initials "S.M.W." (Stella's maiden name initials) written on the back. Inside, there were three pages of foolscap with Joe's handwriting scrawled across them. The first page began with the word "Confidential" underscored. It then read, "The following money is due me from the persons named. Get in touch with them for they will surely pay their debts." There followed a list of about twenty debts owed to him, most of which were legal fees due from other lawyers before he was appointed to the bench. Francis Quillinan, Senator Wagner's partner with whom Crater had shared law offices at 120 Broadway, was mentioned. Some upcoming dates also were referred in the writing, including September 1 and September 10, without any year.

In the middle of the list of debts in the message were two relating to the Libby's Hotel matter. One entry, for "a large sum for commissions when accounts are passed" for which "George Frankenthaler is my attorney," clearly referred to his court-approved legal fees for his work as receiver of Libby's Hotel in the first half of 1929. The second entry, however, was confounding: "[T]here will be a very large sum due me for services when city pays the 2-3/4 million in condemnation. Martin Lippman will attend to it—keep in touch with him." On the last page of the missive to his wife, following the list of debts and moneys owed him, there were scrawled the words "Am very" followed by what seemed to be either "weary," "whary," or "wary," then "Love Joe." After that was again written, "This is all confidential," which was underscored.[7]

When District Attorney Crain came to the Craters' apartment later on the day of the officers' visit, Stella, still in bed, was crying hysterically and unable to answer his questions. He remarked afterward, "Mrs. Crater, when she told us of her discovery had all the appearances of a heart-broken woman telling the truth." His opinion was that "someone had access to the apartment and put the money and papers in the drawer" between the time the apartment was searched by the detectives in September and Stella's recent return to the apartment.[8] At the time of the initial search in early September and thereafter, however, the Craters' apartment building had been closely observed by the NYPD and anyone who tried to enter their apartment, including Joe, presumably would have been spotted.

The first newspaper stories about Stella's stunning discovery naturally expressed bemusement at the latest turn in this already bizarre case. "The hypothetical ghost of former Justice Joseph Force Crater...walked yesterday" into the Crater's apartment, began the front-page story in the *Herald-Tribune*. Even Tammany's newspaper joined in, quipping: "The daily happenings reported as occurring in Judge Crater's residence will tend to excite interest in spiritualism."[9] Other articles found Stella's sudden discovery of her husband's will leaving everything to her, the large amount of money that she needed to pay her bills, and other documents necessary to settle his estate a little too coincidental. Stella was facing possible eviction from the Craters' apartment for nonpayment of co-op fees, and she had no other obvious sources of money to live on. A skeptical *Daily News* published an article under the headline, "Wife finds Crater's Will, Too!" It began: "The mysterious hand that thrust, phantom-like, through a day and night police guard to deposit money and documents in the locked 5th Ave. apartment of former Supreme Court Justice Joseph Force Crater, also left a will in which the missing man left everything to his wife."[10] Finding her husband's will also allowed Stella to conveniently apply to the Surrogate's Court to become the temporary administrator of her husband's estate, enabling her to pay her mounting expenses, and to begin proceedings for resolution of his estate.

On January 22, police detectives returned to the Craters' apartment to speak further with Stella. When asked what she believed had happened to her husband, she reportedly replied through sobs, "O what can I think? Leaving his will and that memorandum [of debts] makes me think he was sending a last message....I know he wanted me cared for. He meant everything to go to me." Her lawyer shortly thereafter told reporters, "She regards the finding of the articles in the bureau drawer as a sign that either he is dead or has gone away for a long rest." But she was positive that her husband wouldn't have killed himself.[11]

Joe's meticulously collected will and other key legal documents, money, stocks, and other items of value did have all the finality of a last accounting of his assets and bequest to his wife. There also was his uncharacteristic tone of dejection and weariness in his shaky, handwritten note, sounding very much like he was facing some sort of existential crisis. It seemed Joe had assembled and prepared these papers under great pressure, confronting some dire set of circumstances, from which he was trying to permanently extricate himself. By his actions, one article stated, "he made elaborate arrangements that his wife might not suffer financially in the event he never returned."[12] But the questions remained when and why he had taken these actions and written his despairing, final message to his wife.

Now Stella, for the first time, came forward with her suspicions of what Joe was responding to when he left his final bequest to her. In a sparse statement issued through her attorney at the time, she alluded to events that may have driven her husband to disappear: "At the time he disappeared there was a troubled situation in the courts and she thought [Joe] might just be keeping out of the way for a short time....There were certain politicians who were sniping for him, she knew. She decided to keep her own counsel and await developments."[13] Her reference, without naming names, could plausibly have been to the Healy-Ewald matter, which was on the front pages of all the newspapers when her husband had disappeared in early August 1930 and certainly qualified as a "troubled situation in the courts."

After being advised by her doctor to stay home for several more days because of her nervous condition, Stella finally did come to Crain's office for a further interview on January 30. She brought another envelope with her husband's handwriting on it that she had recently found in his study, which contained some photos and newspaper clippings regarding Tammany's July 4 festivities the previous year and other judges he knew. While the private interview between Crain and Stella apparently took an hour and a half, it was far from the grilling the district attorney had suggested would take place. Crain told the press afterward that Stella still could "give no reason for [her husband's] going away." The next day, Crain abruptly announced that his investigation into Stella's recent discovery was concluded and expressed no further opinion on how the items got into her dresser drawer after the detectives and grand jurors had thoroughly searched the apartment and that dresser drawer months before and not seen any of it.[14]

The next month, Stella, having submitted to the New York County Surrogate's Court Joe's will and other legal papers she claimed to have just found, was formally appointed temporary administrator of her husband's estate. As such, she was able to withdraw money from the estate to pay for her living expenses, including the monthly maintenance fees due on the Fifth Avenue apartment. Her husband's estate, as initially accounted for, was valued at about $50,000, not a large amount considering Joe's high income as a lawyer (and perhaps from other sources) prior to his appointment as a judge.[15]

2

Stella's discovery of her husband's effective last will and testament, together with prior evidence developed in the investigation, should have been sufficient for the police department to determine when Joe had gathered, prepared, and left the items in their apartment. Police Commissioner Mulrooney and his detectives' failure to tie together this evidence, in turn, would deprive them of crucial insight into what the missing man was planning to do on August 6, 1930. To begin with, there were several strong correlations between Joe's known activities on his last day and his assembly of documents and cash that he left in the apartment for his wife. That morning at his judicial chambers, he had received from checks cashed on his bank accounts a total of $5,150 in large denomination bills, which he had pocketed and taken back to his Fifth Avenue apartment. That sum of cash would have constituted the bulk of the $6,690 that Stella stated she found in her dresser drawer in the apartment. It also was reported that some of the large denomination bills she found were matched to those her husband had received that morning.[16]

On that morning, Crater had also packed up two large briefcases and files of papers in his judicial chambers, and with his deputy's help, brought them back to his apartment. Such effort would have been necessary if Joe intended to use those files and papers to compile the list of about twenty different legal matters for which he was owed money, in the confidential note to Stella. Also, a newspaper article reported that when Joe's message came to light in January 1931, Reginald Isaacs, one of the lawyers mentioned in it as owing Crater legal fees, specifically recalled that Crater had called him on the afternoon of August 6 and inquired about the status of the matter that they worked on. Isaacs also remembered asking him in that conversation if he was going back to Belgrade Lakes for the rest of the summer, and Crater merely laughed but did not answer him.[17]

There were further indications that the items Stella found had been prepared and collected by Joe on the afternoon of August 6. Among the assets he left for his wife was a $500 check payable to him, dated August 4, 1930, which he had already endorsed for deposit. References were also made in his missive to loans he had made to others coming due in early September.[18] Then there was the weary, dejected tone of his writing to his wife, which jibed with observations of Crater's mood by the restaurant owner Haas and his friend William Klein on the night of August 6. Such circumstantial evidence strongly suggests that Joe had collected his will, leases, personal papers, and assets and had composed his final message to his wife on the afternoon of August 6, while he was at their Fifth Avenue apartment and before he ventured out to Broadway that evening. Given the private note penned to Stella and the nature of the documents and the assets he had gathered, there was a sense of finality to his actions. With these items in hand, Stella would have a large amount of money she could live on without him, proof necessary to transfer his assets to her and to marshal his estate, and the ability to collect debts owed to Joe.

Yet there remains the puzzling discrepancy between Stella's claims that she first discovered what her husband had left her in January 1931, when both the police and the grand jurors were adamant that they had thoroughly searched through that very dresser drawer and elsewhere in the apartment in September and October 1930, and did not find Joe's bequest to her then. It is unlikely that seasoned detectives scouring an apartment for clues as to why a prominent judge had vanished would have missed a large collection of envelopes and documents, including thousands of dollars of cash and his will. But what if Stella didn't first find Joe's final bequest to her in January 1931 when she returned from Maine? What if she had really stumbled upon what her husband had left for her *before* the police had first searched the Craters' apartment in early September, even before the news of the judge's disappearance had broken on September 3?

In fact, Stella was the one person who did have access to the Fifth Avenue apartment after August 6, when Joe had apparently left his bequest before disappearing that night, and before the NYPD search for the missing man started. At the end of August, she had returned from Maine to the apartment in a frenzied, fearful state of mind, when the initial private search for her husband by his friends and colleagues had failed to locate him and he had failed to preside at the opening of the Supreme Court session. Little is known about what she did in the apartment during her short stay before hurrying back to

Maine in anticipation of the news of her husband's disappearance becoming public. But if, as the evidence strongly suggests, her husband had left his will, other important papers, and cash in Stella's bureau drawer or somewhere else in the apartment on the afternoon of August 6 for her to find, she would have discovered them during that visit, when she had undoubtedly scoured the apartment looking for any possible clues about what had happened to her husband.

An overlooked clue in the NYPD files gives further credence to Stella's having found what her husband had left for her when she was in the apartment at the end of August. When Detective Edward Fitzgerald first interviewed her at the cabin in Belgrade Lakes, Maine, on September 8, she had turned over to him two of her husband's checkbooks containing check stubs for the two checks Joe had written and had his deputy cash on the morning of August 6.[19] Her husband presumably would have brought those checkbooks back to the Fifth Avenue apartment that day, along with the cash in his suit pocket. And he would have gathered these two checkbooks that afternoon along with his will and other collected papers and assets he was leaving for his wife. The only conceivable way that these checkbooks could have made their way from the Craters' city apartment after her husband had disappeared, to Stella in Maine where she turned them over to Detective Fitzgerald on September 8, was if she had brought them back with her after her brief stay in the apartment at the end of August. That Stella took the documents to Maine in early September also jibes with why the police and the grand jurors failed to find these things in her dresser drawer or anywhere else in the apartment in September and October 1930.

If, as it appears, Stella first found what Joe had left for her when she came back to their apartment in late August, she must have surmised that he had been confronted with a dire and irremediable threat and had disappeared for good. His despondent handwritten note especially would have impressed on her the grave situation he was facing as well his admonition at its start and end that its contents were "confidential."[20] Still, her initial frantic efforts to find her husband were quite revealing. As the Healy brothers' testimony and phone records provided to the Crater grand jury later showed, Stella had placed two telephone calls from the Fifth Avenue apartment to the Healys' summerhouse in Long Island, one in the middle of the night, in which she desperately sought some answers. Martin's brother William, who answered one of the calls, testified that she hysterically asked where her husband was, and that if "he was hiding out anywhere to protect [Martin Healy], she wanted to know it and be in on it." He perceptively described her tone on the call as "sound[ing] as if she had just learned that her husband was dead."[21]

Presumably terrified of the malevolent forces she suspected were responsible for her husband's disappearance and heeding the extremely confidential nature of his note to her, Stella understandably must have foresworn going immediately to the police at the end of August with her discovery of what he had left her in the apartment three weeks before. Instead, she took Joe's confidential message and collection of papers and assets back with her to Maine right before news of his disappearance broke, along with her suspicions that powerful political forces had caused him to vanish for good. Back in Maine, these suspicions of her husband's apparent flight, or perhaps demise at the behest of powerful and dangerous people, no doubt contributed to Stella's nervous prostration, confinement in bed, and general refusal to communicate with the police, the grand jury, or the press in the early weeks of the search for her husband.

By the time she returned from Maine in the middle of January 1931, Stella had to have realized the trouble she would face for withholding from the authorities such significant evidence when she had first found it before they were even aware Joe was missing. She also understood she would need to use the collection of her husband's will and other records he had left her to start proceedings in court to administer Joe's estate. So, to protect herself, she risked fabricating the story that she first discovered her husband's bequest when she returned from Maine, almost five months after she actually did. She could not have anticipated that the detectives and grand jurors would have such specific recollections of their search of her bedroom dresser. As time passed, she would, when pressed, slowly back away from her fabricated story.[22]

3

When Crater's handwritten missive to his wife was turned over to the police department and made public, much attention quickly focused on Joe's cryptic reference to "a very large sum due me for services when city pays the 2-¾ million in condemnation" of Libby's Hotel. While District Attorney Crain quickly shut down his investigation of Stella's puzzling discovery of her husband's bequest, this cryptic reference and the large amount of money mentioned would spawn new speculation about what services Crater actually did provide in the foreclosure and condemnation proceedings in that matter and whether they were responsible for his vanishing, voluntarily or otherwise.

In the months before, the Libby's Hotel matter sporadically had come to the attention of those investigating Crater's disappearance. On September 20, 1930, Crain did announce his intention to have his grand jury look into the several receiverships the missing man held before he became a judge, including that of Libby's Hotel, but it apparently never did. In October, Leonard Wallstein, a special counsel appointed by the city to look into several allegedly excessive condemnation awards to be paid by the city, went back to court to challenge and reopen Justice McCook's preliminary Libby's Hotel condemnation award of approximately $2.85 million that spring as being well in excess of the hotel's real value. But Justice McCook reaffirmed his preliminary award, concluding that a hotel with Russian-Turkish baths for Jewish clientele was actually suitable for the Lower East Side, and that its value had to be determined at the time of the actual condemnation of the property in August 1929, which was just before the stock market crash and onset of the Depression that fall.[23]

At the end of 1930, detectives on the Crater case interviewed some lawyers knowledgeable about the Libby's foreclosure and condemnation. One attorney believed "that there must have been something that was not just right about the condemnation proceedings." Another source, an owner of a chain of hotels, told the police that something was "radically wrong in the Libby Hotel matter in that the award was far in excess of the valuation." He thought that due to the growing scrutiny of the condemnation award and financial difficulties experienced by the Moores' companies in the summer of 1930, a deal over the award that had reached between Crater and the Moores fell apart, and they "might have put the problem up to Crater," and the judge, "fearing the exposure, disappeared."[24]

At the end of January 1931, when Stella had disclosed Joe's confidential message, Wallstein summoned for questioning Martin Lippman, the Moores' chief lawyer, whom Joe's message stated would "attend to the matter" of the "very large sum due" him from the condemnation of the hotel. Lippman said he had no idea what Crater could be referring to since his friend "had nothing whatsoever to do with the condemnation of the property." He had offered Joe only the opportunity to be appointed as the receiver of the hotel at the start of the foreclosure proceedings and had given him the necessary paperwork to have a judge appoint him to that position. Lippman was certain that the only money owed to Crater were his outstanding receiver's fees amounting to about $10,000, which was also mentioned in the confidential note to his wife.[25] The Moores' lawyer did admit though that as receiver, Joe had crucially turned over to him the hotel's income for several months, which likely was sufficient to pay off the Moores' outstanding mortgage bonds and thereby obviate the need for the foreclosure proceeding, but was never so applied.[26] After their meeting, Wallstein voiced his suspicions that Crater's involvement with Libby's Hotel went beyond his official post as receiver, since it was unlikely "that Judge Crater would have made this statement in a perfectly private memorandum if he had not believed that he had a claim," and "[w]hatever his relations to the transaction may have been, it does not appear to have been an ordinary legal one."[27]

So what extralegal services might he have provided to Lippman and the Moores in the foreclosure and condemnation proceedings over the hotel? Of course, he had close ties with Tammany leaders as well as with Mayor Walker's administration, which were beneficial to Lippman and his clients in a number of ways. To start with, at the time Lippman filed the foreclosure action against the hotel in February 1929, the Chrystie-Forsyth street-widening project had been cancelled two months before by Mayor Walker, and it appeared there would be no condemnation award for the hotel. Since he didn't publicly resurrect the project until the month before the city was to officially condemn the hotel and other buildings in the area in June 1929, the Moores probably received advance knowledge of when the city's plans for the project would go forward. With such knowledge, they could start the foreclosure lawsuit with enough time to complete it right before Walker and the Board of Estimate would finalize the property's condemnation. Crater was an obvious source for ascertaining from his many contacts in the Tammany administration if and when the Chrystie-Forsyth public improvement would be revived.

Another striking facet of the Libby's Hotel legal proceedings were the numerous connections between Crater and Tammany officeholders, lawyers, and judges who were key players. When appointed receiver of the hotel, he had chosen as his counsel George Frankenthaler, brother of Justice Alfred Frankenthaler, his friend and Tammany colleague. He also would have had easy access to Referee Quillinan, another connected lawyer working with him in Senator Wagner's law office, who oversaw the actual foreclosure hearing held at the office and the auction sale of the hotel. While it is not known whether it was by design or by chance, Justice Frankenthaler happened to be the judge assigned to consider the former hotel owners' last effort to overturn the foreclosure and sale of Libby's and restore ownership to them. He ultimately denied the relief sought by the former owners in all material respects, rejecting their numerous and seemingly weighty objections to the hotel's foreclosure and sale.

Furthermore, as was reported at the time of the disclosure of his confidential message to his wife at the end of January 1931, Crater had reappeared after the end of his hotel receivership in a new capacity. He now was representing Lippman's law firm employee, Mary Lyons, who was the nominal owner of the hotel property when the city had acquired title to it before condemning it. Charles Craig, a former city comptroller who was representing other hotel creditors in one of the litigations spawned by the debacle, said Crater had approached him on behalf of Lyons in the fall of 1929, well after his position as receiver for the hotel had ended. He proposed to Craig that the Tammany city treasurer in Mayor Walker's administration might be willing to pay Lyons about $3 million for the hotel property, some of which could be used to pay off Craig's clients.[28] Nothing came of those discussions apparently because as La Guardia, the Republican candidate in his first run for mayor that fall, charged at the time, part of the deal was "a good, fat, juicy lease to a couple of Tammany politicians" in the interim before the hotel's demolition.[29]

The Libby's Hotel foreclosure litigation additionally seemed to bear Crater's mark as a skilled litigator. From start to finish, the foreclosure and sale of the hotel were a seamless piece of litigation art, which the brilliant lawyer was capable of planning, directing, and assisting on behalf of Lippman's clients. There was the institution of foreclosure actions although the hotel was not truly insolvent, the exquisite timing of the foreclosure sale right before the city's condemnation of the property, and the overriding of good reasons to postpone the sale and auction. The latter was accomplished by the rapid submission of voluminous and convincing motion papers in opposition to the former owner's applications, one of Crater's special talents. Also, while as Lippman told Wallstein, the missing man did not officially participate in the legal action in the Supreme Court, his claim to a substantial part of the condemnation award as compensation for his prior efforts was plausible. After all, his legal and political maneuverings in the foreclosure and sale of the

hotel may have been essential to the Moores ultimately obtaining the condemnation award in April 1930, and they or Lippman conceivably could have
promised him a "very large sum" for those sub rosa services from the expected
windfall award to come.

4

But the question remains whether Joseph Crater's involvement in the Libby's Hotel saga was the direct impetus for his disappearance. For a number
of reasons, this often cited, but never fully explored, explanation of why he
vanished doesn't hold up under scrutiny.

First, consideration must be given to the lax ethical and legal standards
and the rampant exploitation of foreknowledge of confidential governmental
plans for private gain that were prevalent in the Tammany-controlled municipal government in the 1920s. By these standards, Crater's actions as a lawyer
in the Libby's Hotel proceedings probably were not so outlandish as to cause
him professional humiliation or disbarment. The Moores' efforts to obtain
ownership of the hotel by foreclosing and buying it themselves before the
city finally condemned it for the Chrystie-Forsyth project were a variation on
Tammany's honest grafting schemes that had been well-accepted for decades.

Nor, despite Lippman's embarrassment at the appearance of his name in
Crater's confidential writing, did his legal practices employed in the foreclosure and sale at auction of the hotel run afoul of the norms of the times. Lippman was a well-respected real estate lawyer in a prominent law firm, which
was probably why the Moores retained him on this and other matters in New
York courts. For instance, the purchase of the hotel at auction in the name of
someone other than the true purchaser was not improper, as Lippman even
admitted in a court case in the early 1920s, stating that "in the majority of
real estate sales the actual purchaser is seldom mentioned" and that in some
sales "uninterested persons' names are used."[30] Lippman and Crater, who had
often worked together in other cases, were very much part of the city's legal
elite, and their conduct in the foreclosure and sale, even though conflicted by
current professional ethical standards, was not so egregious or improper as to
warrant his disappearance in order to avoid professional disgrace.

The context of Joe mentioning the Libby's condemnation award in his
confidential note to Stella further suggests that his conduct and state of mind

on the afternoon of August 6 were not the result of any concerns he had about the Libby's Hotel matter. If fear of his involvement in those proceedings were motivating his apparent flight from the city, why would he have mentioned the "very large sum" of money owed to him in passing in the midst of his listing of several otherwise seemingly legitimate legal debts due him? It would have been uncharacteristic of him to direct Stella to go to Lippman to collect the substantial sum he believed came from a shady, illegal deal. Despite his obsessive philandering, Joe was protective of his wife throughout their marriage and was careful to keep her ignorant of any information that might endanger her.

Nor do Crater's whereabouts and activities in the days preceding his disappearance correlate with any newly breaking developments in the Libby's Hotel condemnation proceedings. At the end of July 1930, Special Counsel Wallstein did announce that he would challenge as excessive the tentative award for the hotel issued that spring. But Crater seemed quite unconcerned by this news, as he went on a trip to Atlantic City with some friends and women escorts for a few days, and then left the city for his Belgrade Lakes cabin on August 1, where he intended to stay for most of the rest of the month. Nor does it seem likely that his unexpected sudden return to the city on August 3, which was precipitated by the call he placed in the Maine village to someone the night before, would have concerned the Libby's condemnation award, whose court rehearing wouldn't occur until that fall. While the Crater grand jury's Preliminary Report did find that he had lunch with his friend Justice Frankenthaler on August 5, he had already ruled months before at the end of the foreclosure proceedings in favor of Lippman's clients, which was being appealed, and had nothing to do with the hotel's condemnation lawsuit that was before Justice McCook.[31]

The only parties to the Libby's Hotel scheme that conceivably might have been threatened by Crater's sub rosa involvement in one way or another were the Moores themselves. These proceedings, however, were not an anomalous event for the Moores and their companies but rather a standard business practice. They were engaging in similar schemes with other real estate development projects during this time, where they foreclosed on their mortgage bonds for minor defaults in payments by the owners and then bought the properties for a pittance at auction. In fact, the ABMC was simultaneously executing such plans involving the Sherman Square Apartments being built on West Seventy-Third Street on the Upper West Side in Manhattan. Crater perhaps was involved with Lippman providing legal services for the Moores in the foreclosure of that development, for another entry in his confidential message to his wife stated he expected "there will be a large sum due as counsel" from Quillinan and Lippman on that project.[32] During their heyday in the late 1920s, the Moores' businesses clearly employed aggressive litigation in the courts to further their interests, and they had the resources to hire quite reputable and connected lawyers, like Lippman, Crater, and Quillinan, to represent them.

With the onset of the Depression in the fall of 1929, however, the Moores' business empire began to unravel. As real estate values securing their mortgage bonds plummeted, the ABMC could not pay the amounts becoming due to their bondholders. Contemporaneously, committees of these bondholders as well as creditors had begun to file lawsuits against the Moores and their companies across the nation, trying to wring any value out of the investments they had made in the boon days of the 1920s. On the very day of Crater's disappearance on August 6, 1930, it was reported in the *Times* that the day before, "[c]ontrol of the American Bond and Mortgage Company of Chicago, which has underwritten real estate bond issues aggregating more than $150,000,000, has been placed in the hands of five voting trustees chosen by committees representing holders of preferred stock and debentures."[33] The Moores likewise must have been concerned, by the summer of 1930, of the increasing attention focused on the foreclosure and condemnation proceedings as well as the inflated award for the property. Under such scrutiny, they could no longer unobtrusively pocket their anticipated over $1 million windfall from the award. Such financial shenanigans at the expense of city taxpayers, would attract increasing scrutiny with the onset of the Great Depression.

Given these developments in the summer of 1930, the Moores could not have seriously entertained the additional risk of trying to silence or get rid of a prominent sitting judge. When Crater's private note to his wife and its cryptic reference to the Libby's matter surfaced in late January 1931, the Moores and their counsel were ready to wash their hands of the whole matter. Asked whether Mary Lyons, his employee, still currently owned the rights to the city's condemnation award, Martin Lippman told reporters that she could do "whatever her heart desires" with it. One newspaper article joked about lucky "Cinderella Mary" who would make a million dollars, while the "circle of prominent and influential men" surrounding her, including Lippman, Quillinan, and Justice Frankenthaler, "say they want none of it."[34] Whatever reasons were driving Joseph Crater to act in his despairing and depressed manner on August 6, 1930, they did not correlate with his role in the demise of Libby's Hotel.

In May 1931, ABMC creditors filed suit in federal court in Maine to put the company in involuntary bankruptcy and have an emergency receiver appointed to prevent the dissipation of the company's assets. The primary impetus for the immediate appointment of a receiver was said to be the Libby's Hotel matter, where there was an imminent danger that the city's condemnation award "having been already so concealed is in danger of being improperly distributed."[35] The creditors, in other words, were likely concerned that the Moores would abscond with the entire $2.85 million award for the hotel without paying off the bondholders still holding the first mortgage on the hotel.

Shortly afterward, the US Justice Department obtained broad-ranging indictments against William J. Moore, the former president of ABMC, and his sons and stepsons, including Charles C. Moore, for mail fraud in connection with the sale of $58 million of their bonds and stocks that financed their real estate empire of developments across the country. They were charged with falsely representing that the bonds were adequately secured by the properties, using false property appraisals, not setting aside enough of the bond proceeds to finish construction of the buildings, and paying off the outstanding principal and interest delinquent on their own bonds in order to establish them as safe investments for the public. The Libby's foreclosure was not included in the fraudulent scheme charged, probably because of the added complications wrought by the city having already condemned it. Tried on some of the counts in 1932, William J. Moore, Charles C. Moore, and other family members were found guilty, but the convictions were reversed on appeal.[36]

Under such pressures, the Moores ultimately were forced to concede that the entire Libby's condemnation award of $2.85 million should be paid to the mortgage bondholders of their now bankrupt corporation. After extensive litigation in the courts, the city ultimately did pay that award, plus 6 percent interest, to the ABMC's receiver in 1933. Paying off the outstanding mortgage bonds in full, the receiver gave the remainder of the award to satisfy the claims of the ABMC's bond and stockholders that were not invested in the hotel.[37]

During these years of deepening depression and economic retrenchment, the city's original plans for the Chrystie-Forsyth project to revitalize the Lower East Side, launched in more prosperous times, had become financially untenable. After the structures, including Libby's Hotel, had been demolished and removed in early 1931, the city had received proposals from five prominent architects for the low-income model housing that was part of the original proposal. Yet graft intruded even in the Walker administration's selection from the proposals. The winning proposal was from the respected firm of Sloan Robertson, which to do business with the city, had to contribute over $20,000 to Tammany Hall candidates in recent years and to make inflated bids on other architectural public projects, part of which were kicked back to politicians.[38] But by the time of the contract award to the architectural firm in 1933, the low-income housing project could no longer feasibly be developed. The city had run out of money to finance construction of it, having spent more than anticipated on such things as the extravagant condemnation awards for the Libby's Hotel and other properties torn down for the site. In any case, even those low-income workers who were fortunate to still have jobs by this time could not possibly afford such expensive housing that had been priced for the prosperity of a few years before.

Shortly after coming into office, Mayor La Guardia announced new plans to turn the large vacant space into a park and recreation area for children. On September 14, 1934, with the residents cheering from their windows and fire escapes in the old tenements ringing the open space, the mayor personally opened the partially completed eight-acre park with its playgrounds and wading pools. Describing the new park as "the transforming of a 'mistake' by his predecessors into something beautiful and useful," La Guardia emphasized the work done by nearly a thousand public relief workers as part of his administration's efforts to combat the Depression.[39] The park would be named after President Roosevelt's mother, Sara D. Roosevelt (a name it bears to this day), and he sent a message from Washington thanking the city for the honor which was read at the ceremony.

The naming of the park had both pragmatic and symbolic aspects. Mayor La Guardia was intent and ultimately successful in aligning his administration with Roosevelt's New Deal public works projects and developing a steady pipeline of funding from the federal government for rebuilding the city's infrastructure. The coming decade would see a vast change in its landscape, with the addition of highways, bridges, tunnels, municipal buildings,

and an airport (to be named after the mayor). Not only would these feder-
ally funded public works projects provide much-needed work for the unemployed but also their construction, for the most part, would be more professionally run, honestly awarded, and efficiently administered.

At the same time, the park's naming also represented a turning away from
the system of public improvements of the Tammany-controlled city government over the previous decades, marked by exorbitant costs and incompetent planning, rampant graft and waste, and the corrupt use of politically
connected firms and labor. Deprived of its honest grafting from the city's
munificent treasury after La Guardia's election and the economic contrac-
tion brought on by the Depression, Tammany Hall had produced one of its
last public works, an inadvertent and misbegotten park in the midst of the
Lower East Side.

Searching for Judge Crater

CHAPTER NINE

Disappearing in the Great Depression

I

The search for Joseph Crater would continue, though somewhat abated, through the 1930s in a nation devastated by the biggest depression in its history, with its attendant financial distress, unemployment, dislocations, and migrations. It in turn would be amplified by an increasingly national culture of news and entertainment distributed through a more widespread media network of newspapers, magazines, and radio, and by his ubiquitous missing person circulars. During these years, the search for the missing man became a part of American culture—mentioned in theater and films, a butt of jokes and public amusement, and the object of a sustained craze to find him for reward or otherwise.

The public's fixation with the judge's disappearance during the 1930s may have had multiple sources. The vanishing of a prominent man, a judge, under suspicious circumstances, suggesting that he was either killed or fled his life because of some scandal, was bound to be grist for the nation's audience at any time. But solving the mystery may also have been a welcome antidote to the misery, isolation, and want brought on by the Great Depression, especially during the first years of the decade when a monetary reward was offered. Or perhaps it represented a nostalgic return to the fun and frivolity of the previous decade, which the missing man so fully embodied. The decade of the 1930s also would see great changes in New York City itself and the disappearance of many aspects of life there that were fundamental parts of Crater's world.

For a man often described by those close to him as singular and unusual looking, there was no shortage of purported sightings of Crater. The overwhelming response was prompted by his iconic missing person poster, tens of thousands of copies of which were distributed over the years throughout the nation and abroad, and posted in police departments, post offices, hotels, transportation facilities, courts, ships, consular offices, and other public accommodations. Reports of the missing man typically would spike right after the anniversary of his disappearance, August 6, as Crater's picture would often appear in newspapers and magazines, along with articles about the still unsolved case.[1]

From the start of the investigation, the NYPD received handwritten and typewritten letters and notes, postcards, telegrams, wires, and phone calls from people certain they had seen Crater in a variety of circumstances and places. Some of these communications have been retained in the Crater case file and give a sense of what the police had to respond to. In November 1930, a passenger on a cruise ship sailing from New York to Galveston, Texas, noticed a man who resembled Crater from his photographs was keeping company with a woman who did not appear to be his wife. When the passenger reported this to the police upon the ship's return to the city, detectives showed Crater's picture to the crew of the ship, and they all confirmed that this passenger appeared to be the same person. A detective then traveled to the address in Boston the passenger had registered under and found him to have a "full face resemblance to the judge" and to be about the same age, but when the man stood up to greet the detective, he was a few inches shorter than Crater.[2]

Soon after the search for the missing man had started, the sheriff of New Brunswick, Canada, telegrammed the police department with what sounded like a good lead. A person believed to be Crater had just arrived at an inn there in a Franklin sedan with New York license plates and complained that he was tired after "travelling all night through the woods of Maine." The inn proprietors and a maid had identified him from a photograph in a New York newspaper, estimating he was about five feet, eleven inches, "175 lbs., slim build, clean shaven, about 45 years of age." He had signed in under another name, and "seemed to be worried over something." The telegram admitted that the innkeepers had the "reward in mind." The police were saved a long trip to Nova Scotia, however, when a copy of the man's signature was sent by wire to the NYPD, and a handwriting expert determined the signature not to be Crater's.[3]

Another sighting in Canada was reported in a letter to the police chief from a woman in Quebec, where there was news "in the Montreal papers for some time about the missing Judge Crater." The letter related that the writer's daughter resided in a small town nearby and recently had rented a room in the back of her house to an American resembling the missing judge. The renter raised suspicion because he "seldom goes out" and "when he goes he dresses up kind of rough with his hat pulled down and collar up high as if he was trying to disguise himself." For this unpromising tip, a detective was dispatched to the Canadian town in the dead of winter, and interviewed the boarder, who had come up to Canada because of his poor health, and "explained that due to his illness he very rarely leaves the house." The detective reported that while the man's height and weight were similar to Crater's, and he also had "false upper and lower teeth," and "his features are entirely different."[4]

The expenses incurred in the NYPD investigation into the disappearance quickly reached unprecedented levels. Within its first few months, the unheard-of sum of $200,000 was expended, much of it spent on detectives tracking down the tremendous number of reported sightings of the missing man, including in Maine, Canada, upstate New York, New Jersey, and Pennsylvania. At first, as tips of potential encounters poured in, the Missing Persons Bureau detectives doggedly pursued the leads. "But skeptical as we might be regarding a rumor or a tip, we could not overlook the chance of finding our man, and accordingly we ran them all down," Commanding Officer John Ayres later wrote. "We worked on each piece of information until we were convinced that the person in question was not Judge Crater, and had definitely established the identity of the 'double.'" After the initial weeks of the investigation, the police department resorted to sending telegrams and copies of his missing person poster to local police chiefs in distant parts of the country and abroad to enlist their help in pursuing leads. To emphasize the point, the Missing Persons Bureau issued an internal memo to detectives in 1933, warning "[t]here is no fund available for the defraying of expenses for a trip to look for" the missing judge.[5]

The department reported the receipt in 1932 of 2,500 tips of Crater's whereabouts. Four years later, the detective in charge of the case pointed to a huge pile of letters, postcards, and telegrams, and commented, "These are the clues we've had in the Crater case. Thousands of them. Every time a word is written about the judge, people from all parts of the country write in that they have seen him." Because many of the purported sightings of the missing person were men who lacked some physical attribute of the missing man, life-size standing silhouettes of Crater were used in questioning possible witnesses and distributed to post in public places.[6] The detectives quickly became more discerning of the quality of tips coming in about the missing man. Letters began to be tagged with notes in the files such as the following: "The attached anonymous letters are presumably of persons of low mental condition or cranks and contain nothing of any material interest."[7] But, as another record in the files shows, the police eventually were driven to try rather unorthodox strategies in finding their man. Captain Ayres responded by letter to a William L. Von Edelkrantz of Alameda, California, who had sent his conclusions about the judge's whereabouts based on his extrasensory analysis of photographs, stating, "I feel that if you, through the employment of your instruments, or by any other means, could put us on the Crater trail, it not only would be rendering to us a service, but it would demonstrate to the World at Large, that there is real merit in your particular calling."[8]

Some people sought publicity just by associating themselves in some way with the case. There was Joseph Lesser, a prisoner, who frequently wrote to Stella, claiming that her husband had visited him in prison after his disappearance, and that he could tell her his whereabouts. Lesser claimed to have been referred to Crater as a lawyer who could fix his criminal case and to have paid him to do so, but he was double-crossed and ended up being convicted. A few years later, he admitted that he had made up the story of Crater's postdisappearance visit in an attempt to get back the money he had paid the missing man.[9]

Then there were tips from those harboring personal animosities. Early in the search, an anonymous letter claimed that Crater kept a woman in an apartment building at an address in Manhattan and that the superintendent was aware of it. After a detective spoke to the superintendent and determined the tip to be unfounded, he wrote that "it is possible some well intentioned person saw [someone resembling Crater] enter the house and wished to aid this department and so desired to inform us. However it appears to be more like spite toward [the superintendent]." Another anonymous tip stated the Crater was currently staying at a specific room in a Canadian hotel. The local police burst into the room only to find a honeymooning couple in bed. Other information came from apparent pranksters. In 1935, the NYPD received a tip that the body of a prominent man who had disappeared several years before could be found in the basement of an abandoned theater on the Upper East Side of Manhattan. On a sweltering summer day, two squads of policemen commenced digging up the basement floor, as a crowd of five hundred watched. The police finally quit when convinced it was all a practical joke.[10]

With the advent of nationwide media, including the radio, moving pictures, and magazines, the mystery of Joseph Crater was propagated to a larger and larger audience across the nation and throughout the world. It became part of popular culture and entertainment, a common lingua, that the public could jointly consume and take part in solving. Walter Winchell, one of the originators of celebrity gossip news, predicted Crater's imminent return a few times in his gossip column during the 1930s.[11] In the stage version of "Animal Crackers," Groucho Marx exited a scene saying he was going to "step out and look for Judge Crater." In 1933, Warner Brothers promoted the release of a movie, "Bureau of Missing Persons," by offering the missing judge $10,000 if he identified himself at the New York box office.[12] Contemporary comedians used as a reliable punch line, "Judge Crater, call your office." To "pull a Crater" became part of the lexicon, especially on Broadway, for someone who had suddenly vanished.

While the city's monetary reward for any information leading to the discovery of the missing man was in effect in the early years, people saw it as akin to winning the lottery in the midst of the Depression. A letter in the NYPD files suggests the game or prize-like aspect of the hunt. A man from New Hampshire having learned of Crater's disappearance in *Detective Magazine*, wrote he "had reasons to believe that [Crater] is here" and referred to an unidentified man who "answer[s] your description" with his "index finger of the right hand somewhat mutilated," as described in his missing person circular. The writer went on to admit his reasons for the letter, stating, "I am a married man and have a wife and two children and mother to support so you see I will be very glad to get the reward. I am out of work and it will put me on my feet."[13] The police understandably took no action on this tip.

As years passed, the missing man was sighted abroad in Europe, Cuba, Asia, and Africa. In October 1933, the NYPD received a letter from an expatriate woman living in Shanghai, China. After recently seeing Crater's missing person circular in a magazine offering a reward, she recalled that "a man whose appearance and description is identical with the one given in the poster was living in Shanghai" at a hotel two years earlier. She remembered that "he was always alone, yet seemed to be a convivial sort," and "spoke English at times, but at others spoke to the attendants in what I thought at the time was fairly fluent German." The chief inspector of the police department quickly dismissed the sighting, replying by letter that "Judge Crater did not speak, at the time of his disappearance, any foreign language."[14]

A great deal of publicity was given to the news in August 1936 that an old, bushy-bearded prospector named Lucky Blackiet told the Los Angeles police he had recently run into a bedraggled prospector in the mountains and desert area east of San Diego who looked like the missing judge and had also told him that he had come from New York with $5,000. Other people in the area also reported seeing "a wandering prospector strongly resembling Mr. Crater." The LA police department and newspaper reporters mounted a search into the barren area but saw no sign of the prospector. After further communications with the LA police and Stella, the detectives dismissed Lucky's story.[15]

Early on, the intricacies of the Crater mystery even inspired satire in a *New Yorker* article titled "The Great Disappearance Movement (1934–1937)." The story begins with the sudden disappearance of General A. Livingston Griff, who had been lunching at the Poison Gas and Chemical Warfare Club, and "at precisely 2:41 (according to the testimony of Patrick Jannis, the veteran doorman) he had emerged from the club, entered a taxi, and driven off. He was not seen again." Similar to the speculation concerning why Crater had acquired certain sums of money at critical times, it was discovered that "on the very day of his disappearance, Griff had extracted from his safe-deposit box the sum of eighty-four thousand dollars in cash— exactly the price paid two months previously by the Trustees of the Metropolitan Museum of Art for a magnificent painting by Rousseau." There were sightings of Griff, like Crater, in a variety of comical circumstances—that he was "washing dishes in the kitchen of an Evansville eating-house, that he was incarcerated in a Bavarian insane asylum suffering from the delusion that he was Lindbergh; that he was exhibiting his war wounds and begging for alms on the Pont Royal...—these and countless other reports quickly gained credence."[16]

After General Griff's sudden disappearance, other prominent celebrities follow suit, and then persons of all types and classes succumb to the popular craze until "the entire populace was throwing itself fervently into the great disappearance movement." Perhaps anticipating the great migrations and dislocations of people throughout the nation during the Depression, the disappearance movement creates "striking changes in the social and economic structure." Urban areas, such as New York City, where disappearing "achieved its wildest popularity," are soon vacant of their populations. A few years later, when General Griff reappears in the city, and all the others that have disappeared return to resume their old lives, the "back of the disappearance movement was broken." But with the influx of people back, the city is transformed, it being "decided to demolish the Chanin, Lincoln, and Empire State Buildings in order to make room for modern skyscrapers."[17]

There were many predictions that Crater, like General Griff, would return home once whatever exigencies forced him to flee had subsided and the threat to him diminished. One author, amidst Samuel Seabury's investigations into Tammany corruption in 1931, predicted that "Judge Crater will be found suffering from some brain disorder, referred to as 'American disappearis' when judicial things resume a state of normalcy."[18] Or by the end of the decade, when Tammany Hall was in disarray and no longer posed the same threat to the missing judge, he supposedly would safely return and resume his life, though his exile may have disqualified him from regaining his cherished judicial position.

Still, the tips kept coming in from all parts of the country. At the end of 1936, a detective filed a report of "communications...received at this bureau since the last report in this case." The communications were attributed "to Publicity given this matter in the Public Prints and Magazines," and most of the letters contained photos of the missing man that the writers had viewed. Letters came in from Boston, Massachusetts, Seattle, Washington, Rock Island, Ohio, and Richmond, California, all stating they had recently seen Crater in different locations. The detective requested that all the letters "be answered by...having the writers interviewed by their various Chiefs of Police to ascertain just how much information of value is attached to these communications."[19] The manhunt had long exceeded the capabilities and resources of the police department had to be farmed out to local law enforcement agencies to pursue.

Most remarkably, not one of the thousands of tips received by the NYPD over these years came from someone who had any firsthand knowledge about what had happened to the missing man after he vanished on August 6, 1930. Five years later, the department began "a complete reinvestigation of the disappearance of Joseph Force Crater," trying "to examine anew every scrap of evidence...in the hope that something, previously overlooked, may shed new light on one of New York's most baffling mysteries."[20] No new light was shed by the effort.

2

Martin Healy and members of his Cayuga Club occasionally resurfaced in the news of the 1930s. There were reports in the early years of the Depression, that Tammany leaders were misusing the city's public relief funds to aid those politically loyal to the machine. One of Healy's campaign letters to Cayuga Club members and supporters in 1931 was said to have promised, "Tammany is determined that no deserving member of the party shall suffer acute want."[21] Tammany district leaders' traditional gifts of food, clothing, and toys to the neighborhood residents at Christmastime now were reportedly allotted to those who had been politically vetted.

Shortly after the Healy-Ewald charges had been dismissed, new suspicions of judicial office-buying in the Cayuga Club surfaced from an unlikely source. In April 1931, Annie Matthews, Healy's coleader of the Nineteenth Assembly District (every Tammany district leader had a woman coleader who was largely responsible for the club's social events) gave an unusually candid talk before a meeting of the League of Women Voters about how judges were made in the city. In a burst of honesty reminiscent of George Washington Plunkitt, Matthews asked why, given that district leaders of the parties were not paid for their efforts, would anyone "do this difficult and trying work just for the love of country." The example she used to justify a district leader's compensation struck particularly close to the Cayuga Club. She posited that such a leader "gets a chance to recommend a man for the position of judge, at $25,000 a year for fourteen years, and if he is a Democrat here...he is sure of reelection and that he practically has the position until he retires for age." So, she rhetorically asked, "[i]f somebody offered a thing like that would you just say 'Thank you,' and not leave him a present?...Would you really be such a rotter?"[22]

Matthew's comments clearly referred to nominations for a New York Supreme Court seat, whose annual salary had recently increased to $25,000. They revived speculation about why Crater had accumulated approximately $22,500 one month after being appointed to his temporary seat on the Supreme Court in April 1930. As Matthews implied in her talk, Crater could have paid that money to his boss Healy or higher ups in Tammany Hall to assure his nomination and reelection to a full fourteen-year term that fall and to pay for any campaign expenses incurred in the process. While it was never determined by investigators to whom that money went, Tammany Hall did have a long-standing practice that judges (as well as other officeholders) would have to put up as "campaign expenses" one year's salary in order to gain its backing for nomination and election to that position. Decades before, District Leader Plunkitt had said much the same in one of his bootblack talks— that "[e]ven candidates for the Supreme Court have to fall in line" and "when nominated, to help along the good cause with a year's salary."[23]

If Crater had paid the $22,500 in cash to Tammany higher-ups, it would have been money well spent. At the time, Tammany did maintain complete authority over the nomination of Supreme Court justices in New York County and through its control of Manhattan voters, the ability to practically guarantee their election. His payment of such campaign expenses to Tammany therefore would not have been considered at the time the purchase of judicial office or a crime, nor would it have been cause for him to disappear. He was, as Matthews put it, simply not being an ungrateful rotter.[24]

In one of its series of profiles of current Tammany district leaders in 1933, the *Evening Post* recounted some of the misdeeds attributed to Martin Healy, the "Tammany leader, who held a city job and represented a book company trading with the city, who was a director in a stock venture of doubtful soundness, who raised $10,000 for a new house from a woman whose husband he helped to get a magistracy, and took a little present of $2,000 and a diamond bracelet from another man whom he urged for City Marshal." Despite his removal by Mayor Walker from his post as a deputy city department head and his two criminal trials for judicial office-buying in 1930, the article stated incredulously, Healy "still goes rolling on, still exercises the prerogatives of district leadership, still holds his place in the councils of the Hall." The reporter snidely noted that at least Tammany had not bestowed any new city job on Healy since his tribulations.[25]

The denouement of the Healy-Ewald prosecution played out against the backdrop of dramatic changes in the municipal government resulting from the election of Mayor Fiorello La Guardia in 1933. Shortly after his assuming office, Bertha Ewald, whose family was said to be on the verge of destitution, brought a lawsuit against Martin Healy claiming that he had never repaid any of the $10,000 loan for his Long Island summerhouse, which had been the purpose presented in their criminal trial for the moneys she had paid to him. She then obtained a default judgment of $11,042 against Healy, who claimed to have no income or property with which to pay the judgment.[26]

At a hearing in his wife's lawsuit, ex-magistrate George Ewald expressed his disillusionment with the political system he had been part of. "Today, after being for years a faithful follower of Tammany Hall," he stated, "I have been dispossessed from my home..., my wife who stood in the shadow of prison for months to save Martin Healy is an invalid, and my children scarcely know where their next meal is coming from." He revealed his district leader's further demands of him once he had become a magistrate: "Healy not only asked me to go light in scores of traffic violations, but in cases of a more serious nature. The job of city magistrate, when you owe it to a district leader, is enough to drive one to nervous prostration." Perhaps tilting to the new political winds, he even endorsed La Guardia's plan to reorganize the lower criminal courts so as to take away the power of appointment from the mayor and the district leaders.[27]

A year later, Healy finally was deposed from his position as Democratic district leader of the Nineteenth Assembly District by the whirlwind of new political forces rising in Harlem. For a decade, Healy and his segregated Cayuga Club had ruled with an iron fist over a community that had become predominantly black, making up 70 percent of the district's residents by 1930. While he was still in power in 1933, for instance, a "Negro political club" in the district filed a lawsuit alleging that Healy had unfairly named only white candidates to be party committeemen in districts "populated almost wholly by Negroes" and that the Board of Elections had improperly refused to accept a petition of their candidates for those positions.[28]

But by 1935, Healy faced opposition both from within Tammany and from an insurgent African American club, the Progressive Democratic Club, headed by Ferdinand O. Morton. Morton, the longtime leader of the UCD, the African American Democratic organization, was now one of the highest-ranking minorities in the municipal government, a member of the Municipal Civil Service Commission, and had the political support of President Roosevelt and his administration. At a tumultuous meeting for nomination of district leader in July 1935, which prompted fistfights among the white and black committeemen and required the presence of the police to restore order, Tammany Hall was able to barely keep another white candidate, Harry Perry, as district leader in place of Healy.[29]

This was the beginning of the end of Tammany's control of Harlem. In 1936, the first African American Democratic district leader, Herbert Bruce, won in the adjoining Twenty-first Assembly District in Harlem, also a predominantly black district. By that time, Harlem's black government officials also included two municipal judges, two aldermen, two state assemblymen, and a few assistant district attorneys and assistant state attorney generals. In 1939, what was left of Tammany Hall finally agreed to the election of the first African American district leader for the Nineteenth District, Daniel Burrows, a local realtor.[30]

Shortly after Healy was deposed, the Cayuga Club had left its stately clubhouse on West 122nd Street and soon dissolved. In a transfer symbolic of the replacement of Tammany district clubs by governmental agencies in the provision of jobs and social welfare needs in the city, its brownstone was leased to the Works Progress Administration, a New Deal agency responsible for creating millions of jobs on public works, infrastructure projects, the arts, and in other areas. It now would be used as a "domestic science school" for girls.[31]

Martin Healy's last years were spent in genteel poverty in a large brownstone on West 141st Street in the Harlem Heights section of Harlem, where his family and his brother's family were living. Having been ousted from politics for good, no longer having the means or connections to get any public employment, and with his finances bankrupted by his legal fees in defense of the Healy-Ewald prosecutions and by the hard economic times, Healy suffered his own personal depression. He no doubt felt distraught about his abject fall from power and wealth and his irrelevance in the new metropolis.

According to a relative, Healy spent most of his time inside, sitting behind a large wooden desk on the top floor of the brownstone, perhaps his one from the clubhouse, playing cards, smoking, reading newspapers, and passing time. Also suffering from kidney failure in his last years, he was sometimes able to sit with the rest of the family on chairs in front of their home on summer evenings, and neighbors passing by would be respectful, tipping their hats to him in tribute, and stopping to chat with him. At the end, his circumstances seemed a parody of when, as the Tammany district leader of the Nineteenth Assembly District, he received lines of voters, businessmen, politicians, and neighbors at the Cayuga Democratic Club twenty blocks south and attempted to bend the levers of power to give them what they wanted—jobs, city contracts, licenses, a turkey for Thanksgiving, clothes for winter, or freedom from the criminal justice system.

Martin Healy died at home in 1942, aged fifty-nine. His brief obituary in the *Times* focused on his "being accused of having 'sold' a magistracy to

George F. Ewald for $10,000, but after two trials in which the juries disagreed, the indictment was quashed." No mention was made of the Cayuga Club or its prominent still-missing member who was so closely tied to him.[32]

3

The 1930s were bitter years for Tammany Hall, the longest running political machine in American history. While the Seabury investigations and the resignation of Mayor Walker in the fall of 1932 were perhaps the most visible sign of the political machine's collapse, there were larger historical forces at work. The most significant and immediate was the onset on the Great Depression. During the prosperity and hoopla of the 1920s, the city's citizens could laugh at the Tammany Hall circus, its colorful characters and their grafting ways, complaisant with the knowledge that the politicians, like everyone else, were just trying to make some money. But as an article on Tammany in the *New York Times Magazine* a few years into the Depression put it, "It is one thing to be careless with other people's money in good times; it is something else to waste public funds at a time when people are starving."[33] Nor was it acceptable when in the hard times, its district leaders like Martin Healy were distributing the scant available city work and assistance to the politically loyal, who often were not even needy.

Beyond the corruption and the economic hard times, the tremendous changes in the city and its demography were rendering the political machine increasingly obsolete. Its traditional source of new recruits, poor European immigrants, were no longer coming to the city in great numbers nor settling in ethnic enclaves in Manhattan as they once had. The much smaller numbers of new immigrants were from all over the world, and when they reached Ellis Island, often disbursed beyond Manhattan and the other boroughs of the city, into the suburbs and beyond. Where racial or ethnic communities did grow in Manhattan, as in Harlem, they increasingly began to vote for their own political leaders.

The election of the Fiorello La Guardia as mayor at the end of 1933 sealed the machine's fate. As one historian of his administration has written, "La Guardia's coalition of reformers, Republicans, social democrats, and leftists rebuilt New York's local state, chasing the functionaries of the city's fabled Tammany Hall political machine from power and implanting a cohort of technical experts committed to expanding the scope of the public sector."[34]

Under his relatively nonpartisan administration, new government agencies and policies spawned by the Depression now provided the work, jobs, benefits, assistance, and welfare for the city's unemployed and impoverished citizens, which Tammany previously had covered.

The new mayor was able to effectively sever its lifelines of patronage and perquisites necessary to keep the organization alive. As more jobs exempted from the civil service laws were eliminated, the machine was shut out of thousands of municipal jobs that were crucial to reward its members and supporters. His appointment of competent and professional officials to lead his administration and its boards and agencies additionally deprived Tammany of its ability to access valuable inside information about the city's plans, to influence its decisions in favor of its interests, and to aggrandize business opportunities through "honest graft." Nor with Tammany's loss of control of Manhattan's Democratic electorate did it have the power to nominate and elect state and local judges, ceding the influence it once held over the judiciary.

La Guardia also vigorously attacked Tammany's newest source of support and income, most of which was now generated by dishonest graft, from organized crime. A district leader's selection in 1931 was at the behest of Charles "Lucky" Luciano, a Mafia kingpin involved in prostitution and the drug trade in the city. With the NYPD under new leadership and totally divorced from its influence, the mayor led a war on gambling in the city, some of it still under the auspices of the machine's district clubs, with the mayor personally taking a hammer to slot machines for the press. Aggressive city prosecutors, such as Manhattan District Attorney Thomas Dewey, who were also free from Tammany taint, pursued broad racketeering prosecutions against organized crime figures and their political allies. At the end of the decade, district leader James Hines, whose district was adjacent to Healy's, would be convicted and imprisoned for participating in rackets in Harlem, run by Dutch Schultz and his henchmen.[35]

And President Franklin Roosevelt, now Tammany's bête noire, also had a role in the political machine's demise. Because of the city's insolvency during the early 1930s, Roosevelt, in implementing his New Deal measures, funneled through Mayor La Guardia's administration huge amounts of federal funds for public works projects and for jobs and businesses in the city. He also gave out all federal patronage jobs to the Democratic Party leaders of the Bronx and Brooklyn, who were no longer under its control, further marginalizing the machine. But most fundamentally, as a historian of the Roosevelt-La Guardia partnership has concluded, "By linking citizens to the government in new ways, by enabling citizens to 'see' government differently," Roosevelt's New Deal "helped alter the political culture of New York....The New Deal had made possible a new standard of municipal government; it had also catalyzed a rapid and far-reaching change in popular expectations for public sector production."[36]

The precipitous decline of the great political machine was amply on display at its Independence Day festivities on July 4, 1936, which celebrated the 150th anniversary of its founding as a patriotic society. On the surface, the celebration appeared similar in substance to the one Joe Crater had attended just six years before. Hundreds of boisterous Tammany loyalists crowded into the flag-bedecked auditorium in the stately Wigwam on East Seventeenth Street, while an overflow crowd of one thousand gathered in Union Square Park outside. The program followed its traditional format, including a recitation of the entire Declaration of Independence, "long" and "short" speeches by prominent names, patriotic music and songs, even a rendition of "An American's Creed," the pledge Justice Crater had proudly recited in the summer of 1930. One obvious difference was the open enjoyment of alcoholic refreshments by the celebrants, for the Prohibition Amendment to the US Constitution had been repealed in 1933.[37]

While the people taking part in the festivities that day were well known to him, their shifting prominence, allegiances, and fortunes in a changing political landscape would no doubt have surprised him. President Franklin Roosevelt, running for his second term that fall, sent a brief message of congratulations, which was read from the stage and broadcast by radio. Having praised Tammany as a source of progressive governmental reform while seeking its support as governor, now as president, he had little practical need for the machine. But Roosevelt did try to enlist it in his reelection campaign that year, in which he would attack the business community and malefactors of wealth, whom he referred to now as "royalists," because of their opposition to the New Deal. Comparing contemporary events with those when Tammany had come into being after the Revolutionary War, he graciously stated, "In this day, as in the days of its founding,...is on the side of popular rights and against the exploitation of the many for the benefit of a favored few." As Roosevelt well knew, while Tammany prided itself as being on the side of popular rights, the machine for the past decades had been operated for the benefit of a favored few.[38]

One of the honorary "long talks" was delivered by Crater's mentor and friend, Senator Robert Wagner, who spoke in a more nostalgic, almost eulogistic mood. He fondly recalled Tammany's Independence Day celebration as a "tradition glowing with the warmth of our friendship," and why "on this day above all others, I return with ever growing sentiment and affection to Tammany Hall, where I began my political career." Alluding to his own impoverished youth as an immigrant on the Upper East Side, he said to hearty applause, "Here I learned that no one was too poor or strange or obscure to win recognition, if he had the power and the inclination to render public service. Here I tested the true meaning of friendship, of loyalty, of liberty and of democracy."[39]

But all of Wagner's references were to Tammany's sentimentally imagined past, not to its present or future relevance. He had quickly outgrown the political machine after becoming a US senator ten years before, and was now in the forefront of progressive reform, a congressional leader of Roosevelt's New Deal and the proponent of landmark laws protecting labor unions and the rights to collectively bargain as well as championing social security for the elderly. Much of the rest of his speech was devoted to his friend in the White House, the "great leader...in keeping with our times," who "has guided us from panic to recovery, and during the next four years...will lead us to heights not yet attained." Many of the "economic rights" referred to by him and others in his speech that day—freedom from "want and destitution," freedom from "degrading influences in the worst of the slums," freedom from "the fear of destitution in their old age" and from "insecurity of jobs in the prime of their life"—would now be responsibilities of government, especially the federal government now implementing the New Deal, instead of private or local institutions such as Tammany Hall.[40]

Al Smith was present that day on the dais, still one of the Tammany sachems, but he played no part in the proceedings. For the Happy Warrior had travelled a bitter political path since his disillusioning and humiliating defeat in his presidential bid in 1928 and his perceived rejection by Governor Roosevelt of his advising and contributing to his administration. Over the intervening few years, while remaining a Tammany figurehead, Smith had served as the largely ceremonial position of president of the company constructing and owning the Empire State Building and had become increasingly involved with conservative business groups who were rabid opponents of Roosevelt and the New Deal. Smith and his new allies would castigate Roosevelt as trying to impose a centralized Soviet-style communist dictatorship in this country. The divergence and antagonism between the two men during the 1930s was in part due to legitimate differences in their conceptions of whether the federal or state government should be predominant in enacting progressive reforms to meet the needs of its citizens. But Smith's growing antipathy toward President Roosevelt seemed equally motivated by the deep personal hurt caused by his former political friend and protégé whom he believed had betrayed his trust and friendship, as well as depriving him of his dream of attaining the highest office in the land, by fortuitously running in an election when a Democrat could win.[41]

Other participants at Tammany Hall on July 4, 1936, had played bit parts in Crater's life and the investigation into his disappearance. Thomas T. C. Crain, who as district attorney had led the grand jury investigating his disappearance, still sat on the stage as a sachem and also held an honorary position as "Father of the Council" of the Tammany Society. Frank Quillinan, the referee of the Libby's Hotel foreclosure and a law partner of Senator Wagner in whose offices Crater had practiced, made a traditional appearance dressed up as "Uncle Sam" and was accompanied by a real Cherokee Indian as "Chief Tammany." Justice Alfred Frankenthaler, Crater's friend and the judge who had dismissed the final objections of the Libby's Hotel former owners to its finagled foreclosure and sale, turned up on some committees. Martin Healy, who had been deposed as district leader the year before, was not listed among the approximately five hundred members of the Tammany General Committee composed of Tammany leaders and notables, and it is unclear if he attended the festivities. Presiding over the festivities was Sachem James Foley, Boss Murphy's son-in-law and a respected Surrogate's Court judge, who would shortly play a further role in the settling of Crater's estate. Former Mayor Jimmy Walker, perhaps also trying to distance himself from his old allegiances, was busy and could not attend.[42]

As Chairman Foley must have realized, his final words to close the festivities —"Long Live Tammany"—already amounted to a lost cause.[43] Little more than a decade after Crater had ascended the stage of Tammany's majestic new headquarters overlooking Union Square Park on July 4, 1930, an insolvent Tammany Society was forced to sell it and move into small rental offices uptown. There would be subsequent attempts to resurrect the legendary machine in the city's politics, notably by an Italian American, Carmine DeSapio, in the 1950s, and by an Caribbean American from Harlem, J. Raymond Jones, in the 1960s. But with La Guardia's administration, modern municipal government had finally emerged in New York City, and the most successful and seemingly invincible political machine in American history had vanished as precipitously as its acolyte Joseph Crater.

CHAPTER TEN

Stella Speaks Out

I

From the start of the investigation into her husband's disappearance, Stella had kept silent about what she thought might have happened to him. While initially pledging her full assistance to Police Commissioner Mulrooney in the search for Joe, she had remained ensconced in their cottage at Belgrade Lakes and then at a hotel in Portland, Maine, through the fall and early winter of 1930. Even her brother-in-law, at the instigation of the NYPD, cajoled her in a letter sent early in the investigation to "break your long silence and not remain neutral any longer" and to return to the city to tell what she knew, for "later developments may take a turn which might make things unpleasant for you and place you in an awkward position."[1] Yet she adamantly refused requests by District Attorney Crain to come before his grand jury and answer numerous pressing questions. The Crater grand jury's Preliminary Report in November 1930 expressed its exasperation, stating, "We have fruitlessly endeavored to induce Mrs. Crater to appear before us and give testimony," adding she was the only non-appearing witness who "could give testimony in aid of our inquiry." Only once the grand jury had been officially disbanded in January 1931, did she come back to the city.[2]

For the next seven years, she vigilantly maintained her silence, not speaking with the police nor publicly about the burgeoning mystery of what had happened to Joe. But with her husband fast becoming a national joke and causing notoriety or herself, she decided to have him declared legally dead, whether he actually was or not.[3] In addition to having pecuniary motives to break her silence in 1937, Stella no doubt welcomed the chance to express her long-suppressed thoughts about what had happened to her husband and to settle some personal affronts.

Under New York state law, there was (and still is) "a general presumption that a person who has been continuously absent from his home or place of residence, and unheard from or of by those who, if he had been alive, would naturally have heard of him, through the period of seven years, is dead." The purpose of the rule, which dated back to feudal times in Europe, was to settle the rights and estates of people who had long been absent from a town or community, a frequent occurrence back then that was becoming increasingly rare in modern times with the advances in travel, communications, and transmission of information. Before the presumption of death could be applied, however, the evidence "should remove the reasonable probability of his being alive at the time."[4]

By 1937, Stella also had fallen on very hard times herself. As the executor of her husband's estate since 1931, she had been living off periodic payments from the estate, which by now had dwindled to only a few thousand dollars in assets and property, as well as life insurance policies with a face value of $30,000, which she desperately needed to collect on. Facing eviction from the Fifth Avenue apartment because she had fallen behind on maintenance fees, she had moved in with a friend who had a small apartment in Greenwich Village, and did spot work she could find in the midst of the Depression.[5]

Before filing proceedings to declare her husband dead and probate his will, Stella, at the request of her attorney, Ralph Fay, at last submitted to an in-depth interview about Joe's disappearance for a reputable New York newspaper. The first article appeared on the front page of the *New York World-Telegram* (a successor newspaper to the *World*, which had gone bankrupt years before) on July 21, 1937, under the banner headline, "MRS. CRATER TALKS." Interviewed by one of its reporters in the bucolic setting of her cottage on Great Lake in Maine, she said it was "time to talk...about the rottenness there is in politics." Her long-held belief, which she had been fearful of expressing up to then, was "that her husband was murdered and that his murder was directly connected with his political career as a Tammany judge." She still was "afraid to talk about this thing" because "the same sinister something that took Joe away from me might come after me if I talk too much." Perhaps referring to Joe's confidential message which she said she had found with his will and collected papers and assets in her dresser drawer in the Fifth Avenue apartment in January 1931, she felt that "someone's will is warning me to say nothing; warning me that if I talk something dreadful will happen."[6]

She did mention her husband's involvement in the Libby's Hotel matter as a possible reason for his disappearance. But she was specific in attributing her husband's hasty return from Maine to the city on August 3, 1930, to his "advising Martin J. Healy in the Ewald case" and that "some of the Democratic leaders were a bit worried." When Joe failed to return to Maine as promised for her birthday the next week, she had not worried at first, thinking he was "tied up in [the Healy-Ewald] investigation." If he had felt betrayed by Tammany, she surmised, "[h]e might have been killed because someone thought he knew too much and would tell what he knew."[7]

After finding her husband's despondent confidential note and bequest in her dresser drawer, Stella said she understood "that Joe was going away" and had "straightened out his affairs and left me cash, so that I would not be left stranded." She discounted that he would have committed suicide because "Joe could take a blow [and] would fight back," but "[t]he threats might have been so strong that he feared he might be killed." She was "convinced that Joe is dead" and "that he went away because of a sinister something that was connected with politics."[8]

What made her especially suspicious that his disappearance was connected to Tammany politics was how her husband's political friends and associates had behaved toward her afterward, seemingly refusing to assist her in any way. She repeatedly referred to Senator Wagner, her husband's "political sponsor" and a "close friend," who avoided talking to her whenever she contacted him after Joe's disappearance, one time even letting her sit in the waiting room of his senate office in Washington for hours before she left. She now believed that Wagner distanced himself from her because "Joe was involved in a political scandal and that the Senator did not want to get mixed up in it." She also mentioned her meeting at Tammany Hall with Boss John Curry, who, with a lawyer present, told her, "I am a good Catholic. I go to church every Sunday. I don't know any more about Joe's disappearance than a baby." She added that almost all of the people listed in his handwritten missive to her as owing money to him had disclaimed the debts or refused to pay them off.[9]

During her interview, Stella was especially critical of the NYPD's efforts to find her husband, claiming the detectives initially sent up to Maine to investigate had not been diligent, spending much of their time hunting and fishing in the vicinity. Crucial clues, she thought, had not been pursued, such as the identity of the taxi driver who picked him up outside Haas' restaurant the night of August 6. She recalled going to Police Commissioner Mulrooney upon her return from Maine in early 1931, complaining "they weren't trying to find my husband because of politics."[10]

The next day, another banner headline on the first page of the *World-Telegram* read, "CRATER CASE LINKED TO JOB BUYING." Former prosecutors in the Healy-Ewald case were interviewed and all agreed that Crater would have been a key source of information and possibly a star witness if he cooperated in the prosecution of that case or other related investigations into Tammany corruption. According to the prosecutors, Crater also "was a close associate of Mr. Ewald and a friend of Mr. Healy," and there was undisclosed evidence that "[w]hen the Ewald investigation was underway, Judge Crater conferred with Tammany about the best way of meeting the situation."[11]

The reporter who had interviewed her the day before offered his impression that "[s]he is afraid of Tammany Hall, as fearful as the wife or widow of any Tammany man during the days of its supreme power in New York City," for "Tammany leaders could do almost anything during those late years of the 1920s and the early years of the next decade." The first article had mentioned that at the time of her huband's disappearance, "[a]ll racketeers had their political connections," and "politics in those days was closely affiliated with gangsters, gunmen and professional killers." Also, the "professional killers of the rackets knew how to dispose of bodies," and "if professional killers were used to dispose of Judge Crater, they probably were extremely careful about getting rid of the body."[12]

Despite the seven years that had intervened after Joe's disappearance and the precipitous decline of Tammany Hall, the immediate outcry from her first public interview probably surprised Stella. District Attorney William C. Dodge, one of the few remaining municipal elected officials loyal to Tammany, quickly dismissed Stella's recent pronouncements to the press as "pure bunk." He offered to reopen the Crater investigation but demanded that "[i]f [Stella] has any basis of facts on which her statements are made it is her duty to come here, or to the police, and tell what she knows." Dodge further questioned other aspects of what Stella had said in her interview.[13]

Coincidentally, Simon Rifkind and his wife were vacationing in Maine at the time, and when they saw the articles in the *World-Telegram*, they drove to Stella's cabin and spoke in private with her for more than an hour. Afterward, Rifkind told a reporter, "she doesn't know anything about Joe's business or political activity." Obviously fearful of District Attorney Dodge's threats to reopen Joe's disappearance and that his Tammany cronies were still around, Stella quickly recanted almost all of what she had expressly stated in her interview days before. Another newspaper quoted her as saying, directly contrary to her interview, that she had never "mentioned murder in connection with his death, and I don't know of anyone who would have murdered him."[14]

A NYPD officer was dispatched to Maine to question her about her recent interview. In his very thorough report to the assistant chief inspector, Stella blamed the newspaper article which, "in many respects, does not clearly reflect her opinion, and that the writer, by exaggeration and distortion creates inferences which she feels are not justified." She denied telling the reporter "that politicians were responsible for her husband's death" or that she "knew [or] suspected any individual or group of individuals who might be responsible," yet at the same time, reiterated that "her husband's alleged activity in the Healy-Ewald case, the Libby Receivership and other such matters...might have been a contributing factor." In contrast to what was reported in the *World-Telegram* article, she "denied that she is afraid to talk about the case" and asserted that "she was never threatened, persuaded, or advised against giving to the authorities any information she might have that might be even remotely responsible for her husband's disappearance." The officer's memo also reassured his superiors that as for the detectives who were assigned to Belgrade Lakes at the start of the search, "Mrs. Crater said she feels that they did everything reasonabl[y] possible in the matter, that they thoroughly searched the cottage and woods, in the vicinity and called on her occasionally with regard to developments."[15]

But in another publication later that same year, Stella reaffirmed her understanding of what had happened to her husband. Understandably attracting less attention, the new article appeared under her name in the tabloid *True Story* magazine. The magazine was one of the few remaining pieces of the short-lived publishing empire of the eccentric entrepreneur and self-promoter Bernarr Macfadden. Starting in the 1920s, Macfadden had published sensational pulp magazines and newspapers that proselytized, among other subjects, physical exercise, health foods, true love, and plenty of sex. His most successful newspaper, the *New York Evening Graphic*, introduced the notorious "cosmograph," a picture created by combining an actual person's face on someone else's body in often embarrassing situations.

Stella's article, in the first-person confessional format of the magazine, bore the title, "Why My Husband Disappeared: Judge Crater's Wife Tells All." Given the periodical and its audience, much of the article was devoted to Stella and Joe's romance and abiding love, their wonderful marriage, and her devastation and solitude caused by his sudden departure. But parts of the article turned to her husband's involvement in Tammany Hall politics. She remembered that it was after her husband's growing involvement in Tammany that she noticed a change in their relationship. He increasingly kept his political affairs to himself, and she became a "politician's wife," who could plead ignorance of any knowledge of political goings on that might prove dangerous to her. She was aware, though, that by the late 1920s, "Joe began to find himself more and more the recipient of profits which come naturally to people in contact with those high in political life." In words reminiscent of District Leader Plunkitt's praise of "honest graft," she observed that "one may be honest in character, and thoroughly law-observing in practice, and yet benefit handsomely through contacts."[16]

Her article in *True Story* also clearly specified what was troubling her husband in the last days before he disappeared. She stated that by the beginning of August 1930 "there was only one thing to vex Joe" — the investigation into George Ewald purchasing a magistrate seat by paying $10,000 to Martin Healy. "Joe was one of the men who, as prominent lawyers of the party were advising Healy," she added. Once he had rushed back from Maine to the city by train on August 3, and he failed to return the next weekend as promised, Stella initially was not so concerned, since "I knew, too, that Joe was taken up with the Ewald case and I supposed something very urgent had come up, so urgent that it had made Joe forget even my birthday."[17]

2

In December 1938, Stella Kunz, having quietly remarried earlier that year and represented by a new attorney, Emil Ellis, filed Joe's will for probate in the New York County Surrogate's Court. Her petition stated that her husband had "departed his life in New York County at a time unknown, having disappeared on August 6, 1930, under such circumstances as to afford reasonable grounds for belief that he is dead." The proceeding was assigned by happenstance to Surrogate Judge James A. Foley, the Tammany sachem who had presided as master of ceremonies at its July 4 festivities two years earlier.[18]

Months later, Stella had her deposition taken in her new apartment because she felt too uncomfortable to testify in a courtroom or law office. Her
attorney and Judge Foley's law secretary asked her a series of questions meant
to establish that her husband was presumedly dead. But her testimony was
evasive and incomplete. For example, when she was asked repeatedly whether
Joe appeared "agitated or worried" or had "any problem on his mind" when
she last saw him in Maine on August 3, she replied he did not, failing to mention the telephone call he had made the night before causing him to suddenly
return to the city, which directly contradicted her statements in her *True
Story* article of the year before.[19]

A significant amount of Stella's testimony during her deposition that day,
which was presented verbatim for several pages in her memoir, concerned
whether in fact she had first found her husband's will, insurance policies,
and assets left in her bedroom dresser in the Crater's Fifth Avenue apartment
when she returned from Maine in January 1931, as she previously had maintained. When questioned about her prior visit to the couple's apartment at
the end of August 1930 before news of Joe's disappearance had broken, she
first stated she did not "find any note of any kind" then nor did she make any
"particular search of the apartment."[20] The same dresser in which she had said
she found Joe's collection of papers and assets happened to be present in the
apartment she was now living in, and was the subject of further questions.
When confronted by Judge Foley's law secretary with the discrepancy posed
by the NYPD detectives' statements that they had opened that particular
drawer in September 1930, and there were no such papers and assets there
then, Stella seemed to back away from her claim that she had found those
items in January 1931. When he finally asked her, "[D]o you say definitely
whether on August 29, 1930 [during her initial visit to the apartment], those
papers were or were not in the drawer where you found them?" she replied,
"I can't say."[21]

When asked the foundational questions for establishing her husband's
death under the New York statute, Stella responded more firmly that she not
"heard in any matter whatsoever in any shape or form, from the Judge" at any
time since August 3, 1930. She knew of no "reason why Judge Crater should
desire or decide to have absented himself deliberately from [her]...[or] absent
himself from the City of New York." She believed that "if Judge Crater were
alive today he would have communicated with [her]." But in response to the

question of what she thought had happened to him, she simply said, "I don't know."[22]

In a rather cursory decision given the great publicity surrounding the puzzling and notorious disappearance, Surrogate Judge Foley ruled, on the basis of the uncontradicted evidence, that Joseph Force Crater should be presumed dead under New York law. The bulk of the decision described the massive worldwide search for Crater over the past years: "The most widespread publicity was given through the newspapers and magazines of this country to the circumstances surrounding his disappearance not only at the time, but over the period of years that have elapsed"; the NYPD had "distributed thousands of circulars with his photograph and accurate description of him" throughout the United States and the world; the continuing police search had involved "investigation of literally thousands of communications as to his alleged existence," but "[n]o trustworthy clue to the existence or whereabouts of the absentee has been developed." Finding "the evidence is without contradiction and is not susceptible of conflicting inferences," Judge Foley ruled, "The prominent position which he held, his expectation of election as a Supreme Court Justice at the general election of 1930, his failure to communicate with his wife and his parents and the very comprehensive but unsuccessful investigation made throughout the world by official agencies, all support [the] conclusion" of the "presumption...of the death of the absentee."[23]

But while Foley's decision allowed the probate of Crater's will and distribution of the few remaining assets in his estate to Stella, it did not establish legally that he was dead for purposes of collecting the remaining $30,000 in his life insurance policies that he had left for her. Stella would have to bring a separate lawsuit against the life insurance companies and prove that Crater was in fact dead. So in July 1939, her lawyer Ellis filed a complaint against the two insurance companies that had issued the policies, alleging, "The circumstances of the disappearance of the said Joseph Force Crater indicate that he met his death by 'accident or violent external means'" and, upon information and belief, "his body was disposed of by cremation or otherwise, making the corpus delicti impossible to produce." Proving that he was involuntarily killed would entitle Stella to double the face value of the policies ($60,000) under the policies' "double indemnity" clauses. The life insurance companies responded to the complaint by asserting that Crater was in fact still alive somewhere but could not presently be located, and thus his wife could not collect on the policies.[24]

Ellis claimed that Joe had been murdered in an attempted blackmail extortion over his relationship with yet another chorus girl named June Bryce, who had reportedly disappeared herself a couple of weeks after he did. While mentioned in the police files, Bryce had not been a focus of the grand jury or police investigations. Stella's lawyer finally was able to locate Bryce at a sanitarium in Long Island on the verge of death from advanced tuberculosis. She was so ill that she could not respond to any questions posed by Ellis in person, and when Ellis sought a court order to open a locked trunk in her room, the judge denied him access to the trunk in order to protect her privacy, finding there was insufficient evidence to connect Bryce with Crater's disappearance.[25]

Realizing the futility of proving that her husband was murdered, Stella shortly thereafter entered into a settlement with the insurance companies for the face values of the policies of $20,561 (one of the polices having lapsed because of nonpayment of premiums). The companies, however, were protected in the event her husband would be found alive by a bond posted by Stella to reimburse the insurance companies. Based on the amount of the premium posted for the bond, the bonding company estimated that the chances of her husband's being found alive were about 1 in 35.[26]

With the passage of time, Stella appeared to once again become reticent about why her husband disappeared. Perhaps the years may have dimmed her memory, or she was disinclined to stir up a hornet's nest by naming names. Her memoirs, *The Empty Robe*, published in 1961, raised interest again in the very cold case, at a time when most of her husband's friends and associates were dead and the Tammany machine defunct. But it shed no further light on what she believed had happened to Joe. While describing her husband as "an intimate of [Martin] Healy's," the district leader was otherwise mentioned only in passing in connection with the Healy-Ewald prosecution. Distancing herself from any accusations, she inaccurately claimed that "the District Attorney [Crain] was reported to have speculated that Joe possibly could have vanished when [the Healy-Ewald] investigation began on August 6 because he was involved."[27]

Her memoirs devoted more space to the possibility that her husband's involvement in the Libby's Hotel proceedings led to his vanishing as well as to recent developments in the case during the previous decade.[28] But in her final words on the subject, she retreated to a vague notion that "it was all due to politics" and that she would "never forget how most of Joe's political so-called friends dodged me after his disappearance." As if to underscore the point, her coauthor added in an epilogue, "There is no question but that she knows absolutely nothing about what happened to her husband and kens no more now than she did the day he went away."[29]

CHAPTER ELEVEN

The Westchester House and the Dutch Psychic

I

Almost twenty-five years after Crater had vanished, the most expensive, extensive, and lengthy active manhunt in US history to date had made practically no progress in finding out what had happened to the missing man. In an article in 1950, John Cronin, the head of the NYPD Missing Persons Bureau, expressed complete frustration with the investigation. Of the 29,000 missing person cases handled by the bureau since its inception in 1917, only two hundred remained open and unsolved, and the Crater case was unquestionably the most famous and confounding. "We actually haven't got a hot clue in the whole file," he admitted. "We haven't even been able to establish a good reason for his disappearance."[1] That was about to change, however, and the NYPD would be handed their last and best opportunity to crack the case. Like much about the unusual case, the new clues were improbably developed independently by two very different investigative sources, the police department and a famous clairvoyant in the Netherlands.

For the first time since the early days of the investigations, new clues linked the missing man with Westchester County, which is situated above the northern border of the Bronx. From the start, investigators had been perplexed by Crater's remark, as his court attendant Joseph Mara was leaving his Fifth Avenue apartment on the afternoon of August 6, 1930, that he was going later that day "up Westchester way." In the first days of the hunt, detectives had checked out sanitariums and hospitals in Westchester County to see if he had been admitted, suffering from injuries or amnesia. They had also inquired at the Larchmont Boat Club of which he was a member, but no one had seen him there recently.[2] None of the searches there had panned out, and Crater's words to Mara that afternoon were soon forgotten.

In April 1954, a man gave a deathbed confession of sorts in the kitchen of his apartment in East Harlem. Detective Peter Golemboski, a twenty-five-year, highly decorated NYPD officer who had been stationed in the precinct for years, was asked to come up to talk to a man he knew well from the neighborhood, Henry Krauss, who wanted to "get something off his chest."[3] In his mid-eighties, Krauss had retired after working as a butcher in Harlem for many years, and was residing nearby in an apartment building he owned.[4] Once inside his apartment, he told the detective it was about the Crater case. He insisted, however, that if his wife came into the room, they should stop talking about it because she knew nothing of what he was about to reveal. Golemboski also was directed not to take any notes of their conversation. Nor could he tell others about what Krauss said until after he died, which he expected to be soon; otherwise, Krauss would deny everything he was going to tell him. The detective made no promises about what he would do with the information, but Krauss proceeded nonetheless.[5]

The story Krauss told was sketchy. In 1930, he had owned a "mansion" in Bronxville, New York, which was in the southern part of Westchester County. He would go to his Westchester house on weekends while living during the week in Harlem. His brother-in-law, whose name was not revealed, was staying at the house most of the time as a caretaker. Back then, Krauss had been friendly with Peter Eckert, who owned a local delicatessen in Harlem close to the Cayuga Club, and was the father of Bertha Ewald, who was married to George Ewald.

On one visit to his Westchester house, George Ewald had asked if he could use the Westchester house for parties with his political friends, and Krauss gave him a key. He "was always active with the Democrats" and "knew the Cayuga clubhouse boys pretty good." In addition to Ewald, he knew Martin Healy and Joe Crater, who was then president of the club.[6] He further said that Ewald, Crater, and Healy often brought some women, including on occasion prostitutes, to his Bronxville house for parties. One time, he remembered the three men had brought to the house more than $90,000 in cash and negotiable bonds, which they had gotten "in a crooked deal involving the Municipal Building," and they had buried the proceeds in a box beneath a rose bush in the backyard of the house.[7]

Krauss then recounted to Golemboski in 1954 that "[o]n a Thursday of the week Crater disappeared" in early August 1930, he tried to call his brother-in-law at the Westchester house a few times, but no one answered. He became concerned and drove up to his house on the following Sunday to check if everything was all right. When Krauss entered through the back door into the kitchen, he saw "the place was a shambles; broken glasses and liquor bottles and bloodstains all over the kitchen." His brother-in-law was gone, and he never would see him again. Looking in the backyard, he saw that the ground near the rose bush in the backyard was dug up, and the box with the cash and notes was gone. Uncertain of what had happened there, he cleaned up the bloodstains and mess in the house and drove back to the city.[8]

About a week after his discovery at the Westchester house, Krauss "received a telephone call to meet Ewald" in the back room of his father-in-law Eckert's delicatessen located on Lenox Avenue. When he arrived there, he met Ewald and Healy in the back of the store. Healy told him "there might be some trouble," and he might be questioned by the "District Attorney," but he "should deny he ever knew Crater" and not mention that Crater, himself, or Ewald had ever visited his house or that any money had been buried in the backyard. After Crater's disappearance had been publicly disclosed in early September 1930, he remembered that he "was subpoenaed before the Grand Jury" and "was called to the District Attorney's and questioned," but he "followed Healy's instructions" and was not questioned further.[9]

After Krauss finished his story, Detective Golemboski pressed him for details, asking where exactly his house was in Westchester County, what the name of his brother-in-law was, and why he thought Crater had been at the house around the time he disappeared. He refused to say anything more, only repeating a few times, "Crater is dead, he's buried in Bronxville." He promised to get in touch with the detective the following week and told him "to say nothing to anyone in the meantime."[10] The next week, Golemboski learned that he had entered a hospital for a brief stay. Days after coming home, Krauss suddenly died, before speaking again to him. The detective then suffered a heart attack, which kept him out of work until the following year.[11]

Golemboski later told a journalist that he found Krauss' confession that day in his kitchen to be trustworthy. "He was in pretty good shape. He seemed to me like a man trying to get something off his chest," he said. "I had known him twenty-five years and everything I knew about him made me pretty sure that he wasn't the kind of crackpot who would make up a story like that just to get a little attention." He also recalled that on several occasions over the years before his final meeting with Krause, "whenever there'd be any talk of the Crater case, [Krauss would] always chime in with a flat, 'Oh, he's dead and buried up in Westchester,' the way someone else might say, 'Oh, he's in China.'"[12]

As Captain Cronin recognized in his memorandum to the chief of detectives in December 1955 about the unusual story, the chronology of his account, if accurate, was striking. He had said his disturbing discovery of the disarray and blood in his Bronxville house was on the Sunday after the week Crater was last seen, which would have been on August 10, 1930. And his meeting with Ewald and Healy in the back of Eckert's delicatessen took place about a week after his discovery at the house, which would have been in the middle of August. As Cronin pointed out in his memorandum, "It should be noted here that no one at this time knew Crater was missing; his office staff thought he was with his wife at his summer house in Belgrade Lakes, Maine; his wife there thought he was staying in New York." Further, the news of Joe's having vanished did not become known to the police department and the public until September 3, more than two weeks after Krauss' purported meeting with Healy and Ewald in the back of Eckert's delicatessen. If his account was true, their warnings to him not to disclose any knowledge of Crater being at the Westchester house meant that they possessed personal knowledge that something had happened to him at the house before anyone else knew he was missing.[13]

Cronin and others on the case, however, failed to draw a link between Krauss' story about his house in Westchester and Crater's elliptical remark to his deputy clerk on the afternoon of August 6, 1930, that he was going up "Westchester way" later that day. Certainly, with an obscure clue developed in the case years before, failing to make this association is understandable. But this would prove to be the first in a series of oversights and errors in the NYPD's follow-up of his lead that betrayed a general lack of knowledge of the underlying historical facts of the missing man's life and relationships.

After much painstaking work going through old records at banks, realtor's offices, and the town clerk's office in Westchester County, the detectives did locate what they believed to be the house Krauss said he had owned there. A white eight-room Dutch Colonial built in the early 1920s, it was located at Palmer Avenue, in Yonkers, roughly three miles north of Westchester County's southern border with the Bronx and about two blocks west of the current Bronxville city line, where Krauss had told Golemboski his house had been.[14] The detectives further learned from sources that he in fact had no brother-in-law who lived at the house back in 1930. Rather, it appeared that he, his first wife (who died in 1933), and their daughter lived in the Westchester house at the time.[15] Presumably, if Krauss was residing in the Palmer Avenue house in August 1930, and not just intermittently visiting his brother as he had told Golemboski, he likely would have had more direct knowledge of what had resulted in the bloody shambles in the kitchen there. It appeared Krauss had made up his brother-in-law as the house's caretaker in order to distance and absolve himself from whatever had happened there.

Acquaintances interviewed by the police additionally said that Krauss had a reputation as a shady, vicious, and immoral character. He had been involved in bootlegging and in other rackets with corrupt politicians in the 1920s. He made no secret of having girlfriends and chasing women, which the respectable German butcher community in Harlem tolerated because they liked his first wife. He had held a gun license for a revolver since 1928, which he later reported missing in 1932. Those who knew him thought he was capable of committing murder. His second wife told police after his death in 1955 that although her husband did not tell her anything about his business and political matters, he acted in his last years "as if he had something on his conscience."[16]

2

During the NYPD's ongoing investigation into Krauss and his Westchester house, Captain Cronin was shown a letter from Murray Teigh Bloom, a journalist, stating that "as a result of some fairly weird experiences, I've come back with what might or might not be a good lead on the Crater case." When Cronin met him for lunch in August 1955, Bloom described the trip he had made earlier in the year to meet an acclaimed Dutch psychic and crime solver named Gerard Croiset.[17]

An unassuming, middle-aged grocery clerk with an otherworldly look to him, Croiset had by this time earned an international reputation for his uncanny ability to inexplicably solve crimes, find missing persons and property, and explain vexing mysteries. His clairvoyant abilities were so amazing that scientists at the Parapsychology Institute of the University of Utrecht documented and analyzed his extrasensory abilities in solving crimes to eliminate other possible explanations. His biographer referred to him in 1964 as the "most gifted" and "most tested clairvoyant" in the world, who had "assisted the police not only in the Netherlands, but in a half-dozen countries...in solving many crimes." He was believed to have often employed "object reading" or "psychoscopy" to solve mysteries, a process whereby he "'knows' a person he has never met by simply holding something belonging to [the person]," such as a photograph.[18] Deciding to put Croiset's abilities to the test with the hopelessly unsolved Crater case, Bloom set up an appointment with him at the University of Utrecht but gave no advance indication of the matter he would be asking him about. Crater's disappearance twenty-five years before had attracted little attention in the Netherlands, and the clairvoyant, in his early twenties at that time, had not yet discovered his gift.

In February 1955, Bloom met Croiset and an academic assistant in a room at the Parapsychology Institute in Utrecht. As the journalist later described the scene in a 1959 article in *Harper's Magazine*, he placed a photograph of Crater that he had brought with him face down on the table in front of the psychic and asked him what he could tell about the man. Croiset began to rub his fingers over the backside of the photo facing him and stared into space. As Bloom cheekily observed, "It was my first séance and I felt rather cheated. It had nothing in common with the old-fashioned bravura performance that percolated with groans, grimaces, writhing and stentorian breathing. He simply appeared lost in thought....When he spoke it was with his own normal voice." His first words were: "This man is not alive. I see him sitting on a chair raised above the floor...two men sitting below him, one on each side. He has to do with criminals but not as a lawyer...ah, a judge...he was murdered long time ago...maybe twenty four, twenty five years ago."[19]

Croiset then grabbed a pencil and quickly drew a rough map of the five boroughs of the City of New York. He drew an "X" about one-third of the way up the length of the salami-like shape representing the island of Manhattan, pointed to the mark, and stated, "The judge was kidnapped... enticed...tricked away...from here." This "X" was in Manhattan's midtown area, roughly where the Broadway theater district is located. He next placed another "X" just above the top border of the rough blob he drew north of Manhattan where the Bronx is situated, in what would be the southern part of Westchester County. Pointing to that mark, he said, "Here is where he was killed. It is a farmhouse, a Dutch farmhouse, not far from the city. First, two men talked to him in a room on the first floor of the farmhouse. Then they took him to the cellar and shot him...the man who planned the killing was not there." The clairvoyant said that Crater's body was then buried in the cellar of the house, which had a partial dirt floor. He also gave a detailed description of the man who had planned the killing and that he was from Chicago but not his name.[20]

Bloom described in his article Cronin's reaction when he was first shown the map Croiset had drawn at their lunch meeting in Manhattan: "When he saw the crude drawing Cronin's face became bloodless. He blinked, shook his head, and looked steadily at me for a few moments before he spoke. 'Up until a minute ago,' he said slowly, 'I thought I was the only man on earth who knew about the house in Westchester.'"[21] Cronin and Bloom did venture up to see Krauss' old house on Palmer Avenue in Yonkers. The present owner of the house, who was the widow of the man who foreclosed on his mortgage years before, reluctantly gave them a tour of the house. She told them that when Krauss owned it, the dirt floor in the cellar had been cemented over, and the basement had been extended under the backyard to house a wine cellar. When the owner showed them the backyard, she remembered that her husband used to grow the largest vegetables in the backyard. Cronin glanced at Bloom and muttered, "It figures."[22]

But Cronin, believing that there was no probable cause to believe that Crater was still buried on the premises, figured a court would not issue a search warrant to dig up the property. Bloom offered the widow on the spot a small amount to do his own digging in the backyard as a private citizen. The widow's lawyer, fearing that the discovery of a body would have a detrimental effect on the value of the property, told him that he could buy the property and dig all he wanted, which Bloom lacked the funds to do.[23]

All in all Croiset's performance was remarkably accurate in his perceptions of the basic facts of Crater's disappearance—that he was a judge who disappeared in 1930 (exactly twenty-five years before the meeting in Utrecht) and that he was last seen in the Broadway district of Manhattan. While Bloom made a point of not telling Croiset in advance of what the subject of their meeting would be, the journalist may have been somewhat naïve. Croiset could have surmised that Bloom was coming to ask his assistance about a famous disappearance or mystery in the United States, and there was none more prominent or unsolved than Crater's at the time. By doing some simple research in advance, Croiset could have learned such basic facts as that he was a judge who disappeared in 1930, and he was last spotted getting into a taxicab in midtown Manhattan.

What is inexplicable, however, is how Croiset could know the rest of the information, which was not in the public record, regarding Krauss confession and the NYPD's contemporaneous investigation of it which was proceeding in secrecy. The clairvoyant was able to somehow divine that Crater was "enticed" away or "kidnapped" from the Broadway area up to a farmhouse, which was situated in Westchester County just over its border with the Bronx as drawn on his map at the meeting, and that he was killed in the house and buried in the backyard, consistent with what Krauss had told Golemboski. (Croiset's description of the house as a "farmhouse" even meshed with the police investigators learning that the area around his house was referred to as the "Farm" in the 1920s.) Nor could Croiset have psychically "read" Bloom's mind at their initial meeting in Utrecht because that was before the journalist knew of the police investigation into his story. Given the only physical link between the psychic and Crater at that meeting was his photograph, perhaps Croiset, as his scientific overseers maintained, had some inexplicable ability to "object read," to know "a person he has never met by simply holding something belonging to him."[24] Or perhaps it was all sheer coincidence.

3

By October 1955, the NYPD's investigation of the lead had made substantial progress. The police had located the Westchester house, determined that he and his family were living there at the time of Crater's disappearance, and learned from those close to him that he was an unsavory character capable of murder, who seemed to have something on his conscience at the end of his life. But two months later, in his December 1955 memo to his superiors, Cronin raised serious concerns about the credibility of Krauss' account based on what he thought were inconsistencies between it and the other evidence that the police had uncovered.

First, in Cronin's initial memorandum in October 1955 to his superior about the Krauss revelations, he had identified the man who, with Ewald and Crater, had used the Westchester house for parties with prostitutes, as "Magistrate Ellsworth Healy." Also, the memorandum, when describing his account of having been summoned to the backroom of Eckert's delicatessen, had referred to "Judge Ewald and Judge Healy" as warning Krauss that there might be trouble concerning Crater having been at his house.[25] There was in fact a Magistrate Ellsworth J. Healy, who had sat on the Court of Special Sessions in the Bronx since 1922 and was a Democratic district leader in the organization of Edward Flynn, which was allied with but independent of Tammany Hall. (Flynn, a longtime associate of Franklin Roosevelt, would become one of his top advisors and his local boss in the city when Roosevelt became president.) But, as the detectives learned, Magistrate Healy was very sick by 1930 (he would die three years later), was paralyzed, and had limited sexual capabilities. On this basis, Cronin's memo discredited Krauss' "[s]tatement that Healey [sic] had attended parties with loose women at [his Westchester house]...as [h]e was paralyzed from the waist down since 1924, suffered from paresis and was impotent."[26]

But while Ellsworth Healy had no apparent ties to Joe Crater, there was another Healy with whom the missing man had such a close relationship that he was called the other man's "brains" and the two were known to be intimate cohorts and friends, namely Martin Healy. The police investigation into what Krauss had told Detective Golemboski made clear that he was referring to Martin, not Ellsworth, Healy. The detectives had learned that he "was closely connected with political figures in Harlem," one of the most powerful at the time being Martin Healy.[27] The "Judge Ewald" to whom Krauss referred as using his Bronxville house with Crater and Healy for parties, clearly was George Ewald, who also had close ties to Healy and Crater in the Cayuga Club, as shown by Crater serving as master of ceremonies at the party held for Ewald when he was appointed a city magistrate in 1927.

His recounting of his meeting in the back of Ewald's father-in-law's delicatessen also supports *Martin* Healy having been there. The delicatessen, which was located on Lenox Avenue in Harlem, would have been close by the clubhouse on West 122nd Street. Additionally, Peter Eckert, who was Ewald's father-in-law, was called as a witness at the Healy-Ewald trials because he had helped his daughter Bertha get together part of the $10,000 that was paid to Martin Healy when Ewald was being appointed a magistrate. Lastly, Krauss' account of Crater, Ewald, and the third man hiding the proceeds of a corrupt deal involving a municipal building in the backyard of his house meshes with the evidence that *Martin* Healy was engaged in many grafting schemes as leader of the Cayuga Club, to which Crater often was privy. So it appears Cronin mistakenly had conflated the judicial titles of Magistrate Ewald and Judge Crater with Martin Healy in relating the story to his superiors, coming up in his memorandum with "Judge Healy."[28]

Cronin's December 1955 memo to the chief of detectives also mistakenly discredited the account for a second reason. In his two memoranda to his superiors in October 1955, Captain Cronin reported that Krauss had told Golemboski that he "was called to the District Attorney's and questioned" and "was subpoenaed by the Grand Jury," but made no mention of what had happened in his Westchester house in early August 1930 as Healy and Ewald had directed him. In one memo, Cronin wrote it was unclear "[w]hether [Krauss] testified before the Grand Jury or not." But in his third memo two months later, he further discounted Krauss' revelations because "[p]erusal of Grand Jury minutes shows no record of Kraus[s]'s ever being questioned."[29]

But the references to the "grand jury" in his story were surely to the Healy-Ewald grand jury, not the contemporaneous Crater grand jury as Cronin and the police presumed. Their warning to Krauss in the back of the delicatessen that he might be called for questioning by the "District Attorney" took place in the middle of August when Crain was bungling his grand jury's investigation of the Healy-Ewald accusations. The district attorney was not removed from that prosecution by Governor Roosevelt until the end of August, and he did not begin leading the grand jury that was looking into Crater's disappearance until September 15. Thus, his recollection of what Healy and Ewald told him in the back of the delicatessen makes perfect sense. Once Governor Roosevelt put Attorney General Ward in charge of prosecuting the Healy-Ewald matter, it appears that Krauss, identified as a "friend" of Ewald, did testify before Ward's grand jury on October 1, 1930. Subsequently in early November, the prosecutors had sent out subpoenas to banks to disclose bank accounts held by a list of persons and entities, many of them connected to the Cayuga Club. These included Healy, Ewald, Crater, some Cayuga-named entities, and "Henry Krause." The interest that the prosecutors took in Krauss at the time attests to his relationships with Healy and Ewald.[30]

Whether Krauss knew Crater, as he had told Golemboski, is more difficult to ascertain. George Ewald, who still practiced law in a small office on lower Fifth Avenue when he was interviewed by Bloom for his *Harper's* article, vehemently denied that he had anything to do with him. Ewald ridiculed the idea, saying, "Parties with Healy and Crater? You crazy?...Crater was a very high type man. What the hell would he have to do with a crummy butcher like Krauss...[a] slimy, tricky conniver."[31] But some evidence suggests otherwise. Krauss had told Golemboski, according to Bloom, that he knew Crater as president of the Cayuga Club (after 1928) and was close to the "Cayuga clubhouse boys." If so, he was bound to have interacted with Crater, who was a mainstay at the small brownstone clubhouse, Healy's advisor and crony, and regularly attended meetings there even after he became a judge. Also, in the NYPD files, a handwritten note on one of Cronin's memos in October 1955 states that in one of Crater's personal checkbooks still in its possession then, there were entries for two checks written to "Enery Krause."[32]

So Krauss' confession to Detective Golemboski in his Harlem apartment in 1954 checked out in significant respects. But lost in minor contradictions in his story, like whether he was subsequently called to testify before a grand jury or not, the NYPD investigators insufficiently considered the inherent plausibility of his account of being hauled before Healy and Ewald in the backroom of Eckert's delicatessen in the middle of August 1930. By that time, approximately ten days after Crater had been last seen, both the district leader and the magistrate were in immense legal and political peril. Over the previous two weeks, well-publicized allegations had surfaced, supported by convincing evidence, that Ewald had bribed Healy for his appointment as a magistrate in 1927. At the time of the meeting in Eckard's deli, a sitting grand jury (albeit one led by the incompetent District Attorney Crain) would have been considering whether to indict the two men on criminal charges of bribery and the sale of judicial offices. And both men had strong reason to fear the extensive knowledge and uncertain intentions of their longtime confederate and now Justice Joseph Crater. In their meeting with Krauss according to his account, the two men intimated personal knowledge that something had already happened to Crater to obviate that danger, and demanded that Krauss conceal any connection the judge had with his Yonkers house. But twenty-five years later, the police department, finally aggressively pursuing the first lead arguably based on personal knowledge, was sidetracked by a lack of detailed knowledge of the chronology of events surrounding Crater's disappearance.

After 1955, there are no further memos remaining in the NYPD files regarding the butcher's story and the inquiries flowing from it. The false discrepancies between his story and the facts the police investigators had found seem to have brought this part of the investigation to a premature end. Admittedly, with these clues only surfacing so long after his disappearance, the primary witnesses and suspects having died, and Crater's body never found, the police would still have had an uphill battle trying to establish who was responsible for his disappearance. But time also had dimmed the NYPD's collective memory of the case, its evidence, its central figures, and the vanished days of Tammany Hall's ascendency at the end of the Twenties.

In the initial years after Crater vanished, the political machine, through its influence over municipal officials as well as its unforthcoming witnesses, had sufficiently stymied the grand jury and police investigations to ensure that they would be unsuccessful. Threatened by what the missing man could divulge about its secrets and crimes, Tammany, through District Attorney Crain, Mayor Walker, Martin Healy, George Ewald, and others were strongly motivated not to want to find Crater nor to learn what had happened to him. Yet by 1955, long free of any such restraining political influence, the NYPD failed to find him because of inadvertent mistakes, ignorance of the facts, and confusion about the key figures in the very cold case, rather than from willful blindness or complicity.

4

The publication in 1959 of Bloom's article did cause a resurgence of public interest in whether Crater was still buried on the premises of the house on Palmer Avenue (now Palmer Road) formerly owned by Krauss. He traveled back to Utrecht with a picture of the house seeking further information from Croiset. After again going into an "almost imperceptible trance," he perceived that while Crater had been shot and initially buried in the basement of the house, his body had subsequently been reburied "near water not far from the house" in front of three trees. Bloom's article mentioned that Cronin had learned that a small pond and three trees adjacent to it had been added in the backyard of the house a couple of years after Crater disappeared.[33]

With Cronin apparently still believing there was no probable cause to have a search warrant issued for digging in the backyard of the Yonkers house, *Life* magazine financed a very limited excavation of a corner of its backyard. The largely pictorial article titled "Weird Clue in the Crater Mystery: A huge hole gets dug in search for judge's body," appeared in the magazine's November 16, 1959, issue. Ringed by photos of Crater, Krauss, Cronin, Croiset, Bloom, and others, the article briefly recounted what Krauss told Golemboski, as well as the Dutch clairvoyant's extrasensory revelations. It also referred to a new witness, Krauss' daughter, who confirmed that their family was residing in the house around the time Crater disappeared, but she naturally could not re-member where she and her family were back then, almost thirty years before. The present owner of the house was photographed standing over a deep hole dug in a small corner of his backyard that had turned up nothing.[34]

Croiset was still on the case, psychically searching for Crater in June 1964. After the Missing Persons Bureau reached out to him for further assistance, the Dutch mystic now "perceived" that his body had been moved from the backyard of the Palmer Road house to the side of an abandoned road then leading to the house, again near a pond with three trees, in a shallow grave. Westchester County Sheriff John Hoy was asked to assist in pursing this neb-ulous clue. Hoy remarkably found a spot on the side of an old road with a drained pond bed with three trees, which was across from the Spring Lake Golf Course, about two miles north of the house. In a reprise of the early days of the search when even implausible tips of Crater's whereabouts were thoroughly pursued, he and his men spent four days digging an area of five thousand square feet to a depth of three feet in scorching summer heat. The sheriff finally called a halt to the excavation, quipping "There wasn't even a bone some dog might have buried for future reference."[35]

Occasional references to the missing man were still appearing in the popu-lar culture by then. The theater-obsessed Crater would have been pleased by the inclusion in the 1960 Broadway musical "Fiorello" of a character "Judge Carter," whose name intentionally was misspelled to avoid a defamation suit in case he was still alive thirty years after his disappearance.[36] *MAD* magazine featured a spoof on "TV's Wonder Dog" Lassie, including a comic of "Lizzie" finding the missing man. He was the subject of joking references in television shows in the 1960s, including episodes of *The Dick Van Dyke Show* and *Rocky and Bullwinkle*. Sportswriters seemed to invoke his name more often in their journalism, typically when referring to an athlete who temporarily had lost athletic abilities, like a star hitter in baseball who was in an uncharacteristic slump. Of course, whenever people have inexplicably vanished of late, Cra-ter's name perennially appears, along with those of his cohorts in vanishing, Amelia Earhart, Jimmy Hoffa, and Ambrose Bierce.[37]

With no new developments, psychic or otherwise, in the Crater case for several years, the NYPD decided in 1971 to contact the "principals" still living in order to update their files. Naturally, one of those sought was Crater's legal colleague and friend, Simon Rifkind, whose name appeared under "Name of

Complainant" with his address listed as "120 Broadway" on every DD-5 re-port in the NYPD files. The Missing Persons Bureau had difficulty initially contacting Rifkind about the cold case, however, because its letter to him was addressed to the New York County Bar Association. Upon learning that the police had been looking for him, Rifkind, one of the city's top litigators and a name partner in the megafirm, Paul, Weiss, Rifkind, Wharton & Garrison, quipped from his office in a high-rise building on Park Avenue, "If they can't find me, how could they ever find Crater?" The police department officially closed the case as unsolved in 1979.[38]

Crater's fictional debut in a bit role in Vincent T. Bugliosi's *Lullaby and Good Night* in 1987 was not a flattering one. Based loosely on Judge Seabury's investigation into corruption in the Vice Squad of the NYPD, the heroine, who has been falsely set up by her Tammany-connected ex-husband to be arrested by a Vice Squad officer for prostitution, becomes a call girl to earn money to overturn her conviction, get back custody of her daughter from her ex-husband, and strike a blow at the machine. One of her frequent cli-ents is Judge Crater (not a stretch by any means) who suffers from a severe foot fetish. In one session in his judicial chambers, Crater fondles the her-oine's feet and high-heeled shoes while giving a slightly garbled account of his role in the Libby's Hotel saga—his having made a lot of money by serving as "referee for the appraisal" for "this old hotel on Canal Street" which the city has bought for $3 million to use as a highway.[39] A few years later, a much more sanitized version of Joseph Crater's life appeared in a children's book, *What Happened to Judge Crater?*, in the History's Mysteries series. remark-ably providing a juvenile account of Tammany Hall, Healy, Krauss, the Lib-by's Hotel scheme, Sally Lou Ritz, and other figures in the Crater case. The author's answer, in a succinct rendition of less than fifty pages, is as inconclu-sive as that of the NYPD: "Perhaps someday someone will shed new light on Judge Crater and his strange disappearance. For now he remains hidden in the shadows."[40]

In the new century, the first and only adult nonfiction treatment of the Crater case was published, Richard J. Tofel's *Vanishing Point*. The slim volume sets Crater's disappearance within the broader context of Samuel Seabury's subsequent investigations into Tammany corruption and its downfall. While ably presenting the basic facts of the case, Tofel relies heavily on contempo-rary news articles, which often were inaccurate and in which some of the key witnesses gave different accounts of events than what they told the police or the grand jury. Tofel skillfully analyzes the available public evidence in the case and comes to some similar conclusions as reached here (for instance, when Stella first came upon her husband's bequest). But on the ultimate question of what happened to Crater, his book has little to say, and ends with a previous unsubstantiated speculation that he died from a heart attack while otherwise engaged in Polly Adler's brothel.[41]

In 2005, the Crater case did have a brief resurrection before a public largely unaware of the legendary unsolved missing person case. The new clue recapitulated the long history of tips from persons of questionable sanity, or who sought a momentary brush with celebrity and fame by claiming they had seen or knew what had happened to him. On August 19, 2005, the front page of the *New York Post* blared, "I KILLED JUDGE CRATER, Vanish mystery 'solved.'" The NYPD Cold Case Squad had received a handwritten note left by a recently deceased Queens woman that had been discovered among her belongings by a relative. The note stated that her husband (who was long deceased) told her at some point that he had heard from a friend who was a police officer and his brother, a taxi driver, that they were the ones who had picked up Crater outside Haas' Chophouse on the night of August 6, 1930. According to their story, they had driven him to Coney Island, where he was killed and buried under the boardwalk, at the future site of the New York Aquarium. The writer of the *Post* article couldn't resist adding at that if the information in the note was accurate, "he's been sleeping with the fishes all these years." The woman left no explanation of a motive nor any relationship between the people involved and the missing man.[42]

Despite the fading popular recognition of the frozen case, the initial story was covered extensively in the media—on television and online news, on the front page of the *Times*, and in other newspapers.[43] But the Cold Case Squad was unable to confirm any details of the deceased woman's story, which had been related to her by others long dead. There were reports that several bodies had been discovered while the foundations of the aquarium were being dug in the 1950s, but no one knew where those bodies were now. "As far as we know, the story we have is speculative," one investigator remarked. "It may be some lady's scribbling."[44] Shortly thereafter, the police department returned the Crater case to closed and unsolved status, presumably this time, for good.[45]

What Happened to Joseph Crater?

I

With the addition of the last pieces of the puzzle cast by the developments in the case in the 1950s, Joseph Crater's perplexing behavior and movements in the days leading up to his final appearance on the night of August 6 begin to come into focus. An understanding of what led to his getting into the taxicab on West Forty-Fifth Street that night, in turn, will help elucidate where he was headed afterward, the reasons why, and what ultimately became of him. What follows is the author's conjecture about what Crater and others were thinking and doing in the days leading up and after he vanished. Barring unlikely future revelations such as the discovery of Crater's body, only a hypothesis based on the very limited evidence now available can be ventured.

In the days leading up Crater's disappearance, the first pivot point in his behavior was the phone call he placed to an unknown party on Saturday night, August 2, from Belgrade Lakes Village, that precipitated a radical change to his plans to stay in Maine until the end of the month.[1] In her memoirs, all Stella would recall of what Joe told her immediately after the call was that he had to return immediately to the city "to straighten out a few people." But in 1937, closer in time to the event, she gave a more specific reason both in her *World-Telegram* interview and her confessional article in the pulp magazine True Story—that Joe suddenly returned to the city in order to advise Martin Healy and George Ewald regarding the breaking allegations that in 1927, the Ewalds had paid $10,000 to Healy to arrange for George's appointment as a city magistrate.

Stella's belatedly expressed belief of what had driven her husband back to the city the next day makes sense chronologically. Having just arrived at the Crater's cabin in Maine on Saturday morning after an overnight drive from the city, Joe placed a phone call to someone in New York that same night in town, suggesting that he had learned of something urgent and pressing while in the city that necessitated a long-distance telephone call on the first day of his extended vacation. The only news that could possibly have warranted such great concern about what was happening in the city in the doldrums of the summer was US Attorney Tuttle's rapidly developing inquiry into the Healy-Ewald matter. The day before, Healy had barely escaped Tuttle's efforts to subpoena him to testify before a federal grand jury about the money he received from the Ewalds, when a federal judge ruled that he had legitimately asserted his privilege against self-incrimination. So, the most likely recipient of the call Crater placed in Belgrade Lakes on Saturday was Healy, Ewald, or someone on their behalf. The message conveyed must have been that the two men had dire need of his immediate return to the city to assist them, both legally and politically, in defending against Tuttle's criminal investigation. That Crater was a sitting justice, with a wealth of ties to and influence with other judges, prosecutors, and elite lawyers in the city, would naturally been of immense help to Healy and Ewald.

In coming back to the city, Crater surely contemplated the dangers of his assisting Healy and others in a very prominent criminal proceeding. Tuttle and his prosecutors were well aware of the close bond between Healy and Crater in the Cayuga Club, and that the judge probably had extensive knowledge of what was being investigated. As reported in the newspapers, Crater was an obvious person to be questioned or subpoenaed in the Healy-Ewald matter because he knew how things were done in the Cayuga Club. Confirmation of Crater's concern about the federal prosecutor's interest in him and his records appears in Tuttle's obscure, privately published memoirs. Tuttle recalled that a few days before Crater's disappearance, "a prominent lawyer" with whom he was friendly asked for a private meeting. The question he had for Tuttle "diplomatically put, was whether...I was contemplating subpoenaing Judge Crater's bank accounts." Tuttle refused to answer his visitor, but by the time of his memoirs had an explanation for the judge's disappearance—he "found that the price of silence, however high, must be paid."[2]

When Joe arrived back at his Fifth Avenue apartment on the morning of Monday, August 4, Crater happened to run into his maid, who was there cleaning. As she later told Crain's grand jury, he instructed her to return to clean the apartment that Thursday morning, suggesting he would no longer be around by that time. After likely consulting with Healy and perhaps others about Tuttle's investigation that day, however, Joe's behavior on Monday night does not suggest an undue concern about the situation—or he was very adept at compartmentalizing the various parts of his life. He had dined with his friend William Klein, Klein's girlfriend Sally Ritz, and Ritz's parents at Haas' Chophouse on West Forty-Fifth Street. Joe seemed in good spirits that night, Klein later told police, and said that he would be going back to Maine in a day or two, which was consistent with what he told his maid that morning. After dinner, Crater continued to exhibit a relaxed frame of mind, visiting a girlfriend who was dancing at the nightclub Club Abbey and staying there until early in the morning.

But on the next day, Tuesday, August 5, worrisome new developments in the Healy-Ewald matter appeared that would keep Joe in the city longer. It was reported that the day before, Tuttle had written a private letter to District Attorney Crain, transferring the investigation of the office-buying charges to Crain for prosecution. The reason given for the transfer was that the crime of buying a city judicial office was a violation not of federal law, which Tuttle had authority to enforce, but of New York State law, which he did not. Included with Tuttle's letter was evidence his investigators had developed so far in the matter, and the promise of the name of a witness who had heard George Ewald brag about his payments to Healy to make him a magistrate.

Though Healy and the Ewalds must have breathed a sigh of relief that Crain, a Tammany loyalist of questionable competence, would now be in charge of the investigation into the office-buying allegations against them, the district leader likely would have demanded Joe's assistance there even more. Healy undoubtedly knew that Crater's connections and influence with Crain as well as his brethren sitting on the State Supreme Court, who might be presiding over an upcoming trial of the charges, would be essential to his beating the charges. But for Crater, the growing publicity and prominence of the Tammany judicial scandal, and the real possibility that he could be called to testify or provide records in the inquiry had to be deeply disconcerting, clouding his recent appointment to the bench and endangering his otherwise certain nomination and election to a full fourteen-year term as a justice that fall.

The details of Joe Crater's activities on August 5 are sparse. According to the Crater grand jury's report, he was seen in the vicinity of his courthouse downtown and had lunch with his friend Justice Frankenthaler. That evening, he had dinner at the home of Dr. Raggi, his personal doctor, who was treating his finger (recently crushed while he was in Atlantic City), and Raggi's wife, followed by a game of bridge. When interviewed by the police, Raggi seemed defensive of his friend, stating the judge had seemed in his usual good spirits and that he was planning on returning to Maine in a day or two to join Stella.[3] But it is possible that Crater, seeking a distraction from Healy and Ewald, was in a good mood that night.

Yet by the time Joe Crater returned to his Fifth Avenue apartment and went to sleep that Tuesday night, he seems to have considered his options and made up his mind as to what he would do the next day, August 6. If he stayed in town to continue to advise Healy and Ewald, he would certainly become further mired in the judicial office-buying accusations against his Cayuga Club cronies. Returning to his vacation with Stella in Maine, as he said he would to Klein the night before and Raggi that night, would not be a viable alternative since the prosecutors could always subpoena him back to the city to testify. His highly coveted reputation and future on the bench, as well as conceivably his license to practice law, were at stake.

Crater also must have been harboring some real concerns about tying himself so closely to Healy's personal interests. In the many years he had spent with the district leader at the Cayuga Club, serving effectively as his consigliere and "brains," he could not have missed the ruthless, avaricious, and thuggish side of his friend's character. In addition to the current allegations against Marty, Joe would have known all about, and sometimes participated in, many of his grafting, bribery, "contracts," and other schemes, information the district leader would not allow to be divulged at any cost. Moreover, some of Healy's grafting was of the dishonest type and may have involved organized crime figures up in Harlem, with whom the judge had no intention of getting involved. Joe also no doubt was well aware, from his many years at the Cayuga clubhouse, of the violent and criminal propensities of some of the "Cayuga boys," men like Henry Krauss and Herman Bitterman, who was alleged to have been involved in the killing of Magistrate Macrery the year before.

When Crater emerged from his Fifth Avenue apartment on the morning of August 6 and traveled to his judicial chambers, he methodically began to implement his plan to leave his life in the city for good. Once at his judicial chambers, he secretively collected papers and folders from his chambers to take with him, disposed of others, and cleaned out his desk and cabinets. He had his deputy Mara cash checks at his banks for more than $5,000 in cash, which he took home, along with some work files. When leaving the 60 Centre Street courthouse, as his deputy Mara later told police, the judge quickly descended the long, wide, stone steps into a taxicab, furtively glancing around to make sure he wasn't seen taking final leave of his judicial office.

After the two men had arrived back at the judge's apartment around noon with his bags and folders of documents, Crater spoke his cryptic parting words to Mara, that he was going up "Westchester way" later that day. From the start of the search, these words had been dismissed as meaningless banter on a steaming hot day. But in light of later revelations about Henry Krauss's house in Westchester County and his story of Healy, Ewald, and Crater's use of it for parties and hiding illicitly obtained money, perhaps Joe's parting words were intended to be of more significance. What if he was planning to go to Krauss's house that night to retrieve some of the money stashed there to use in fleeing his present life and starting another? Because Crater very well could have been apprehensive of going up to the isolated farmhouse in Westchester County, possibly in Healy's company, perhaps his parting words to Mara were intended to leave clues, like a trail of breadcrumbs, as to where he would be going, in case something went wrong up at Krauss's house. He may have thought that Mara would remember his boss's parting words that afternoon if his boss disappeared. In fact, even though a whole month went by before the police actually questioned Mara, a longer time than Crater probably thought would pass before his disappearance would be disclosed, he was able to recall his boss's parting words. If Crater's journey to Westchester were to lead to his demise, at least those looking for him might have a place to begin a search.

After Mara left his boss alone in the apartment, it is more obvious what Joe did for the rest of the afternoon. He spent the next hours methodically putting his legal affairs and assets in order to provide for Stella after he departed. He gathered together about $6,690 in cash, which mainly came from the $5,150 he had withdrawn from his bank accounts that morning, as well as his will, life insurance policies, deeds to his properties, bankbooks, stock certificates, and other documents. He normally kept many of these items in his safety deposit box at the building where Senator Wagner's law office was located; he could have brought them home over these last days. He also composed, in what Stella would later describe as unusually shaky handwriting, the confidential message to her listing the debts that lawyers and clients owed him, likely using as references the files and papers he had just brought home from his chambers. In fact, one attorney listed in the letter later remembered that Crater called him on the afternoon of August 6 to confirm that the debt was still owed. Leaving their marriage for good, Joe made every effort to provide her with whatever assets, properties, insurance policies, and debts he was owed, so that she had the financial wherewithal to survive when he was gone.[4]

Like his earlier parting words to Mara in his apartment, Joe's misspelling of the valediction of his confidential note before he signed it may have been intentional and designed to drop a clue to apprise his wife of what, or whom, was causing him to leave her in despair and fear. By signing off as what looked like "Am so whary, Joe," an obvious misspelling of "weary" which Stella would know her literate husband would not normally do, he could have been subtly signaling to her that Martin Healy, whom she knew as her husband's close crony, was behind his hurried flight from the metropolis. And when, as the evidence does support, Stella first found Joe's confidential note and the rest of his bequest in their apartment at the end of August 1930, before news of his disappearance had broken, one of the first calls she tried to make was to Healy at his Long Island summerhouse. His brother William answered one of Stella's phone calls, placed in the middle of the night, in which he later testified that she sounded hysterical and demanded to know what had happened to her husband and whether he was now in hiding to protect Martin.[5]

At some point that day, Crater also must have learned through his Tammany contacts or perhaps from Healy himself that Mayor Walker had just suspended his good friend, without pay, from his municipal job until the charges of the judicial office-buying scheme against him were resolved.[6] This was the first time Walker had felt enough pressure to remove a senior official in his administration for alleged corruption, and a powerful Tammany district leader no less. Though he may not have read it, an editorial in the *World* that day seemed to confirm Crater's greatest fears of being a witness in the Healy-Ewald matter, observing that in Crain's prosecution, "[i]t will be important to see how far Tammany is willing to go in locating missing witnesses and in compelling reluctant witnesses to testify."[7] Joe Crater had no intention of becoming one of those missing or reluctant witness compelled to testify against his political boss in this prosecution or any others involving the Cayuga Club or higher-ups in the machine. It was simply too dangerous, and would obliterate his once so-promising career and future in New York City.

Before Joe left his apartment around 6 p.m. that day, he took one more action demonstrating his intent to depart the life he had made in the city for good. He left behind on his bureau his personal items which bore his name or initials: his monogrammed calling card case, pocket watch, and pen, which the police would find there when they first searched his apartment. Such items, which he always carried on him, would not be needed and could be harmful when he established a new identity elsewhere.

2

Crater's erratic conduct after he left his apartment in the early evening and headed to Broadway is more difficult to explain. If he was planning to permanently leave the city, then why intentionally go to a part of the city where he would be recognized and see people he knew, and make it that much easier to track his flight? He went to his friend Gransky's ticket office and asked for a ticket for a show he had already seen with him, raising a red flag. The judge then proceeded to his favorite chophouse where he knew he could run into his friend Haas, the proprietor, and while there, he unexpectedly and embarrassingly also ran into William Klein. Both Haas and Klein noticed the judge seemed dispirited. If he had hoped to savor for one last time his adored Broadway and its nightlife before he departed, he did not seem to be enjoying it.

But perhaps Crater's confused conduct on the night of August 6 reflected his last-minute indecision about whether he should follow through with his plans to abandon his life and everything he had accomplished. He must have realized that fleeing under these circumstances would raise suspicions of wrongdoing on his part, that his name would ever afterward be associated with scandal and impropriety, which is precisely what happened. Being an egotistical and proud man, he must have considered this seriously. His other option was to stay in the city and face what was coming, to prepare to be called as a witness and to provide incriminating evidence in the Healy-Ewald prosecution and other future ones involving Tammany corruption. And if Healy or Tammany turned against him and tried to make him a scapegoat, he certainly knew enough about such corruption, especially involving the Cayuga Club and lawyers and judges, to fight back. If he had remained in the city, one of his friends later remarked, "he was a headstrong man who might have smashed a political house of cards with a few words from the witness stand if he felt that he was being made a 'goat' in an investigation."[8]

Yet ultimately, a little after 9 p.m., Joe left his friends outside Haas' Chop-house and got into a taxicab headed west on West Forty-Fifth Street. Where the cab was headed was never ascertained because the driver was never iden-tified. The taxi did not take Crater to the theater nearby where a ticket was being held for him because the cab was headed in the opposite direction and he never picked up the ticket.

If Crater intended to go to Krauss's house in Westchester that night be-fore fleeing for good, it seems improbable that he would have taken the taxi-cab from West Forty-Fifth Street directly there. That would have entailed a long and expensive trip along backroads through the Bronx and into Yonkers, which would have given the taxi driver a good chance to observe and remem-ber the odd-looking passenger in the backseat. So, the taxi he was riding in probably was headed on a trip somewhere more brief and local, which would also help explain why the driver never came forward when the news of the judge's disappearance first appeared a month later.

Some speculation is necessary at this point, as there is no evidence one way or the other to help us. If Crater's ultimate destination that night was Krauss's house north of the city, where he wanted to pick up some cash stashed there and begin his journey to a new life, it seems likely he would have apprised Healy of his plans at some point during that day. So perhaps he was taking the cab to meet up with and bid a final goodbye to his friend at the Cayuga clubhouse located on West 122nd Street. This would be consistent with the taxicab Joe got into heading west along Forty-Fifth Street toward the far west side of Manhattan bordering the North (now the Hudson) River, where there were less-trafficked roads that paralleled the river that could have been used to drive north to the clubhouse in central Harlem.

If so, Marty Healy may have greeted Joe at the Cayuga Club. At the least, the two men, who had formed an unlikely but strong partnership and friend-ship over the years, would have wanted to take leave of each other. They prob-ably would have agreed that to avoid the danger of Joe being called to testify in the prosecution against Healy and Ewald, it was imperative for him to flee and avoid the city for a long while. They also perhaps discussed Crater's plans to stop at Krauss's house.

By this time, however, Healy must have considered his options and also made up his mind. Having been humiliatingly suspended from his city of-fice earlier that day by his friend Jimmy Walker, Martin understood that the charges of judicial office-buying were not going to be easily dismissed, even with incompetent District Attorney Crain now in charge of the prosecution. Knowing Joe well, Healy may have entertained doubts that he, who had recently achieved his life's ambition of becoming a judge and was extraordinarily proud of his newfound stature in the city, could pull off his disappearing act and stay away from the metropolis for long. Maybe Healy thought the judge's prominence or his singular appearance would give him away if he attempted to assume a new life somewhere else, and he would be brought back to bear witness against him and Ewald. Or perhaps he was concerned that Crater, in a fit of rectitude or revenge, would voluntarily return and try to bring down the district leader and the political machine. In either case, if Crater came back, he simply knew too much about the crimes and corruptions of Healy and other higher-ups in Tammany Hall, and the risk that he would talk was just too great. A man desperate to retain his power and wealth as well as his freedom, which were all under serious challenge, Healy could have coldly calculated that Joe Crater had to be silenced because he knew too much. With him out of the way, there was a better chance that he and Ewald could beat the office-buying charges against them.

If the plan was to go up to his house in Yonkers, Henry Krauss may have been at the clubhouse too, and driven with Crater up there, perhaps with others from the clubhouse. Joe may not have known what was in store for him there and probably went voluntarily, believing this was the first step in his escape to a new life. As Croiset perceived it, the judge was "enticed" or "tricked" into going to Krauss's house, perhaps still believing or hoping those driving him to the house were there to assist him. If Croiset is given any further credence, Healy, the man who likely had plotted what was to unfold at Krauss's house, did not accompany Crater up to the house. He naturally would have wanted to have an alibi if a murder was going to take place there.

Krauss's wife and daughter, who were living at the Westchester house at this time, would have been away somewhere that summer. His farmhouse was in a secluded area, with few houses nearby or people present to notice what was occurring. Once Krauss, Crater, and possibly others arrived at the butcher's house, there may have been drinking, according to Krauss's last confession, although the judge wouldn't have been a big participant. It very well might have been Krauss who shot and killed Crater with the pistol he kept for his bootlegging activities (and he later reported missing), either in the kitchen (as Krauss suggested) or in the cellar below (as Croiset did). On a perhaps macabre note, Krauss, the butcher, could have employed his skills to dismember the judge's body so that it could more easily be disposed of. At least initially, the body may have been concealed beneath the earthen cellar floor or in the backyard of the farmhouse, though if Croiset is to be believed, it was subsequently moved elsewhere.

3

If Healy was the one responsible for silencing Crater, his decision seemed to pay off at first. In the days after his disappearance, Crain's grand jury was convened and heard the Healy-Ewald charges, and embarrassingly did not return any indictment. After the November elections, State Attorney General Ward and his prosecutors, who were put in charge by Governor Roosevelt and were no friends of the machine, still were unable to convict Healy, the Ewalds, or Tammany in three trials on the judicial office-buying charges, though there were suggestions that jury tampering also was employed to ensure the result. Healy and his codefendants, though spending tremendous amounts on their legal fees, were able to claim some vindication, and the district leader still retained his powerful post as district leader of the Nineteenth Assembly District in Harlem for several years. Tammany Hall, whose leaders figured prominently in the Healy-Ewald trials, came out scathed but not defeated. After all, Tammany had its rocky moments before in its long reign, and appeared capable of righting itself again.

But greater political, economic, demographic, and social forces were again transforming the metropolis in so many ways that, if Joe Crater had returned to his city just a few years later as many predicted he would, he would have barely recognized it. The political machine that had controlled the city when he disappeared, and that had facilitated his rapid ascension to power, wealth, and status there, was in shambles two years later. Despite the unsuccessful Healy-Ewald prosecutions, the investigations into Tammany's corruption and stranglehold over the municipal government had only accelerated. Judge Seabury's investigations starting soon after Crater vanished would remove or imprison district leaders, judges, police officers, and municipal officials, culminating in the resignation of Mayor Walker in the fall of 1932.

By the latter half of the 1930s, the progressive administrations of Mayor La Guardia and President Roosevelt had starved the tiger of its fuels of patronage, handouts, and votes. The new mayor had replaced the Tammany district leaders and loyalists in the higher echelons of the municipal government with activists, nonpartisan, and capable officials. With the federal, state, and city governments now being the purveyors of social welfare benefits and protections from exigencies, especially for the unemployed and the aged during the hard economic times, the machine had lost one of its chief reasons for garnering votes and staying in power. By the end of the 1930s, what was left of Tammany Hall was engaged in dishonest grafting with organized crime.

If he could have returned to New York a few years later, Crater would also have been amazed and perhaps dismayed by other changes wrought by the Depression years on the city of the Roaring Twenties. With the new austerity and large numbers of the unemployed, grafting schemes involving the government and business no longer were viewed as entertaining or acceptable because everyone seemed to be striking it rich on the stock market or otherwise during that decade of excess. New government regulation of business and the professions with the concomitant changes in morality, ethics, and concepts of conflict of interest ended the days of District Leader Plunkitt's honest graft, inside information, and "opportunities" for the taking. While a fourteen-year employment at $25,000 a year if Crater had been elected to a Supreme Court seat that fall would have given him security during the Depression, changing judicial and legal ethics would have ensured that Joe would not have enriched himself on the bench, as he had boasted to Stella.

Larger demographic and political forces additionally had swept away the white bastion of the Cayuga Democratic Club in Harlem. Marty Healy, the reason for Joe's attempted escape from the city and for his demise according to the hypothesis presented here, was deposed as district leader in 1935 by the new political forces of the African American community which rejected Tammany's direction. Shortly after that, the Cayuga Club itself was disbanded and its clubhouse, once the site of widespread grafting, ironically would be rented out under the auspices of a New Deal government agency. If Joe Crater had returned then to reveal all the damning information he possessed about Healy, the Cayuga Club, and Tammany Hall, he could only have given a history lesson.

What certainly would have been a major disappointment to Joe was that the years of the Depression had extinguished the bright lights of Broadway and the halcyon days of his beloved theater, with even the mighty Shubert brothers' companies driven into bankruptcy. The swanky, risqué nightclubs and the ribald, hedonistic nightlife he had so enjoyed had been replaced in the following decade by more sedate and cheaper clubs geared to larger audiences and more generic patrons. And the subsidence of the sexual revolution unleashed in the 1920s and disappearance of the eponymous flirtatious chorus girls and flappers he coveted would have severely hampered his lifestyle.[9]

So perhaps it is fitting that Joe Crater never made it back to the modern metropolis being born. A man consummately of his time and place, Manhattan in the Roaring Twenties, he had skillfully made his way in the great city and achieved success and prominence in its upper strata far beyond his dreams. Yet along the way, he had availed himself of New York City's dirty politics, its crooked businesses and legal system, its sybaritic nightlife, and its fun and theatricality. In the year of his disappearance, a foreign writer, perhaps sensing that the end of the Jazz Age Manhattan was near, became nostalgic:

> If the planet grows cold, this city will nevertheless have been mankind's warmest moment....Night is abolished. How could anyone rest amid all this light, all these spasms and combustions?...People hustle each other good-humoredly. Everything is cheerful yet terrible. Broadway's lights and fanfares are not destined to make one forget life, but to intensify it tenfold. Distractions are set alongside toil, as in a gold rush. The wear and tear is terrible, people fall and are carried off, the game goes on....Suppose it were only a dream, a prodigious attempt, an Avatar, a fleeting renaissance, a superb purgatory?[10]

So Justice Crater remains forever frozen at that moment on the night of August 6, 1930, when at the prime of his life, nattily dressed, a man out on the town, he hailed and entered a taxicab in the middle of Broadway that took him away forever. Having been thoroughly enthralled and entangled by the pleasures, prerogatives, and corruptions of his scintillating and seductive place and time, he did not possess the wherewithal and resources to escape or outlive it. Crater's real feat was to vanish from that grand, forgotten metropolis right before it disappeared as completely and irretrievably as he did.

NOTES

Introduction

1. "Wagner Joins Crater Search As Clews Fail," *New York Herald-Tribune* (hereafter "*Herald-Tribune*"), Sept. 7, 1930, 1, 6.

2. George M. Hall, "Justice J.F. Crater Missing from His Home Since Aug. 6," *New York World* (hereafter "*World*"), Sept. 3, 1930, 1, 4.

3. "Preliminary Report of the Grand Jury," Court of General Sessions of the County of New York, Oct. 31, 1930 (hereafter "Preliminary Report"), Case File No. 13595 (hereafter "NYPD Files"), reviewed at New York City Police Department, Headquarters, 1 Police Plaza Path, New York, NY. The NYPD case file was obtained by the author through a request under the New York State Freedom of Information Law.

4. Morris Markey, "The Vanished Judge," *New Yorker*, Oct. 11, 1930, 43.

5. See Ariel Lawhon, *The Wife, the Maid, and the Mistress* (New York: Doubleday, 2014); Peter Quinn, *The Man Who Never Returned* (New York: Overlook Press, 2010).

6. Author Peter Quinn had access to the NYPD file on the Crater case in writing his fictional account of Crater's disappearance.

7. "Judge Crater," *New York Daily News* (hereafter "*Daily News*"), Oct. 3, 1930, 39.

1. When Last Seen...

1. Advertisement, *New Yorker*, Jan. 19, 1929, 67; "Real Estate Notes," *New York Times* (hereafter "*Times*"), March 13, 1929, 56.

2. "Mercury Goes to 93 on Hottest Aug. 5," *Times*, Aug. 6, 1930, 1, 2.

3. Robert A. M. Stern, Gregory Gilmartin, and Thomas Mellins, *New York 1930:*

Architecture and Urbanism Between the Two World Wars (New York: Rizzoli International Publications, Inc., 1994), 97.

4. Mrs. Joseph Force Crater, "Why My Husband Disappeared," *True Story*, Nov. 1937, 26, 117.

5. DD-5, Sept. 10, 1930, 1; DD-5, Sept. 11, 1930, 1; DD-5, Sept. 13, 1930, 2–3, NYPD Files.

6. DD-5, Sept. 10, 1930, 2, DD-5, Sept. 13, 1930, 3, 5, NYPD Files.

7. DD-5, Sept. 13, 1930, 5, NYPD Files.

8. DD-5, Sept. 10, 1930, 1, DD-5, Sept. 13, 1930, 5, NYPD Files. Another detective who interviewed Mara reported in his DD-5 that he said that Crater told him he "was going swimming in Westchester [that day] and would see him in the morning" at his chambers. DD-5, Sept. 11, 1930, 1, NYPD Files. Much of the newspaper coverage likewise quoted Crater as having told Mara that he was going "swimming" in Westchester, which led to ensuing reporting about whether Crater did or did not like to swim. The author will rely on Mara's initial statement to the NYPD, as recorded in the DD-5s, that Crater told him at his apartment that he was going up to Westchester County later that day as the most accurate statement.

9. Stella Crater and Oscar Fraley, *The Empty Robe* (New York: Doubleday, 1961), 26–27, 32–34, 36, 48–49.

10. Crater, "Why My Husband," 116.

11. Crater and Fraley, *Empty Robe*, 66.

12. "Dry Evils Demand a New Declaration, Tammany Is Told," *Times*, July 5, 1930, 1, 5.

13. "Crater Came Here on 'Urgent Call,'" *Times*, Sept. 27, 1930, 10.

14. Crater and Fraley, *Empty Robe*, 77–78; Crater, "Why My Husband," 118.

15. DD-5, Sept. 13, 1930, 8, NYPD Files; "Aide Denies Crater Destroyed Papers," *Times*, Sept. 5, 1930, 6.

16. DD-5, Sept. 8, 1930, and attached "Missing Since August 6, 1930," circular, NYPD Files.

17. DD-5, Sept. 9, 1930, 1–2, DD-5, Sept. 10, 1930, 2, DD-5, Sept. 13, 1930, 8–9, NYPD Files.

18. DD-5, Sept. 9, 1930, 1, DD-5, Sept. 10, 1930, 1, NYPD Files.

19. DD-5, Sept. 13, 1930, 3–4, 6, NYPD Files.

20. In his book on the Crater case, Richard Tofel has suggested that he did not get into a taxi outside of Haas' Chophouse but instead walked away from Klein and Ritz who got in the taxi. Richard J. Tofel, *Vanishing Point: The Disappearance of Judge Crater, and the New York He Left Behind* (Chicago: Ivan R. Dee, 2004), 31–32. But the accounts given to the police by the only eyewitnesses, Klein and Ritz, stated unequivocally that Crater hailed and got into a taxi heading in a west-

erly direction on West Forty-Fifth Street toward Ninth Avenue. See DD-5, Sept. 9, 1930, 1, DD-5, Sept. 13, 1930, 4, 6, NYPD Files.

21. A contemporary travelogue of New York City mentions the starting time of Broadway musicals was twenty minutes before 9 p.m. as a result of a new police regulation. Paul Morand, *New York* (New York: Henry Holt and Co., 1930), 192.

22. Crater and Fraley, *Empty Robe*, 81.

23. Crater and Fraley, *Empty Robe*, 82–84; Crater, "Why My Husband," 118–19; "Mrs. Crater Blocks Maine Police Hunt," *Times*, Sept. 23, 1930, 1.

24. Author's Interview with Simon Rifkind, Aug. 6, 1993, at offices of Paul, Weiss, Rifkind, Wharton & Garrison, New York, NY (hereafter "Rifkind Interview").

25. Tofel, *Vanishing Point*, 95.

26. Crater and Fraley, *Empty Robe*, 83–84; "Mrs. Crater Blocks Maine Police Hunt," *Times*, Sept. 23, 1930, 1, 4.

27. DD-5, Sept. 10, 1930, 1, NYPD Files.

28. DD-5, Sept. 10, 1930, 1, NYPD Files; Crater and Fraley, *Empty Robe*, 86, 88. Lowenthal did recall that while he was there, Stella placed three telephone calls "of a private nature," one to the judge's sister in Massachusetts, one to Belgrade Lakes, and one to Blue Point, NY. DD-5, Sept. 10, 1930, 1.

29. Crater and Fraley, *Empty Robe*, 88–89.

30. "Wide Hunt Is Begun for Justice Crater," *Times*, Sept. 4, 1930, 1, 5.

31. John Brooks, "Profiles: Advocate," *New Yorker*, May 25, 1983, 46, 51–52, 59, 69–70.

32. Rifkind Interview; Brooks, "Profiles," 56. In his interview with the author and as he had stated previously to the press, Rifkind blamed Crater's law secretary Johnson for his false reassurances that he had recently seen his boss when he hadn't. Rifkind Interview. He thought this had the effect of delaying the start of the police investigation into Crater's disappearance for at least a couple of weeks, thus making the ensuing search much more difficult. But even after he informed Stella of Johnson's false reassurances that Crater had been around in the middle of the month, Rifkind was one of those counseling her not to go right to the police when they learned that Joe had failed to appear on the opening day of the Supreme Court term on August 25, a sure sign that something was terribly amiss. As the organizer of the private search for the missing man, he bore significant responsibility himself for a delay of an additional ten days before the NYPD learned of the disappearance, assuring that the trail was colder when the police search began.

33. Hall, "Justice J.F. Crater," 1, 4.

34. Hall, "Justice J.F. Crater," 1, 4.

35. Hall, "Justice J.F. Crater," 1.

2. The Search Officially Begins

1. James Lardner and Thomas Reppetto, *NYPD: A City and Its Police* (New York: Henry Holt and Co., 2000), 55, 71, 126, 203; Arthur Browne, *One Righteous Man: Samuel Battle and the Shattering of the Color Line In New York* (Boston: Beacon Press, 2015), 21–22.

2. "Lexow Committee Report," quoted in M. R. Werner, *Tammany Hall* (New York: Doubleday, Doran & Co., 1928), 374. A detailed account of the Lexow Committee and Mazet Committee's corruption probes into the police department and Tammany Hall, which exposed these unseemly connections, is presented in Werner, *Tammany Hall*, 348–420.

3. Milton Mackaye, "Profiles: Cop's Cop," *New Yorker*, Oct. 24, 1931, 22.

4. Mackaye, "Profiles: Cop's Cop," 25.

5. Lardner and Reppetto, *NYPD*, 201.

6. Captain John H. Ayres and Carol Bird, *Missing Men* (New York: Garden City Publishing Co., 1932), 4.

7. "Crater's Disappearance But One of 70 Vanishing Daily In New York City," *Herald-Tribune*, Sept. 14, 1930, Sect. 2, 3.

8. Ayres and Bird, *Missing Men*, 6.

9. Ayres and Bird, *Missing Men*, 4, 8.

10. "Judge Crater Mystery 25 Years Old," *Herald-Tribune*, July 29, 1955, 13.

11. DD-5, Sept. 9, 1930, 1–2, Sept. 10, 1930, 1–2, Sept. 11, 1930, 1, NYPD Files.

12. DD-5, Sept. 9, 1930, 1, NYPD Files.

13. DD-5, Sept. 10, 1930, 1, NYPD Files.

14. DD-5, Sept. 13, 1930, 2, NYPD Files.

15. Henry F. Pringle, "Profiles: The Janitor's Boy," *New Yorker*, March 5, 1927, 24.

16. Fremont Rider, *Rider's New York City* (New York: Macmillan Co., 1924), 178.

17. "Crater Intended Dropping Out of Sight, Police Say," *World*, Sept. 5, 1930, 1, 4.

18. J. Joseph Huthmacher, *Senator Robert F. Wagner and the Rise of Urban Liberalism* (New York: Atheneum, 1968), 121.

19. DD-5, Sept. 10, 1930, 2–3, NYPD Files.

20. DD-5, Sept. 10, 1930, 3, NYPD Files.

21. DD-5, Sept. 10, 1930, 3 & attachment, NYPD Files.

22. "Father Believes Crater Is Alive," *World*, Sept. 8, 1930, 1, 10.

23. Foster Hirsch, *The Boys from Syracuse* (Carbondale: Southern Illinois Univ. Press, 1998), 125.

24. DD-5, Sept. 13, 1930, 3–4, NYPD Files.

25. DD-5, Sept. 13, 1930, 4, NYPD Files.

26. DD-5, Sept. 9, 1930, 1, NYPD Files.

27. For example, see "Aide Denies Crater Destroyed Papers," *Times*, Sept. 5, 1930, 1, 6; "Missing Justice Crater Sought as Ewald Witness," *Herald-Tribune*, Sept. 4, 1930, 1, 2.

28. DD-5, Sept. 13, 1930, 4, NYPD Files.

29. DD-5, Sept. 27, 1930, & attached "Statement of Mrs. Connie Marcus," Sept. 26, 1930, 3–4, NYPD Files.

30. Hirsch, *The Boys*, 155.

31. "Playbill," *Artists and Models* (Paris-Riviera Edition of 1930), Shubert Archives, New York, NY.

32. Robert Benchley, "Keeping Cool with the Shuberts," *New Yorker*, June 21, 1930, 26, 30.

33. DD-5, Sept. 13, 1930, 3–4, NYPD Files.

34. DD-5, Sept. 13, 1930, 5–6, NYPD Files.

35. DD-5, Sept. 10, 1930, 2, NYPD Files.

36. "Quiz Girls in Crater Hunt," *Daily News*, Sept. 10, 1930, 2, 6.

37. DD-5, Sept. 13, 1930, 8, NYPD Files.

38. DD-5, Sept. 13, 1930, 9–11, & attached "Statement of Miss Marie Miller," Sept. 13, 1930, 1–3, NYPD Files.

39. DD-5, Sept. 8, 1930, & attached "Circular," NYPD Files.

40. DD-5, Sept. 8, 1930, & Circular, NYPD Files.

41. Sept. 8, 1930, and Circular, NYPD Files.

42. Letter from Stella Crater to Captain John H. Ayres, August 16, 1931, 1–2, NYPD Files. In response to the police department's delicately inquiring as to whether or not her husband was circumcised, she stated in the letter, "As to the matter of circumcision to the best of my knowledge + belief I do not think he was—however after giving the matter additional thought I would not care to be positively definite on this point and suggest if you consider it essential you get in touch with his Doctor."

43. "Federal Men Scan Crater Bank Books," *Times*, Sept. 6, 1930, 1, 2; "Jury to Inspect Home of Crater," *World*, Oct. 14, 1930, 8.

44. "Mulrooney Says Judge Crater 'Intended to Drop From Sight,'" *New York Sun* (hereinafter "*Sun*"), Sept. 4, 1930, 1, 2; "Wide Hunt Is Begun," *Times*, 5; "Crater's Wife Intimates She Believes Him Alive," *Daily News*, Sept. 12, 1930, 2, 4.

45. "Hunts Crater Clews in Vain," *Sun*, Sept. 8, 1930, 1; "Crater's Trip Here Spurs Crain Query, *Times*, Oct. 4, 1930, 2.

46. "Supreme Court Justice Crater Has Been Missing for a Month," *New York Democrat* (hereinafter "*Democrat*"), Sept. 6, 1930, 1; "Personal—but not confidential," *Democrat*, Sept. 13, 1930, 1.

47. "The Search for Justice Crater," *World*, Sept. 10, 1930, 10.

3. On the Great Stage of Manhattan

1. "Wagner Joins Crater," *Herald-Tribune*, 6.

2. Commonwealth of Pennsylvania, *Manufacturing and Mercantile Resources of the Lehigh Valley* (Philadelphia: Industrial Publishing Co., 1881), 57.

3. *Portrait and Biographical Record of Lehigh, Northampton and Carbon Counties* (Chicago: Chapman Publishing Co., 1894), 744–45.

4. Catherine Ross, "Missing—Joseph Force Crater," *Sunday Express*, Aug. 5, 1990, 1; Frank Whelan, "The Mystery of Judge Crater," *Allentown Morning Call*, Jan. 15, 1989, B3.

5. *The Rechauffe* [Yearbook] (Easton, PA: Easton High School, 1906), 18, 79; Commonwealth of Pennsylvania, *Report of the Superintendent of Public Instruction* (Harrisburg, PA: Harrisburg Publishing Co., 1906), 181.

6. Commonwealth of Pennsylvania, *Report of the Superintendent of Public Instruction*, 180.

7. Ann Kovalenko, "Easton Recalls Judge Crater," *Allentown Sunday Call-Chronicle*, Sept. 11, 1960, 13.

8. *Rechauffe*, 79.

9. *The Melange* [Yearbook] (Easton, PA: Lafayette College, 1909), 369.

10. Entry in 1910 Lafayette College yearbook reproduced in Whelan, "Mystery of," B3; Kovalenko, "Easton Recalls," 15.

11. DD-5, Oct. 2, 1930, 5; NYPD Files.

12. Kovalenko, "Easton Recalls," 15.

13. Crater and Fraley, *Empty Robe*, 32.

14. DD-5, Sept. 17, 1930, & attached letter from Monty Crater to Joe Crater, dated Sept. 1, 1930, NYPD Files.

15. Department of Commerce and Labor, *Statistical Abstract of the United States, 1910* (Washington, DC: Government Printing Office, 1911), 50.

16. Department of Commerce and Labor, *Statistical Abstract*, 201.

17. Department of Commerce and Labor, *Statistical Abstract*, 96, 694, 696.

18. J. A. Spender quoted in Bayard Still, *Mirror for Gotham: New York as Seen by Contemporaries from Dutch Days to the Present* (New York: Fordham Univ. Press, 1994), 273.

19. "Kent Hall Dedication," *Columbia Alumni News*, Nov. 3, 1910, 119.

20. Staff of the Foundation for Research in Legal History, *A History of the School of Law, Columbia University* (New York: Columbia Univ. Press, 1955), 233.

21. *Report of Special Committee of Law Library at Kent Hall*, Dec. 29, 1910, 2, at Columbia Law School Library, New York, NY.

22. George Martin, *CCB: The Life and Century of Charles C. Burlingham* (New York: Hill and Wang, 2005), 69.

23. Theron G. Strong, *Landmarks of a Lawyer's Lifetime* (New York: Dodd, Mead 1914), 427.

24. George Martin, *Causes and Conflicts: The Centennial History of the Association of the Bar of the City of New York 1870-1970* (Boston: Houghton Mifflin Co., 1970), 188.

25. Martin, *Causes and Conflicts* 185, 217.

26. Rifkind Interview.

27. "Body of a Man Found in Bay Is Not Crater's," *Sun*, Sept. 23, 1930, 1, 2.

28. Winston Murrill, "Mrs. Crater Talks," *New York World-Telegram*, July 21, 1937 (hereafter "*World-Telegram*"), 3.

29. The Federal Writers Project, *The WPA Guide to New York City* (New York: The New Press, 1992), 256; Andrew S. Dolkart and Gretchen S. Sorin, *Touring Historic Harlem: Four Walks in Northern Manhattan* (New York: New York Landmarks Conservancy, 1997), 10–15. The effort to attract blacks to Harlem after the turn of the century is described in Gilbert Osofsky, *Harlem: The Making of a Ghetto* (Chicago: Ivan R. Dee, 1996), 92–123.

30. Ira Katznelson, *Black Men, White Cities: Race, Politics, and Migration in the United States, 1900–30, and Britain, 1948–68* (New York: Oxford Univ. Press 1973), 62–63; Thomas Kessner, *Fiorello H. La Guardia and the Making of Modern New York* (New York: McGraw-Hill Publishing Co. 1989), 204.

31. Katznelson, *Black Men*, 68–69; John C. Walter, *The Harlem Fox: J. Raymond Jones and Tammany, 1920–1970* (Albany: State Univ. of New York Press, 1989), 46–48, 50–51.

32. Warren Moscow, *The Last of the Big-Time Bosses: The Life and Times of Carmine De Sapio and the Rise and Fall of Tammany Hall* (New York: Stein and Day, 1971), 45; Katznelson, *Black Men*, 64; James Weldon Johnson, *Black Manhattan* (New York: Da Capo Press, 1991), 146, 158.

33. Walter, *Harlem Fox*, 35. The Cayuga Club's leaders apparently were indiscriminate in barring non-whites, also denying membership to a lawyer from the West Indies. Walter, *Harlem Fox*, 4.

34. Osofsky, *Harlem*, 257, n. 38.

35. "Tammany Warned of Revolt in Harlem," *Times*, July 12, 1927, 52; Katznelson, *Black Men*, 72.

36. "Accuses Tammany of Ignoring Negroes," *Times*, April 15, 1927, 10.

37. Thomas M. Henderson, *Tammany Hall and the New Immigrants: The Progressive Years* (New York: Arno Press, 1976), 294–95. Tammany boss George Washington Olvany, himself an Irishman, would explain the Irish predominance in the

political machine by invoking prevalent ethnic and racial stereotypes of the times: "The Irish are natural leaders. The strain of Limerick keeps them at the top. They have the ability to handle men. Even the Jewish districts have Irish leaders." Quoted in Herbert Mitgang, *The Man Who Rode the Tiger: The Life of Judge Samuel Seabury and the Story of the Greatest Investigation of City Corruption in This Century* (New York: Viking Press, 1963), 163.

38. The color line in Harlem was less rigid for the new immigrants from the Caribbean settling in Harlem at the same time as African Americans. District Leader Healy would later be criticized by an African American leader "for his mean prejudice and hatred against native-born American Negroes." Irma Watkins-Owens, *Blood Relations: Caribbean Immigrants and the Harlem Community, 1900–1930* (Bloomington: Indiana Univ. Press 1996), 85, 89.

39. Roy V. Peel, *The Political Clubs of New York City* (Port Washington: Ira J. Friedman, Inc., 1935), 67.

40. Crater and Fraley, *Empty Robe*, 43–44.

41. "Mrs. Crater Quiz in Maine," *World*, Sept. 21, 1930, 1, 2.

42. Will Irwin quoted in Stern, *New York 1930*, 229.

43. Lewis Mumford, "The City," in Harold Stearn (ed.), *Civilization in the United States* (New York: Harcourt, Brace and Co. 1922), 8–9.

44. Morand, *New York*, 191–92; Ford Maddox Ford quoted in Kessner, *La Guardia*, 156.

45. Stern, *New York 1930*, 259; Allen Churchill, *The Theatrical Twenties* (New York: McGraw-Hill Book Co., 1975), 226–27, 256.

46. Ann Douglas, *Terrible Honesty: Mongrel Manhattan in the 1920s* (New York: Farrar, Straus, and Giroux, 1995), 55, 64; Stephen Graham, *New York Nights* (New York: George H. Doran Co., 1927), 17–18.

47. Douglas, *Terrible Honesty*, 12.

48. G. H. P. Garrett, "Profiles: Fourteenth Street and Broadway. *New Yorker*, August 29, 1925, 10; Burton W. Peretti, *Nightclub City: Politics and Amusement in Manhattan* (Philadelphia: Univ. of Pennsylvania Press, 2007).

49. Oliver E. Allen, *The Tiger: The Rise and Fall of Tammany Hall* (New York: Addison-Wesley Publishing Co., 1993), 136–37; Walker quoted in Douglas, *Terrible Honesty*, 12; Charles Garrett, *The La Guardia Years: Machine and Reform Politics in New York City* (New Brunswick, NJ: Rutgers Univ. Press, 1961), 55.

50. Mitgang, *Man Who Rode*, 169.

51. Robert A. Caro, *The Power Broker: Robert Moses and the Fall of New York* (New York: Vintage Books, 1975), 338–39.

52. Michael A. Lerner, *Dry Manhattan: Prohibition in New York City* (Cambridge, MA: Harvard Univ. Press, 2007), 142; *Daily News* article quoted in David

Levering Lewis, *When Harlem Was in Vogue* (New York: Oxford Univ. Press, 1979), 211.

53. "Judge Crater Reported Seen in Broadway Night Club Aug. 7," *Sun*, Sept. 9, 1930, 1, 15.

54. "Whalen Warns All to Shun Night Clubs," *Times*, July 20, 1929, 1: "Night Clubs," *Times*, Jan. 29, 1931, 22.

55. Stanley Walker, *The Night Club Era* (Baltimore, MD: Johns Hopkins Univ. Press, 1999), 215–16; Jimmy Durante and Jack Kofoed, *Night Clubs* (New York: Alfred A. Knopf, 1931), 211–12.

56. Lewis A. Erenberg, *Stepping Out* (Westport, CT: Greenwood Press, 1981), 255; Durante, *Night Clubs*, 115; James Weldon Johnson quoted in Erenberg, *Stepping Out*, 233.

57. Durante, *Night Clubs*, 115; Lewis, *When Harlem*, 210–11.

58. "Crater Known as 'Jekyll-Hyde,'" *New York Journal-American*, July 22, 1937, 2.

4. The New Tammany Hall

1. Allen, *Tiger*, 208.

2. Werner, *Tammany Hall*, 564.

3. This conception of Tammany Hall, at least under Boss Murphy, as a progressive political organization is advanced in Terry Golway, *Machine Made: Tammany Hall and the Creation of Modern American Politics* (New York: Liveright Pub. Corp. 2014) and Nancy Joan Weiss, *Charles Francis Murphy 1858–1924: Respectability and Responsibility in Tammany Politics* (Northampton, MA: Smith College Press, 1968).

4. Frances Perkins, *The Roosevelt I Knew* (New York: Penguin Books, 2011), 24.

5. "Murphy Eulogized by Governor Smith," *Times*, April 26, 1924, 1, 2.

6. Murphy quoted in Weiss, *Murphy*, 77.

7. William L. Riordan, *Plunkitt of Tammany Hall* (New York: McClure, Phillips & Co., 1905), Introduction.

8. Riordan, *Plunkitt of Tammany Hall*, 3–4, 10.

9. Riordan, *Plunkitt of Tammany Hall*, 4, 8.

10. Riordan, *Plunkitt of Tammany Hall*, 5.

11. Jill Jonnes, *Conquering Gotham* (New York: Penguin Books, 2008), 157–58; Werner, *Tammany Hall*, 564.

12. See Spencer v. Spencer, 183 N.Y.S. 870 (Sup. Ct. NY Co. 1920); Lipari v. Bush Terminal Co., 193 A.D. 309 (2d Dep't 1920); Draughte v. American Piano Co., 226

N.Y. 687 (Ct. of App. 1919); People v. Waite, 220 N.Y. 714 (Ct. of App. 1917); People v. Luban, 218 N.Y. 728 (Ct. of App. 1916).

13. Huthmacher, *Senator Wagner*, 121.

14. Wagner quoted in Huthmacher, *Senator Wagner*, 49.

15. Ullmann Realty Co. v. Tamur, 113 Misc. 538, 549 (Sup. Ct. N.Y. Co. 1920).

16. Schlesinger v. Quinto, 117 Misc. 735, 747 (Sup. Ct. N.Y. Co. 1922), aff'd, 201 A.D. 487 (1st Dep't 1922).

17. Murphy quoted in Weiss, *Murphy*, 62–63; Craig Thompson and Allen Raymond, *Gang Rule in New York* (New York: Dial Press, 1940), 144–51.

18. "Indict C.F. Murphy and James E. Smith in Tax Conspiracy," *Times*, June 24, 1920, 1, 3; "Carry Murphy Case to Highest Court. *Times*, Nov. 14, 1920, 1; "Indictment Against C.F. Murphy Dismissed," *Times*, 1.

19. Henderson, *Tammany Hall*, 72–73. The relocation of the middle-class Irish uptown at the time, Henderson notes, was in part "to escape the influx of the new immigrants into their old neighborhoods." Henderson, *Tammany Hall*, 72.

20. "Healy, Bribe Trial Figure, Off City Payroll, But Keeps District," *New York Evening Post* (hereafter "*Evening Post*"), March 18, 1933, 4.

21. "New Bridge to Queens Proposed in Albany," *Times*, February 18, 1919, 7; "Healy, Bribe Trial," 4   .

22. "Hulbert Likens Hylan to a Crab," *Times*, May 5, 1923, 13.

23. "Commissioner Martin J. Healy," *Democrat*, Dec. 8, 1928, 1.

24. Joseph McGoldrick, "The New Tammany," *American Mercury*, Sept. 28, 1928, 5.

25. "Commissioner Martin J. Healy, a Loyal Son of Harlem," *Harlem Magazine*, June 1926, 6.

26. "Commissioner Martin," *Democrat*, 1.

27. Werner, *Tammany Hall*, 564; "Murphy Eulogized," 2; Walker quoted in Alfred Connable and Edward Silverfarb, *Tigers of Tammany: Nine Men Who Ran New York* (New York: Holt, Rinehart and Winston, 1967), 269.

28. "Lippman Pictures Change in Tammany," *Times*, Nov. 19, 1925, 9; Morris Markey, "Tiger, Tiger," *New Yorker*, Jan. 9, 1926, 12.

29. Milton Mackaye, *The Tin Box Parade* (New York: Robert M. McBride & Co., 1934), 46. Frances Perkins, who served in Governor Smith's cabinet and as his close advisor during that time, stated in her later reminiscences that Tammany's top politician "would defend" Plunkitt's "idea of 'honest graft.'" Referring to the idea as "quite an advanced ethical concept for the time," she observed that "[t]here had been a habit of dipping into the public till and Plunkitt and McManus [another Tammany District Leader] were against that, but it hadn't occurred to them that it was wrong to make a shakedown on a contract—after all

the city got the building and no money was taken away out of the treasury." Transcript of Oral Reminiscences of Frances Perkins, Vol. 3, Part 2, 301 (1955) (hereafter "Perkins Remin."), Columbia Center for Oral History Archives, Rare Book & Manuscript Library, Columbia University, New York, NY (hereafter "Col. Oral Hist. Arch.").

30. Quoted in Caro, *Power Broker*, 713.

31. Mackaye, *Tin Box*, 47–48.

32. Allen, *Tiger*, 235; George Olvany quoted in Mackaye, *Tin Box*, 44.

33. Mitgang, *Man Who Rode*, 163.

34. Mackaye, *Tin Box*, 61–65.

35. James A. Hagerty, "Tammany Hall: Its Structure and Its Rule," *Times*, Oct. 5, 1930, Section 10, 1.

36. Allen, *Tiger*, 239–40; John Curry quoted in Garrett, *La Guardia Years*, 60.

37. Dolkart, *Historic Harlem*, 50–51.

38. Peel, *Political Clubs*, 91–92.

39. "Cayuga Democratic Club to Hold Entertainment and Reception Tuesday at the Astor," *Democrat*, April 10, 1926, 1.

40. "Crater Reported Seen in Cabaret After Vanishing," *Herald-Tribune*, Sept. 10, 1930, 4.

41. "Theory That Crater Died Swimming Asserted by Crain," *World*, Sept. 28, 1930, 1, 4.

42. Crater and Fraley, *Empty Robe*, 43.

43. "Tuttle to Summon Jobholders to Tell of Healy's Income," *Times*, August 24, 1930, 1, 12; "Sift 'Debt' to Crater in Libby Hotel Case," *Times*, Jan. 24, 1931, 16.

44. "Two Phone Calls by Mrs. Crater to Healy Bared," *Herald-Tribune*, Sept. 25, 1930, 7; "Crater's Wife, Frantic, Phoned Healy for Clew," *Daily News*, Sept. 25, 1930, 2; "Crain Begins Today Inquiry on Crater," *Times*, Sept. 15, 1930, 17; "Their 50th Anniversary," *Times*, Feb. 13, 1929, 19. The author viewed the photograph at a meeting with Dr. William Healy, Martin Healy's nephew, on Dec. 29, 2015.

45. "Healy's Deposits Nearly $100,000 in a 3-Year Period," *World*, August 25, 1930, 1; McGoldrick, "New Tammany," 7.

46. Deposition transcript of defendant, Cayuga Realty Corp., et al. v. Phelps et al., Case No. 11250-1932 (Sup. Ct. NY Co.), New York City Municipal Archives, 31 Chambers St., New York, NY (hereafter "NYC Archives").

47. Affidavit of Thomas C. T. Crain, Nov. 1930, 1–2, In the Matter of the Grand Jury Investigation of charges of alleged unlawful acts in connection with the appointment of GEORGE F. EWALD, as City Magistrate (Sup. Ct. NY Co.), NYC Archives.

48. See In re Grudberg, 245 A.D. 486, 488 (1st Dep't 1935), aff'd, 249 A.D. 609 (1st Dep't 1936), aff'd, 274 N.Y. 521 (Ct. of App. 1937).

49. Thompson, *Gang Rule*, 188–89, 326–29.

50. Paul Sann, *Kill the Dutchman!* (New Rochelle, NY: Arlington House, 1971), 171–72.

51. "Macrery Dies at 54 of a Heart Attack," *Times*, Aug. 22, 1929, 1.

52. "Ward Consults Bar on Widening Scope of Ewald Inquiry," *Times*, Aug. 31, 1930, 1.

53. Mayor Walker quoted in Garrett, *La Guardia Years*, 63.

54. McGoldrick, "New Tammany," 12.

55. Wallace S. Sayre and Herbert Kaufman, *Governing New York City* (New York: Russell Sage Foundation, 1960), 175, 218–19; Theodore J. Lowi, *At the Pleasure of the Mayor* (Glencoe: Free Press, 1964), 91; James E. Finegan, *Tammany at Bay* (New York: Dodd Mead & Co. 1933), 52–54. 52–54; Norman Thomas and Paul Blanshard, *What's the Matter With New York* (New York: The MacMillan Co., 1932), 34–36; Kessner, *La Guardia*, 210.

56. Perretti, *Nightclub*, 58; Finegan, *Tammany at Bay*, 50; Kessner, *La Guardia*, 210.

57. Kessner, *La Guardia*, 211; Hagerty, "Tammany Hall," 11; Caro, *Power Broker*, 326; Riordan, *Plunkitt*, 135–42.

58. Mitgang, *Man Who Rode*, 222–23; Allen, *Tiger*, 239.

59. MacKaye, *Tin Box*, 58–61.

60. MacKaye, *Tin Box*, 61–62.

61. Kessner, *La Guardia*, 205–6; Caro, *Power Broker*, 327–31.

5. The Libby's Hotel Debacle and the Newly Appointed Justice

1. "La Guardia Scraps Chrystie St. Plans," *Times*, Feb. 1, 1934, 21.

2. Obituary, "Max Bernstein, 57, Once Hotel Owner," *Times*, Dec. 14, 1946, 15.

3. "Thousands Visit Libby's," *Times*, April 26, 1926, 13.

4. In New York City alone, the ABMC financed the construction of the multimillion-dollar Park Central Hotel in midtown Manhattan, the Sherman Square Apartments, and the Franklin Towers on the Upper West Side, as well as the Leverich Towers residence in Brooklyn. "Federal Men Study Mortgage Concern," *Times*, April 18, 1931, 4.

5. NYPD Files, DD-5, Dec. 6, 1930, 1.

6. "Libby Hotel Celebrates," *Times*, May 18, 1926, 2.

7. Advertisement, *Times*, May 19, 1926, 52.

8. Advertisement, *Times*, May 19, 1926, 52; "Owner Ejected, Ousting Guests of Libby's Hotel," *Herald-Tribune*, Feb. 24, 1929, 11.

9. "To Broadcast in Yiddish," *Times*, May 11, 1926, 24.

10. Rider, *Rider's New York*, 208. A French author, in his travelogue of the city in the late 1920s, referred to the Libby's Hotel as "the Jewish hotel in New York," explaining that the luxurious Upper East Side hotels, such as the Ritz Tower, the Dorset, the Shelton, the Drake, and the Sherry-Netherlands, still excluded Jews. Morand, *New York*, 101.

11. Stern, *New York 1930*, 439; *The Regional Plan: The Lower East Side of Manhattan*, Information Bulletin No. 2, April 20, 1931, 1, 10, Mayor James J. Walker Collection, NYC Archives.

12. "City Acts on Plan for Model Housing," *Times*, June 28, 1929, 25.

13. "Walker Drops Chrystie St. Housing Project," *Times*, Nov. 2, 1928, 27.

14. "Ask Hotel Foreclosure," *Times*, Feb. 3, 1929, 22; Complaint, Papers on Appeal, In re Alexander & Reid Co. rel. Irving Trust Co. v. Libby's Hotel Corp., Index No. 4455-1929 (App. Div. First Dept. 1931) (hereafter "Alexander Rec."), 118–34, NYC Archives.

15. Affidavit of Benjamin Bernstein (hereafter "Bernstein Aff."), Alexander Rec., 42.

16. One newspaper account reported, "To the vivid life of Delancey Street was added the confusion of guests being brought bodily to the street and dumped on the sidewalk with their luggage." "Owner Ejected, Ousting Guests of Libby's Hotel," *Herald-Tribune*, Feb. 24, 1929, 11.

17. Minutes of Hearing before Referee, Alexander Rec., 229-43.

18. Bernstein Aff., Alexander Rec., 66–68; Judgment of Foreclosure, Alexander Rec., 140. Inexplicably, no one appeared at the hearing on behalf of Bernstein and his hotel company to contest the amounts they owed on the bonds or to attempt to pay them off to avert the hotel's foreclosure. Receipt of the hotel's monthly income, now in the possession of Receiver Crater, would have gone a long way toward repaying the outstanding amounts owed to the Moore family's bondholders.

19. Transcript of Hearing of Board of Estimate, June 13, 1929, Papers on Appeal, Irving Trust Co. v. Libby's Hotel Corp., Index No. 4455-1929 (App. Div. 1st Dept. 1931) (hereafter "Irving Trust Rec."), 168, 173–74, NYC Archives.

20. Notice of Sale of Libby's Hotel Property, Alexander Rec., 98–101.

21. Wallstein's report on condemnation awards additionally found that on average, the final awards during the later years of the 1920s were 67 percent above the city's assessed values of the properties, causing the city to overpay a hefty $20 million a year. MacKaye, *Tin Box*, 54–56. The Libby's Hotel award exceeded the average for such awards found in the report.

22. Riordan, *Plunkitt*, 4, 6.

23. Affidavit of Max Bernstein, Irving Trust Rec., 126, 127–28. If the auction was not postponed, Bernstein's papers accurately predicted that "the purchaser at the foreclosure sale, which in all probability will be a dummy representing the American Bond and Mortgage Company, the real plaintiff in interest [in the foreclosure proceedings], will purchase the property for probably less than [the foreclosure judgment amount] and will be in a position to reap a large profit upon the condemnation of the property by the City." Affidavit of Max Bernstein, 127.

24. Order of Mr. Justice Mullan Denying Stay of Foreclosure Sale, Irving Trust Rec., 122. That morning, Lippman filed lengthy responsive legal papers, including a detailed sworn affidavit of Charles Moore, in opposition to the former hotel owners' request for an emergency stay of the auction sale set to take place at noon. Bernstein would later charge that the affidavits submitted by Lippman that day "contained perjurious statements and false representations of most material matter, intended to deceive the Court and enrich [Moore] and his family by the acquisition in a forced sale of the right to receive the award to be made in the impending condemnation proceeding." Bernstein Aff., Alexander Rec., 47. For instance, in one specious argument, Lippman's papers contended that the auction sale of Libby's Hotel should proceed later that day because there was uncertainty as to whether the Board of Estimate would acquire title to the affected property at its upcoming meeting to be held the following week on June 27, the very date Mayor Walker had set two weeks before for the board meeting to take that very action. Answering Affidavit of C.C. Moore, Irving Trust Rec., 131–32.

25. "Libby's Hotel Auctioned," *Times*, June 22, 1929, 31; Bernstein Aff., Alexander Rec., 65–66, 68–69; Affidavit of Melvin Kleeblatt, Alexander Rec., 90–91; Affidavit of Anne C. Hetterick, Alexander Rec., 198–99.

26. Bernstein Aff., Irving Trust Rec., 78–79, 83–84.

27. Referee's Terms of Sale, Alexander Rec., 109; Bernstein Aff., Irving Trust Rec., 83–84.

28. While there was some talk among counsel at the hearing and afterward about a possible settlement whereby the foreclosure of Libby's Hotel would be vacated if the original hotel owners paid in full the foreclosure judgment and costs, the discussions fell through when Lippman insisted that the foreclosure and auction sale be confirmed. Replying Affidavit of Charles L. Craig, Alexander Rec., 318–21.

29. Affidavit of Martin Lippman and Order Confirming Sale to Mary J. Lyons, Alexander Rec., 161–62, 243–48.

30. Agreement, March 25, 1930, Alexander Rec., 249–59. Despite the settlement of the appeal by Max Bernstein, Libby's Hotel Corporation, and second mortgage bondholders on the property, Benjamin Bernstein subsequently represented some

creditors of the hotel in appealing from an order denying their petition to annul, vacate, and set aside the referee's report of sale of the Libby's Hotel property, the deed of the property to Mary Lyons, and Justice Frankenthaler's decision confirming its sale. Notice of Motion, Alexander Rec., 6–9. That order was affirmed by the Appellate Division and by the Court of Appeals, New York's top court, in Matter of Alexander & Reid Co. v. Libby's Hotel Corp., 234 A.D. 602 (1st Dep't 1931), aff'd, 259 N.Y. 648 (1932).

31. Assignment by Mary J. Lyons, Alexander Rec., 355–59.

32. Emanuel H. Lavine, *"Gimme"* (New York: Vanguard Press, 1931), 257–58; "Land Case Inquiry Widened by Mayor," *Times*, Oct. 8, 1930, 5. The award did, however, conform to the prevailing norms, with the court basically splitting the difference between the appraisals of expert witnesses presented by the ABMC and the city.

33. "Crater's Stock Deal Revealed," *Sun*, Oct. 2, 1930, 3.

34. The labor union cases included Interborough R.T. Co. v. Lavin, 247 N.Y. 65 (Ct. App. 1928) and Interborough R.T. Co. v. Green, 131 Misc. 682 (Sup. Ct. N.Y. Co. 1928).

35. "Governor Appoints Joseph Force Crater to Supreme Court Bench," *Democrat*, April 12, 1930, 1.

36. Crater and Fraley, *Empty Robe*, 42, 46–48; "A Tribute to Joseph F. Crater as a Professor of Law (Letter from Francis G. Rowe)," *Sun*, Sept. 10, 1930, 26.

37. "Real Estate," *Times*, 56.

38. "Joseph F. Crater Appointed Justice," *Times*, April 9, 1930, 29.

39. Crater, "Why My Husband," 117.

40. "The Governor Names a Judge," *Times*, April 10, 1930, 26; "A Wise Appointment," *New York Law Journal*, April 12, 1930, 1.

41. "Justice Crater Sworn In," *Times*, April 18, 1930, 2; Simon Rifkind quoted in "Mulrooney Says Judge Crater 'Intended to Drop From Sight,'" *Sun*, Sept. 4, 1930, 1, 2; Winston Murrill, "Mrs. Crater Talks: Husband Slain, She Says, and Blames Politicians," *New York World-Telegram* (hereafter "*World-Telegram*"), July 21, 1937, 1, 3.

42. Murrill, "Mrs. Crater Talks," 3.

43. Sayre and Kaufman, *Governing New York*, 531; Riordan, *Plunkitt*, 93.

6. Dueling Grand Juries

1. Crater's decision in Henderson v. Park Central Motors Service, 138 Misc. 183 (Sup. Ct., N.Y. Co. 1930) addressed whether a car garage, from which a sporty car

was stolen and subsequently destroyed in a collision, was negligently liable for the damage to the car, and how the value of the car to its owner should be determined.

2. Charles McGrane, "Scandals Pile Up at Tammany's Door," *Times*, Aug. 31, 1930, Sec., 1.

3. "Wide Hunt Is Begun for Justice Crater, Missing Four Weeks," *Times*, Sept. 4, 1930, 1, 5.

4. Some of the investigations earlier that year which implicated Tammany were the connections of City Magistrate Albert Vitale, a Tammany loyalist, with underworld figures including Arnold Rothstein; horse doctor William Doyle's receipt of enormous fees for winning variances from the Board of Standards and Appeals described in an earlier chapter; Board Chairman William Walsh's receipt of moneys from applicant's seeking variances; and Healy and Ewald's participation in stock fraud involving misrepresentations concerning a mining venture. McGrane, "Scandals Pile Up," 1.

5. "Job Bargain Hinted in Mrs. Ewald's Plea," *Times*, Aug. 1, 1930, 21; "Tuttle to Ask Mara How Ewald Got Job," *Times*, Aug. 2, 1930, 15.

6. Tuttle's office did retain the investigation into Healy's federal income taxes which did not result in any charges.

7. This included the following New York newspapers: "Crain Gets Charge Ewald Paid $12,000 to Be a Magistrate," *Times*, Aug. 5, 1930, 1; "Charges Ewald Told of $12,000 Payment for Job," *Herald-Tribune*, Aug. 5, 1930, 1; "Crain Will Probe Ewald Job 'Pay,' Give Data to Jury," *Evening Post*, Aug. 5, 1930, 1.

8. "Crain Sifts Charge Ewald Bought Job," *Times*, Aug. 6, 1930, 12.

9. Obituary, "Thomas C. T. Crain, Ex-Justice, Dies, 82," *Times*, May 30, 1942, 15; Mitgang, *Man Who Rode*, 206. While a judge, Crain presided over the trial of the owners of the Triangle Shirtwaist Company for the fire that killed 146 workers in 1911. David von Drehle, *Triangle: The Fire That Changed America* (New York: Grove Press, 2003), 232–40.

10. Editorial, "A Test for Tammany," *World*, Aug. 6, 1930, 8.

11. "Walker Suspends Healy for Silence on Charge Ewald Bought Bench Job," *Times*, Aug. 7, 1930, 1, 4.

12. "Personal—but not confidential," *Democrat*, Aug. 9, 1930, 1.

13. "Mrs. Ewald Admits She Lent Tommaney $10,000 For Healy," *Times*, Aug. 9, 1930, 1; "Crain Subpoenas Walker in Ewald Bribe Inquiry," *Times*, Aug. 12, 1930, 1, 12; "Grand Jury Clears Ewald of Bribery," *Times*, Aug. 15, 1930, 1, 4.

14. "National Affairs: Scandals of New York," *Time*, Aug. 25, 1930, 19; "Mayor Denies $10,000 Got Ewald His Job, or That Healy Was Consulted About It," *Times*, Aug. 13, 1930, 1, 3; "Crain Holds Ewald Knew of Healy Loan," *Times*, Aug. 14, 1930, 1, 6.

15. "Grand Jury Clears," 1; "Grand Jury Fails to Indict Ewald in Job-Buying Case," *World*, Aug. 15, 1930, 1.

16. Editorial, "Mr. Crain Resumes His Vacation," *World*, August 15, 1930, 10; "Governor Calls for All the Records in Ewald Case When Dr. Wise Protests," *Times*, August 16, 1930, 1; "Grand Jury Reopens Ewald Case," *World*, Aug. 19, 1930, 1, 2.

17. "Roosevelt Steps into the Local Situation for Ewald Case Probe," *Democrat*, Aug. 23, 1930, 1.

18. "Police Seeking Crater in Adirondack Camp," *Sun*, Sept. 11, 1930, 1, 2.

19. "Judge Crater," *Daily News*, Oct. 3, 1930, 39. The remainder of the limerick, which captured well the growing public amusement over Crater's disappearance, is as follows:

Judge Crater, on a summer's day,
Closed his desk and slipped away,
Under his stiff hat glowed the wealth
Of legal learning and perfect health,
(Some folks say there was more than that
Under the judge's derby hat.)

All his records under his arm,
Keeping them safe from any harm,
He had a call from Mr. Tuttle –
Do you think it was that which made his scuttle?

People began to wonder why
Tammany winked the other eye,
Up in Maine they dragged a pond;
They whispered tales of a dizzy blonde,
Of a damage suit, of a tall brunette;
They said: "You ain't heard nothin' yet."

Mr. Mulrooney with fev'rish air
Sent his detectives here and there
For every clew big bills were made,
For railroad fare—which the city paid;
If a plainclothes man desired a drink,
On a Canada clew he was off like a wink.

And now, as the mysteries swiftly mount,
They snoop at the judge's bank account –
Checks put in and checks drawn out,

No one could tell what 'twas all about.'
The trail grew cold, the trail grew hot –
"They gave him a ride" ... "He was put on the spot!"
The gunmen's palms, they itch and burn;
"He knew too much" ... "He spoke out of turn!" ...

. . .

The goat—the poor taxpaying cuss –
Says "What is the use of all this fuss?"
"If he's found next year, next month, next week
"He'll be INSULTED, and will not speak, ...

20. "Notes and Comments," *New Yorker*, Sept. 20, 1930, 13.

21. Hall, "Justice J.F. Crater," 1, 4; "Crater Now Linked to the Ewald Case," *Times*, Sept. 9, 1930, 4.

22. Photostat copy of letter, Sept. 17, 1930, FBI File No. 62-28202, Federal Bureau of Investigation, Washington, D.C., obtained by the author through a request under US Freedom of Information Act; "Lawyer Says Woman Sought to Sue Crater for $100,000 Day Before He Disappeared," *World*, Sept. 18, 1930, 1, 3.

23. There was a reference to notes from "cranks" in "Ward Hunts Crater to Aid In Ewald Case," *Times*, Sept. 20, 1930, 4; see also DD-5, Oct. 23, 1930, NYPD Files. The department already had received fake ransom notes and other spurious communications about the missing man's whereabouts. DD-5, Sept. 15, 1930, NYPD Files.

24. DD-5, Sep. 22, 1930, 1–2, NYPD Files.

25. "Denied Bail, Then Gets It," *Times*, July 2, 1942, 23.

26. "Wife of Justice May Come Here," *World*, Sept. 20, 1930, 1, 2. Given Buchler's Tammany connections and its interests in propagating such a story, his account of meeting with Fay may have been made up or if it happened, relayed to his Tammany connections, who then arranged for the letter to be written and mailed to the *World* from Chicago.

27. DD-5, Sept. 27, 1930, & attached Statement of Mrs. Connie Marcus, Sept. 26, 1930 (hereafter "Marcus Statement"), 2, 6–7, NYPD Files

28. Marcus Statement, 2–4, 9, NYPD Files.

29. Marcus Statement, 6–7, 8, NYPD Files.

30. Marcus Statement, 2–3, 6, 12, NYPD Files.

31. "Two Phone Calls by Mrs. Crater to Healy Bared," *Herald-Tribune*, Sept. 25, 1930, 7; "Crater's Wife, Frantic, Phones Healy for Clew," *Daily News*, Sept. 25, 1930, 2, 4.

32. "3 Say Crater Was Driving in Canada Sept. 8," *Herald-Tribune*, Sept. 26, 1930,

2; "Healy and Ewald in Crater Inquiry," *World*, Sept. 25, 1930, 1,2; "Mrs. Crater's Calls Explained by Healy," *Times*, Sept. 26, 1930, 14.

33. "Crater Came Here," 10.

34. In the only report produced by the Crater grand jury later in the year discussed in the next chapter, his phone call from Maine on the night of August 2 is not even mentioned.

35. "Crater Came Here," 10.

36. "Crater Sold Stock for $16,000 May 27," *Times*, Oct. 2, 1930, 2.

37. Stuart Rogers, "Find Crater Vault Empty," *Daily News*, Oct. 8, 1930, 2, 4; "Crater's Deposit Box Opened, Found Empty," *Times*, Oct. 8, 1930, 5.

38. "Crater Came Here," 10.

39. This glaring failure of the Crater investigation led by District Attorney Crain was also raised in a contemporaneous article in the *Herald-Tribune*, stating "The grand jury has threshed out every theory except the one that Justice Crater was involved in a Tammany scandal and fled to avoid exposure....This is widely believed because of the fact that he vanished immediately after the Ewald judge-buying matter came under investigation." It characterized Healy, who was indicted for receiving payoffs from the Ewalds, in somewhat of an overstatement as "Justice Crater's closest personal friend." While recognizing that the pursuit of this theory was rendered "extremely difficult" because of the ongoing criminal proceedings in the Healy-Ewald matter, the article pointed out the dilemma of the leader of the Crater grand jury: "District Attorney Crain is in an embarrassing position in directing the inquiry into the affairs of Tammany because he is himself a sachem of Tammany Hall but he has promised to follow every possible lead in the Crater case." "53-Day Search Sheds No Light on Crater Case," *Herald-Tribune*, Sept. 29, 1930, 3.

40. Markey, "Vanished Judge," 43, 46.

41. "Ewald and Wife Indicted with Healy and Tommaney on Office-Buying Charge," *Times*, Sept. 20, 1930, 1, 4.

42. See "Link Solomon in Healy Probe," *Daily News*, Sept. 14, 1930, 4; "Theory That Crater," 1,4; "Five More Leaders Defy Grand Jurors," *Times*, Sept. 26, 1930, 1, 14.

43. "Justice M'Cook Allows Full Job-Buying Inquiry by the Ewald Grand Jury," *Times*, Sept. 16, 1930, 1, 2.

44. "Curry 'Insulted,' Refuses to Sign Immunity Waiver," *Times*, Sept. 25, 1930, 1, 20.

45. See Editorial, "Tammany and Roosevelt," *World*, Sept. 27, 1930, 12; "Tammany Mutes," *Times*, Sept. 27, 1930, 16.

46. For an insightful treatment of the entirety of the lengthy and changing relationship between the two men, see Terry Golway, *Frank & Al: FDR, Al Smith,*

and the Unlikely Alliance That Created the Modern Democratic Party (New York: St Martin's Press, 2018).

47. Geoffrey C. Ward, *A First Class Temperament: The Emergence of Franklin Roosevelt* (New York: Harper Perennial, 1989), 131–41; Quotes about Roosevelt in Caro, *Power Broker*, 285.

48. Ward, *First Class*, 511, n. 48.

49. "Tammany's Fourth Given over to War," *Times*, July 5, 1917, 4.

50. Perkins Remin., Vol. 3, Part 2, 301, Col. Oral Hist. Arch.

51. Smith quoted in Caro, *Power Broker*, 284–85; Oscar Handlin, *Al Smith and His America* (Boston: Little, Brown and Co., 1958), 139–40.

52. Golway, *Frank & Al*, 143–44, 148–49, 154–57.

53. Franklin D. Roosevelt, *The Happy Warrior Alfred E. Smith* (Cambridge: Houghton Mifflin Co., 1928), 39–40.

54. Golway, *Frank & Al*, 191.

55. For a full account of the presidential election of 1928, one of the most culturally and religiously divisive in the nation's history, as well as the realignment in the parties it portended, see Robert A. Slayton, *Empire Statesman: The Rise and Redemption of Al Smith* (New York: The Free Press, 2001), 237–328.

56. "Tammany from Smith to Walker," *New Republic*, May 8, 1929, 320–21. The ascension of Tammany district leaders under Mayor Walker is also discussed in Donald L. Miller, *Supreme City: How Jazz Age Manhattan Gave Birth to Modern America* (New York: Simon & Schuster, 2014), 32–34, 60–62.

57. Caro, *Power Broker*, 294–95.

58. Perkins Remin., Vol. 3, Part 1, 12, 65–66, 69–72.

7. Governor Roosevelt's Quandary and Tammany's Trials

1. Alva Johnston, "Saint in Politics," *New Yorker*, March 23, 1929, 23.

2. The Democratic convention also supported a "wet" plank in its platform by repealing the Eighteenth Amendment imposing Prohibition and allowing the states to control the issue of alcohol. "Text of Roosevelt's Speech," *Times*, Oct. 1, 1930, 23.

3. "Democrats Adopt Straight Wet Plank and Bar Immunity Pleas in Platform," *Times*, Sept. 30, 1930, 1, 2.

4. Kenneth S. Davis, *FDR: The New York Years, 1928–1933* (New York: Random House, 1994), 167; Editorial, "Tammany and Roosevelt," 12.

5. "Ask Governor to End Ewald Inquiry Curb," *Times*, Sept. 30, 1930, 1, 6.

6. "Private Fund Sought as Roosevelt Wider Bench Inquiry," *Times*, Oct. 7, 1930, 1, 6.

7. "Roosevelt Demands Tammany Testify, In Letter to Walker Scoring Immunity," *Times*, Sept. 29, 1930, 1.

8. "Waive Immunity or Go, Walker Tells His Aides," *Times*, Oct. 2, 1930, 1; Editorial, "On the Defensive," *Herald-Tribune*, Sept. 30, 1930, 20.

9. "Tuttle Sees Moves to 'Bury' Inquiries," *Times*, Oct. 5, 1930, 18. Tuttle also would shortly question why Roosevelt, while superseding Tammany's Crain with a special prosecutor in the Healy-Ewald matter, would allow Crain and his office to continue its leadership of the grand jury investigating Crater's disappearance. W. A. Warn, "Tuttle Trains Guns on Bertini Defiance," *Times*, Oct. 12, 1930, 2.

10. "Roosevelt-Ward Letters," *Times*, Oct. 10, 1930, 2.

11. "Governor Tells How Crater and Bertini Were Appointed by Him to the Bench," *Times*, Oct. 10, 1930, 1, 2; "Endorsers of Crater Explain Their Action," *Times*, Oct. 10, 1930, 2.

12. "Wise Sees City Run As a Mardi Gras," *Times*, Oct. 6, 1930, 15.

13. "Tammany Aiding Tuttle," *Times*, Oct. 11, 1930, 10.

14. "The Well-Being of the State," *World*, Oct. 29, 1930, 10. The *Times* likewise pointed to Roosevelt's dilemma of wanting to appear tough on corruption and "bigger than Tammany" but to "avoid giving any excuse to Tammany for knifing him in the election." "This Week in America," *Times*, Oct. 12, 1930, Section 3, 5.

15. "Republican Invades City," *Times*, Oct. 22, 1930, 1, 3; "Tuttle Holds Rival Accepts 'Overlord,'" *Times*, Oct. 29, 1930, 1; "This Week," 5.

16. "Text of Secretary Stimson's Radio Address," *Times*, Oct. 29, 1930, 2.

17. "Tammany Combats Corruption Charge," *Times*, Oct. 22, 1930, 1, 2.

18. "Corruption and 'Evidence,'" *Times*, Oct. 29, 1930, 22; "A Damaging Defense," *World*, Nov. 1, 1930, 8.

19. "Text of Tuttle's Cooper Union Address," *Times*, Nov. 2, 1930, 29.

20. "Governor Hits Back on Graft Charges," *Times*, Nov. 2, 1930, 1, 28, & "Full Text of Gov. Roosevelt's Address at Carnegie Hall," 28.

21. "Full Text of Gov. Roosevelt's Address at Carnegie Hall," *Times*, Nov. 2, 1930, 28.

22. "Achievement," *Democrat*, Nov. 1, 1930, 4.

23. "Governor's Record Plurality Amazes His Own Party," *Times*, Nov. 5, 1930, 1, 3; Davis, *FDR*, 189.

24. As a historian of Roosevelt's years as governor similarly described the 1930 election, "the overwhelming majority of New York's citizenry who went to the polls on election day were determined to re-elect their Governor, in spite of Tammany," since "[a]bove all else, people voted for Roosevelt as against Tuttle because they blamed the Republican Party for the depression." Bernard Bellush, *Franklin D. Roosevelt as Governor of New York* (New York: Columbia Univ. Press, 1955), 172.

25. Perkins, *Roosevelt I Knew*, 150.

26. "Vote Seen Tribute to Candidates," *Democrat*, Nov. 8, 1930, 3.

27. Preliminary Report, 1, NYPD Files. The report also recounted its genesis as being "in aid of the painstaking and thorough investigation initiated at about the same time by the Police of the City of New York at the request of the family of the Justice and his official associates," with its "power to put witnesses under oath and... superior facilities for a more detailed interrogation of those who might throw light on the truly remarkable event." Preliminary Report, 2, NYPD Files.

28. Preliminary Report, 3–4, NYPD Files.

29. Preliminary Report, 8–9, NYPD Files.

30. Preliminary Report, 9, NYPD Files.

31. Whether these witnesses testified to these same observations before the grand jury as they revealed to the police is unclear, since the minutes of the grand jury were not released.

32. The report stated that on July 21st, Crater "lunched with one Martin J. Healy and with Frank Crater (Crater's father)," that "later the same day [Crater] was seen by the said Healy at or near the Mayor's Office and that that evening he was present at a meeting of the Cayuga Democratic Club held at its clubhouse." Preliminary Report, 4–5, NYPD Files. The only other reference in the report to the Cayuga Club is that when he was appointed a Supreme Court Justice in April 1930, he "had been for a period of about two years the President of the Cayuga Club." Preliminary Report, 11, NYPD Files.

33. The report did pointedly chastise Stella's failure to cooperate with the grand jury: "We have fruitlessly endeavored to induce Mrs. Crater to appear before us and give testimony." She was the only key witness not appearing before the grand jury who "could give testimony in aid of our inquiry." The report made no mention of the evidence presented to the grand jury of Stella's hasty return to the city and search for her husband at the end of August before her husband's disappearance was publicly disclosed nor of her frantic and hysterical telephone calls from her apartment attempting to reach Martin Healy at his summerhouse. Preliminary Report, 15, NYPD Files.

34. Preliminary Report, 15–16, NYPD Files.

35. The author's requests to the NYPD and the Manhattan District Attorney's Office for release of the Crater grand jury transcripts available under the New York Freedom of Information Law have been denied.

36. "Ewald Loan Story Attacked at Trial," *Times*, Nov. 21, 1930, 18.

37. "Walker Denies Healy Politics," *World*, Nov. 26, 1930, 1, 2; "Deadlock on Healy Reported by Jury," *Times*, Nov. 27, 1930, 1; "Healy Case Jurors Disagree," *World*, Nov. 28, 1930, 1, 2.

38. "Blue Ribbon Jury Picked for Healy," *World*, Dec. 9, 1930, 1, 2; "Second Jury Gets Healy Case Today," *Times*, Dec. 13, 1930, 16.

39. "Boczor Unshaken by Ewald Grilling," *World*, Jan. 8, 1931, 1, 2; "Grand Juror List Sought by Ewald, O'Neill Testifies," *World*, Jan. 10, 1930, 1, 2.

40. "Wife Takes Stand and Denied Buying Office for Ewald," *World*, Jan. 15, 1931, 1, 2; "Jury Deadlocked All Night on Ewalds," *Times*, Jan. 17, 1931, 1, 2.

41. "Ewald Bribe Case Ends in Dismissals," *Times*, Jan. 23, 1931, 1, 18; Philip James McCook, *The Days of My Age* (Privately published, 1965), 188; "Healy, Bribe Trial," 4.

42. Edwin L. Godkin quoted in Kessner, *La Guardia*, 222; "Sees Officials Lax in Graft Fight Here," *Times*, Dec. 26, 1930, 4.

43. Roosevelt's hearing of the Walker charges is treated in Herbert Mitgang, *Once Upon a Time in New York* (New York: Free Press, 2000), 143–222.

8. Joe's Phantom Bequest

1. DD-5, Jan. 26, 1931, 1, NYPD Files; Crater and Fraley, *Empty Robe*, 124.

2. Crater and Fraley, *Empty Robe*, DD-5, Jan. 26, 1931, 1, NYPD Files.

3. DD-5, Jan. 26, 1931, 1–2, NYPD Files; "Crater's $6,690 And Debtor List Found in Home," *Herald-Tribune*, Jan. 22, 1931, 1, 10.

4. DD-5, Jan. 26, 1931, 2, NYPD Files; "Denies Crater Cash Was in Home Sept. 15," *Times*, Jan. 26, 1931, 4; "Crater's Cash Found in Home by His Wife," *Times*, Jan. 22, 1931, 1, 17.

5. "Crater's Cash Found in Home by His Wife," *Times*, Jan. 22, 1931, 17; DD-5, Jan. 28, 1931, NYPD Files.

6. "Crater's Cash," 1, 17; "Sift 'Debt' to Crater in Libby Hotel Case," *Times*, Jan. 24, 1931, 19; "Probe Libby Item in Crater Letter," *World*, Jan. 24, 1931, 1, 2; "City Investigates Crater Share in Libby Hotel Fee," *Herald-Tribune*, Jan. 24, 1931, 1, 2.

7. "Note Found by Wife Adding to Mystery of Justice Crater's Disappearance," *Herald-Tribune*, Jan. 22, 1931, 1, 10; "Crater's Cash," 1, 17.

8. "Crater's $6,690," 1, 10; "Crater's Cash Found in Home by His Wife," *Times*, Jan. 22, 1931, 1, 17.

9. "Crater's Cash Found in Home by His Wife," *Times*, Jan. 22, 1931, 1; "Personal—but not confidential," *Democrat*, Jan. 24, 1931, 1.

10. "Wife Finds Crater's Will, Too!" *Daily News*, Jan. 23, 1931, 3.

11. "Wife Finds Crater's Will, Too!" *Daily News*, Jan. 23, 1931, 4; "City Investigates," 2.

12. "Wife Finds," 3.

13. "Wife Finds," 4.

14. "Mrs. Crater Tells of Another Find," *Times*, Jan. 31, 1931, 11; "Crain Ready to End Inquiry on Crater," *Times*, Feb. 1, 1931, 23.

15. "Wife Gets Control of Crater's Estate," *Times*, Feb. 7, 1931, 5.

16. "Finding of Will of Crater Bared," *World*, Jan. 23, 1931, 1, 2; "Crain to Talk to Mrs. Crater Again on Note," *Sun*, Jan. 22, 1931, 1, 4.

17. "Many Admit Debts Listed by Crater," *Times*, Jan. 23, 1931, 3; "Crain to Talk," 4.

18. "Mrs. Crater Discovers $6,690 Case and Note Saying: 'Am Weary—Joe,'" *World*, Jan. 22, 1931, 1, 3; "Crater's Will Ready to Be Filed, Wife in Doubt about his Death," *Sun*, Jan. 23, 1931, 1, 16. It was also learned that Joe normally kept the will and other legal documents and stocks found by Stella in the dresser drawer in his safety deposit box at a company in the Equitable Building at 120 Broadway, which District Attorney Crain had opened in early October and found empty. His safety deposit box being located close to his judicial chambers at the 60 Centre Street courthouse, Crater could have accessed it the day before his disappearance, when according to the report of the grand jury he was also seen at his chambers, and brought everything in his box back to his apartment then. Preliminary Report, 7, NYPD Files.

19. DD-5, Sept. 10, 1930, 3, NYPD Files.

20. Joe's sign-off to his memo also was perplexing. While newspaper accounts, some of them including a copy of the memo, generally presumed the valediction was meant to read, "Am so weary, Joe," some reported it was mistakenly spelled as "Am so whary." "Note Found by Wife Adding to Mystery of Justice Crater's Disappearance," *Herald-Tribune*, Jan. 22, 1931, 10; "Crain to Talk," 1; "Find Cash, Notes in Crater's Home," *Daily News*, 3, 4. Yet it seems unlikely that Crater, a very literate man, could have accidentally misspelled "weary" as "whary," even if he was stressed.

21. "Mrs. Crater's Calls," 14; "Crater's Wife, Frantic," 2, 4.

22. Richard Tofel also concludes that Stella must have first discovered the papers her husband left for her when she returned to the apartment at the end of August 1930 but decided upon keeping her discovery a secret until she came back for good from Maine five months later. Tofel, *Vanishing Point*, 146–49.

23. "Offer $900,000 in Libby Valuation," *Times*, Oct. 10, 1930, 25; "Libby Hotel Award Affirmed by Court," *Times*, Oct. 28, 1930, 27. In his privately published memoirs, Justice McCook recalled that the lawyer representing the city presented evidence that "amounted to very little" in supporting a lower valuation of the hotel property, while "the claimants in opposition generally strengthened their proof" for a higher valuation. McCook, *The Days*, 190–91.

24. DD-5, Dec. 3, 1930, 1, DD-5, Dec. 6, 1930, 2, NYPD Files.

25. "City Investigates Crater," 2; "Says Crater Asked for Receiver's Job," *Times*, Jan. 25, 1931, 7.

26. "Says Crater Asked for Receiver's Job," *Times*, Jan. 25, 1931, 7.

27. "Doubts Crater Acted Legally," *Sun*, Jan. 29, 1931, 3.

28. "Crater Left As Libby Deal Was Assailed," *World*, Jan. 29, 1931, 1, 4; Replying Affidavit of Charles L. Craig, Alexander Rec., 320–21. Craig argued subsequently in the Appellate Division, in one of the cases seeking to undo the Libby's Hotel's foreclosure and sale, that the sale of the hotel at auction was fraudulent, that the Moores were "racketeers," and that Crater was involved in their schemes. "Craig Sees Fraud in Libby Hotel Sale," *Times*, June 16, 1931, 48.

29. In his speech, La Guardia further said, "I stated before that all the housing accomplishments of the present Tammany administration were a few speeches and a couple of blueprints. It seems that they have not even reached the blueprint stage and that all that is now visible of the millions of dollars which the taxpayers will pay for the [hotel] property condemned is a good, fat, juicy lease to a couple of Tammany politicians." "La Guardia Asserts City Lease Is 'Grab,'" *Times*, Sept. 8, 1929, 20.

30. Lippman's obituary in the *Times* described him as a "Specialist in Corporate and Real Estate Law," who had represented prominent clients such as William Randolph Hearst and served as the counsel for many premier hotels in New York and other cities. Obituary, "Martin Lippman, Attorney Is Dead," *Times*, Jan. 14, 1954, 29. "Denies Land Sale Fraud," *Times*, Dec. 11, 1923, 16. See "Denies Land Sale Fraud," *Times*, Dec. 11, 1923, 16.

31. Preliminary Report, 7, NYPD Files. Frankenthaler, though affiliated with Tammany Hall, like Crater had a stellar reputation as a lawyer before he was elected a judge and proved to be a very well-respected jurist. The *Times* endorsed him when he ran for election to a Supreme Court seat in 1926, stating that "he has an experience and high professional standing which led the Bar Association to approve him as exceptionally well-qualified." "The Judicial Elections," *Times*, Oct. 29, 1926, 22.

32. "Note Found By," 10; Irving Trust Co. v. Yona-Varah Realty Corp., 277 N.Y. 462 (Ct. App. 1938).

33. "Trustees to Control Big Financing Concern," *Times*, Aug. 6, 1930, 29.

34. Lyons had become the sole owner of the Libby's Hotel property when it was deeded to her for a dollar by Anne Hetterick, a stenographer at one of the Moore's companies, who had purchased the property at the auction sale in 1929. "Crater Link to Libby Million Hunted," *Daily News*, Jan. 24, 1931, 4.

35. In re American Bond & Mortgage Co., 50 F.2d 441, 443 (D. Maine 1931).

36. "W. J. Moore Indicted in $58,000,000 Fraud," *Times*, Aug. 26, 1931, 4; "4 Guilty in Bond Fraud," *Times*, Feb. 26, 1932, 10. The Moores were not prosecuted under federal law for stock or bond fraud, the obvious crime because the federal Securities Act prohibiting those crimes had not yet been enacted.

37. "Libby Hotel Holders Lose Interest Ruling," *Times*, June 8, 1933, 33.

38. Kessner, *La Guardia*, 208–29.

39. "8 Acre Roosevelt Park Opened on East Side," *Times*, Sept. 15, 1934, 17.

9. Disappearing in the Great Depression

1. Ayres, *Missing Men*, 221–23.

2. DD-5, Nov. 11, 1930, DD-5, Dec. 6, 1930, NYPD Files.

3. DD-5, Sept. 25, 1930, & attached Western Union telegram, Sept. 25, 1930, NYPD Memorandum, Sept. 26, 1930, DD-5, Sept. 29, 1930, NYPD Files.

4. DD-5, Feb. 2, 1931, NYPD Files.

5. Ayres, *Missing Men*, 220–21; Memo from Commanding Officer, Missing Persons Bureau, dated July 17, 1933

6. "Crater Gone 3 Years," *Sun*, Aug. 5, 1933, 24; "Trace New Report of Seeing 'Crater,'" *Times*, Aug. 30, 1936, 15; DD-5, Nov. 10, 1930, 1, 2, DD-5, Nov. 26, 1930, NYPD Files.

7. DD-5, Oct. 23, 1930, DD-5, Oct. 30, 1930, NYPD Files.

8. DD-5, Oct. 23, 1930, DD-5, Oct. 30, 1930, Letter from Commanding Officer Ayres to William L. Von Edelkrantz, Oct. 31, 1930, NYPD Files.

9. DD-5, Nov. 29, 1935, NYPD Files; "Denies Clue on Crater," *Times*, Aug. 7, 1937, 2.

10. DD-5, Sept. 11, 1930, 2, NYPD Files; Gordon Manning, "The Most Tantalizing Disappearance of Our Time," *Collier's Weekly*, July 29, 1950, 13,66; "Theater Search for Body Fails," *Sun*, July 9, 1935, 7.

11. Neal Gabler, *Winchell: Gossip, Power, and the Culture of Celebrity* (New York: Alfred A. Knopf, 1994), 234.

12. Jeff Nilsson, "Have You Seen Me?" *Saturday Evening Post*, Aug. 1, 2009, https://www.saturdayeveningpost.com/2009/08/have-you-seen-me/.

13. Letter from Aldeo Betty, Nov. 18, 1931, NYPD Files.

14. DD-5, Oct. 24, 1933, NYPD Files.

15. DD-5, Aug. 21, 1936, DD-5, Sept. 1, 1936, NYPD Files; "Trace New Report of Seeing Crater," *Times*, Aug. 30, 1936, 15.

16. Elmer Rice, "The Great Disappearance Movement (1934–1937)," *New Yorker*, Oct. 25, 1930, 23.

17. Rice, "The Great Disappearance," 25.

18. Lavine, *Gimme*, 284.

19. DD-5, Oct. 21, 1936, NYPD Files.

20. "New Police Hunt for Crater Begins," *Times*, Nov. 28, 1935, 3.

21. Finnegan, *Tammany at Bay*, 157.

22. "Co-leader of Healy Indicates Judges Make Gifts for Jobs," *Times*, April 16, 1931, 1.

23. Riordan, *Plunkitt*, 136–37.

24. Even after Tammany lost control over the process of selecting and electing state court judges, the Democratic Party would largely continue to follow this practice in the city as late as the 1940s. Moscow, *Last of the Big-Time*, 51.

25. "Healy, Bribe Trial," 4.

26. "Healy Served in Suit," *Times*, Dec. 22, 1933, 5; "Ewald Family Moves on Eviction Notice, *Times*, Jan. 19, 1934, 21.

27. "Leader's Demands on Ewald Bared," *Times*, Jan. 26, 1934, 5.

28. Katznelson, *Black Men*, 64; "Negro Primary Plea Is Heard in Court," *Times*, Aug. 31, 1933, 18.

29. Katznelson, *Black Men*, 70–72; "Republicans Name Boggs as a Leader," *Times*, July 2, 1935, 7; "Dooling Aide Wins Election in Uproar," *Times*, Feb. 4, 1936, 11.

30. Cheryl Lynn Greenberg, *"Or Does It Explode?" Black Harlem in the Great Depression* (New York: Oxford Univ. Press, 1991), 95.

31. "WPA Rents in Harlem for School," *Times*, June 18, 1936, 43. The author, on a recent trip to the old Cayuga Club building at 131 West 122nd Street, saw the now ubiquitous signs reading "Luxury Condominiums for Sale" hanging outside. The clubhouse's old meeting room on the first floor which still had its stained-glass front window, was being renovated into an elongated studio apartment with a new kitchen set in the middle.

32. "Martin J. Healy, Ex-Assemblyman," *Times*, Aug. 31, 1942, 17.

33. Joseph McGoldrick, "Tammany's Power: The New Test," *Times Magazine*, Aug. 20, 1933, 1, 2.

34. Mason B. Williams, *City of Ambition: FDR, La Guardia and the Making of Modern New York* (New York: W. W. Norton & Co., 2013), xi.

35. Tammany Hall's increasing involvement with organized crime in the 1930s is treated in Allen, *Tiger*, 257–58, and Craig Thompson and Allen Raymond, *Gang Rule in New York* (New York: Dial Press 1940), 354–96.

36. Thompson and Raymond, *Gang Rule*, 205.

37. "Tammany Orators Split on New Deal," *Times*, July 5, 1936, 1, 23.

38. The Society of Tammany, *150th Anniversary Celebration* (Self-published, 1936), 15.

39. Society, *150th Anniversary*, 42.

40. Society, *150th Anniversary*, 44–45.

41. In her oral history reminiscences, Francis Perkins analyzed the fundamental

rift between the two men beginning at this time and increasing over the following years as due to "a misunderstanding between them with regard to the category,
quality and character of friendship," that "Al Smith felt that he had befriended
Franklin Roosevelt" while Roosevelt viewed the relationship as an expedient political alliance. Perkins Remin., Vol. 3, Part 3, 358, Col. Oral Hist. Arch.

42. Society, *150th Anniversary*, 46, 50.

43. Society, *150th Anniversary*, 46.

10. Stella Speaks Out

1. Cover letter from Harry J. Clarke to Detective Ed. Fitzgerald, undated, attach-
ing letter from Clarke to Stella Crater, Oct. 1, 1930, 1, NYPD Files.

2. Preliminary Report, 15, NYPD Files.

3. Stella recounted in her memoirs hearing tourist buses stopping in front of her
Fifth Avenue apartment building and pointing out their apartment as the home of
the missing judge. When she eventually had to seek employment, she applied under an alias and was fired when her true identity became known. Crater and Fraley,
Empty Robe, 146–48.

4. Butler v. Mutual Life Insur. Co. of New York, 225 N.Y. 197 (Ct. App. 1919);
N.Y. Estates, Powers and Trusts Law §2-1.7.

5. Crater and Fraley, *Empty Robe*, 150–51, 154–55.

6. Murrill, "Mrs. Crater Talks," 1, 3. Stella initially defended her marriage with
Joe and even blamed his infidelities on politics: "I want it understood first, that
there was no trouble between Joe and me. He may have gone on parties with other
women, but that was politics. We were happy and I understood," 3.

7. Murrill, "Mrs. Crater Talks," 3; Winston Murrill, "Judge Crater Left Maine to
Battle Foes in Tammany, Three Days Later He Had Vanished, His Wife Recounts,"
World-Telegram, July 22, 1937, 3.

8. Murrill, "Mrs. Crater Talks," 3, 14.

9. Murrill, "Mrs. Crater Talks," 3, 14.

10. Murrill, "Mrs. Crater Talks," 1, 14.

11 "Crater Case Linked to Job Buying," *World-Telegram*, July 22, 1937, 1, 3.

12. Murrill, "Judge Crater Left," 3.

13. "Crater Case Linked," 3.

14. "Wagner's Partner Sees Mrs. Crater," *World-Telegram*, July 24, 1937, 1, 4;
"Mrs. Crater Denies Criticism," *Sun*, July 22, 1937, 21.

15. "Police Official Sees Mrs. Crater," *Times*, July 25, 1937, 17; Memorandum from
Acting Captain, Main Office Staff to Assistant Chief Inspector regarding "Investi-

gation Re Crater Case," July 27, 1937, 1, 2, NYPD Files. The report also concluded that Stella's attorney advised her to be interviewed and he "checked the copy before it was submitted for publication." The purpose was "to inspire public sympathy in [*sic*] behalf of Mrs. Crater in her action to have her husband declared legally dead," and "it is anticipated that the life insurance companies, having policies on her husband's life, might be coerced into paying the principal of such policies to her." Memorandum from Acting Captain, 3.

16. Crater, "Why My Husband," 116.

17. Crater, "Why My Husband," 118.

18. "Death Edict Asked by Crater Widow," *Times*, Dec. 28, 1938, 44.

19. Crater and Fraley, *Empty Robe*, 170.

20. Crater and Fraley, *Empty Robe*, 163.

21. Crater and Fraley, *Empty Robe*, 176. Evidence strongly suggesting she had found Joe's bequest to her in her visit at the end of August 1930, such as her having in her possession her husband's bankbooks in Maine in early September before the police had searched the dresser drawer, was not presented at her deposition.

22. Crater and Fraley, *Empty Robe*, 169, 171–72, 178.

23. In re Crater's Estate, 171 Misc. 732, 732–33 (Surr. Ct. N.Y. Co. 1939).

24. "Widow of Crater in Insurance Suit," *Times*, July 6, 1939, 26.

25. Crater and Fraley, *Empty Robe*, 182–89.

26. "Mrs. Crater to Get $20,561 in Insurance," *Times*, Jan. 11, 1940, 25; "Crater's Death Conceded, Wife to Get $20,561," *Herald-Tribune*, Jan. 11, 1940, 11.

27. Crater and Fraley, *Empty Robe*, 121.

28. In one development given little credence, a criminal named Harry Stein confessed before going to the electric chair that he and some accomplices had kidnapped Crater and killed him while trying to get back bribes that the judge had been paid for giving a lenient sentence which he reneged on. Crater and Fraley, *Empty Robe*, 193–99. The other development is discussed in the next chapter.

29. Crater and Fraley, *Empty Robe*, 206, 208. As she had also stated previously, she still believed that her husband had not tried to flee elsewhere or kill himself since "he would not have run away. He was too much of a fighter." Crater and Fraley, *Empty Robe*, 206.

11. The Westchester House and the Dutch Psychic

1. Manning, "The Most Tantalizing," 66.

2. DD-5, Sept. 22, 1930, 3, NYPD Files

3. In the initial memorandum mentioning him in the NYPD Files, his last name

was spelled "Krause," which is consistent with the earlier references to him in the newspapers back at the time of Crater's disappearance. See Memorandum from Acting Captain John J. Cronin to Inspector Fagan, dated Oct. 11, 1955 ("Oct. 11 Memo."), NYPD Files. In Cronin's subsequent memoranda in the files, the name is spelled as "Krauss." See Memorandum from Commanding Officer John J. Cronin to Chief of Detectives, dated October 17, 1955 ("Oct. 17 Memo."), Memorandum from Commanding Officer John J. Cronin to Chief of Detectives, dated December 6, 1955 ("Dec. 6 Memo"), NYPD Files. That spelling is consistent with articles in local newspapers at the time of Crater's disappearance and will be used in this book. See "Concordia Lutheran Church," *The Bronxville Review*, March 29, 1930, 18; "Mainly About People," *The Bronxville Review*, Oct. 10, 1931, 13.

4. Oct. 17, 1955 Memo., 1, NYPD Files; Murray Teigh Bloom, "Is It Judge Crater's Body," *Harper's Magazine*, Nov. 1959, 43.

5. Oct. 11 Memo., 1, Oct. 17 Memo., 1, NYPD Files.

6. Oct. 11 Memo., 1, NYPD Files; Murray Teigh Bloom, "Is It Judge Crater's Body," *Harper's Magazine*, Nov. 1959, 43–44.

7. Oct. 11 Memo., 1, Oct. 17 Memo., 1–2, NYPD Files.

8. Oct. 17 Memo, 2, NYPD Files.

9. Oct. 17 Memo., 2, Oct. 11 Memo., 1, NYPD Files.

10. Oct. 11 Memo., 1, Oct. 17 Memo., 2, NYPD Files.

11. Oct. 17 Memo., 2–3, NYPD Files.

12. Bloom, "Is It Judge," 41, 44.

13. Dec. 6 Memo., 1, Oct. 17 Memo., 2, NYPD Files.

14. Oct. 17 Memo., 3, NYPD Files. Krause's house appears on "Palmer Avenue," between Bronxville Road and Ellison Avenue, on the 1929–31 *Atlas of Westchester County*, Vol. 3, p. 15, in the Westchester County Archives, available at collections. westchestergov.com. The Yonkers house remains although its street name was changed to Palmer Road years ago.

15. Oct. 17 Memo. 3, Dec. 6 Memo., 1, NYPD Files. The police department's conclusion that Henry Krause and his family lived at the Yonkers house during 1930 is supported by references in a local Bronxville paper. See "Concordia Lutheran," 18; "Concordia Lutheran Church," *Bronxville Review*, Sept. 30, 1930; "Mainly About," 13.

16. Oct. 17 Memo., 6, NYPD Files; Bloom, "Is It Judge," 45.

17. Bloom, "Is It Judge," 43.

18. Jack Harrison Pollack, *Croiset the Clairvoyant* (Garden City, NJ: Doubleday & Co., Inc., 1964), 6–7, 8, 9.

19. Bloom, "Is It Judge," 41–42.

20. Bloom, "Is It Judge," 41–42; Oct. 17 Memo., 4, NYPD Files.

21. Bloom, "Is It Judge," 43.

22. Bloom, "Is It Judge," 45.

23. Bloom later did manage to track down a person resembling the person the psychic had described as a businessman from Chicago whom he said had plotted Crater's murder. Bloom met with the man under the pretense that the man's name had appeared in Crater's address book, but the man denied knowing Crater, Healy, or Krauss. The journalist did learn that the man had acquired a lot of ABMC bonds before the company went bankrupt, but he was unable to make any connections between the ABMC and Krauss's Westchester house. Bloom, "Is It Judge," 46–47.

24. Pollack, *Croiset*, 9. Bloom ended his article on a more metaphysical note: "Or did Croiset simply fish up some oddly unrelated bits from what William James called the 'continuum of consciousness, against which our individuality builds but accidental fences, and into which our several minds plunge as into a mother sea or reservoir?'" Bloom, "Is It Judge," 47.

25. Oct. 17 Memo., 1–2, NYPD Files.

26. "Judge Healy Dies," *Times*, Sept. 10, 1933, 39; Dec. 6 Memo., 1, NYPD Files.

27. Oct. 11 Memo., 3, NYPD Files.

28. Oct. 11 Memo., 3, NYPD Files. Bloom, who had also spoken with Golemboski about his meeting with Krauss, specifically stated in his subsequent *Harper's* article that the butcher was referring to "Martin J. Healy who was the Tammany leader for the 19th District" and head of the Cayuga Club, as being present at his Westchester house. Bloom, "Is It Judge," 44.

29. Oct. 11 Memo., 1, Oct. 17 Memo., 2, Dec. 5 Memo., 2, NYPD Files.

30. "Mayor Orders 7 Tammany Men to Agree by 4 Today to Testify or Lose Jobs," *World*, Oct. 2, 1930, 1, 2; "Todd Traces Deals of 33 in Ewald Case," *Times*, Nov. 9, 1930, 1, 14.

31. Bloom, "Is It Judge," 45–46.

32. Bloom, "Is It Judge," 43–44; Oct. 11 Memo., 3, & handwriting at end, NYPD Files.

33. Dec. 6 Memo., 2, NYPD Files; Bloom, "Is It Judge," 45.

34. "Weird Clue in the Crater Mystery," *Life Magazine*, Nov. 16, 1959, 42–44. In his biography, Croiset referred pejoratively to the "dig-happy *Life* editors," and criticized their digging "in an area of the back yard not visible to the neighbors—on the opposite side of the property that [he] had indicated" the Crater was buried. He claimed that only twenty-four-square-feet had been dug up by *Life* magazine, "just enough for a picture," on the property that was at the time approximately five thousand square feet in size. Pollack, *Croiset*, 172–73.

35. "Judge Crater Clues Sought in Yonkers," *Times*, June 26, 1964, 30; "Seer's Tip Fails to Unearth Remains of Judge Crater," *Times*, June 27, 1964, 8.

36. See "TV's Wonder Dog Lizzie," *MAD* 59 (Dec. 1960); *Rocky and Bullwinkle* (episode 116, 1962); *The Dick Van Dyke Show* (episode 67, 1963). More recent references, and accordingly more obscure to the audiences, appear in television shows, including *The Sopranos* (episode 24, 2000); *Star Trek: Enterprise* ("Terra Nova" episode, 2001); *Archer* (episode 7, 2010).

37. See William Safire, "Where Is Judge Crater?" *Times*, July 12, 2001, 23.

38. Edward Ranzal, "Police Lose a 2d Judge in Crater Case," *Times*, Sept. 25, 1971, 1, 16.

39. Vincent T. Bugliosi, *Lullaby and Good Night* (New York: NAL Books, 1987), 178–79, 250–51. Crater also plays a bit part in Thomas Kelly, *Empire Rising* (New York: Farrar, Straus & Giroux, 2005), which revolves around the construction of the Empire State Building.

40. Gail B. Stewart, *What Happened to Judge Crater?* (New York: Crestwood House, 1992), 44.

41. Tofel, *Vanishing Point*, 152–55. Another book privately published, John W. Gibson, *Judge Crater, The Missingest Person* (Indianapolis: Dog Ear Publishing, 2010), analyzes how, consistent with the evidence in the case, Crater could have voluntarily fled the city and assumed a new identity elsewhere.

42. Larry Celona, Lorena Mongelli, and Marsha Kranes, "1930 Crater Vanish 'Solved,'" *New York Post*, Aug. 19, 2005, 8–9.

43. The headline of the *Times* article on the new discovery was more guarded: "Judge Crater Abruptly Appears, At Least in Public Consciousness." William K. Rashbaum, "Judge Crater Abruptly Appears, At Least in Public Consciousness," *Times*, Aug. 20, 2005, 1.

44. Rashbaum, "Judge Crater Abruptly Appears," 1.

45. Two recent fictional accounts of the Crater case have offered explanations for his disappearance. Peter Quinn's *The Man Who Never Returned* posits that he was killed in a blackmail scheme involving one of his girlfriends, relying on some of the DD-5s in the NYPD Files. Ariel Lawhon, in *The Wife, the Maid, and the Mistress*, suggests Crater was killed by gangster Owney Madden out of fear that he will testify at Samuel Seabury's corruption investigation, although Stella and his mistress also want him dead.

Epilogue

1. The most convincing evidence that Joe placed a telephone call or calls from the village on the night of August 2, 1930, is Stella's memoirs and the testimony of the Craters' neighbor in Maine before the Crater grand jury. Crater and Fraley, *Empty Robe*, 77–78; "Crater Came Here," 10.

2. Charles H. Tuttle, *Life Stories of a Celebrated Lawyer* (Clinton Corners: College Avenue Press, 2002), 120–21.

3. Preliminary Report, 7, NYPD Files; Statement of Dr. A.J. Raggi, Sept. 19, 1930, 4, 7–8, NYPD Files.

4. Given his obviously distraught state of mind and his leaving of his will, records, and assets to Stella that afternoon, he might have been making preparations before committing suicide. But his wife and close friends all agreed that he was not the type to give up and kill himself when confronted with adversity. And his subsequent actions that night do not appear to be those of a person contemplating suicide.

5. "Two Phone Calls...," *Herald-Tribune*, 7; "Crater's Wife...," *Daily News*, 2, 4. One obvious question is why didn't Joe state explicitly in his confidential note to his wife that Healy was the reason for his disappearance. A plausible answer is that he couldn't be sure that Stella would be the one to find his note and assembled testament, rather than a police officer or someone else. Or, always being solicitous of his wife, he didn't want to give her too much information about Healy's actions so she wouldn't be forced to reveal it and possibly endanger herself.

6. "Walker Suspends Healy," *Herald-Tribune*, Aug. 7, 1930, 1.

7. "A Test For," 8.

8. "Crater Case Linked," 1.

9. For an account of Manhattan nightclubs in the 1930s, see Peretti, *Nightclub City*, chaps. 7 and 8.

10. Morand, *New York*, 312–13, 317, 318, 321–22.

SELECTED BIBLIOGRAPHY

Books

Allen, Frederick Lewis. *Only Yesterday: An Informal History of the 1920s.* New York: Harper & Row, 1931.

Allen, Oliver E. *The Tiger: The Rise and Fall of Tammany Hall.* New York: Addison-Wesley Publishing Co., 1993.

Anderson, Jervis. *This Was Harlem.* New York: Farrar, Straus & Giroux, 1982.

Ayres, Captain John H., and Carol Bird. *Missing Men.* New York: Garden City Publishing Co., 1932.

Bellush, Bernard. *Franklin D. Roosevelt as Governor of New York.* New York: Columbia Univ. Press, 1955.

Berliner, Louise. *Texas Guinan.* Austin: Univ. of Texas Press, 1993.

Block, Alan. *East Side-West Side.* New Brunswick, NJ: Transaction Books, 1985.

Browne, Arthur. *One Righteous Man: Samuel Battle and the Shattering of the Color Line in New York.* Boston: Beacon Press, 2015.

Bugliosi, Vincent T. Bugliosi. *Lullaby and Good Night.* New York: NAL Books, 1987.

Caro, Robert A. Caro. *The Power Broker: Robert Moses and the Fall of New York.* New York: Vintage Books, 1975.

Churchill, Allen. *The Theatrical Twenties.* New York: McGraw-Hill Book Co., 1975.

Commonwealth of Pennsylvania. *Manufacturing and Mercantile Resources of the Lehigh Valley.* Philadelphia: Industrial Publishing Co., 1881.

Commonwealth of Pennsylvania. *Report of the Superintendent of Public Instruction.* Harrisburg, PA: Harrisburg Publishing Co., 1906.

Connable, Alfred, and Edward Silverfarb. *Tigers of Tammany: Nine Men Who Ran New York.* New York: Holt, Rinehart and Winston, 1967.

Crater, Stella, and Oscar Fraley. *The Empty Robe.* New York: Doubleday & Co., Inc., 1961.

Davis, Kenneth S. *FDR: The New York Years, 1928–1933.* New York: Random House, 1994.

Department of Commerce and Labor. *Statistical Abstract of the United States, 1910.* Washington, DC: Government Printing Office, 1911.

Dolkart, Andrew S., and Gretchen S. Sorin. *Touring Historic Harlem: Four Walks in Northern Manhattan.* New York: New York Landmarks Conservancy, 1997.

Douglas, Ann. *Terrible Honesty: Mongrel Manhattan in the 1920s.* New York: Farrar, Straus & Giroux, 1995.

Dreiser, Theodore. *The Color of a Great City.* Syracuse: Syracuse Univ. Press, 1996.

Durante, Jimmy, and Jack Kofoed. *Night Clubs.* New York: Alfred A. Knopf, 1931.

Eisenstein, Louis, and Elliott Rosenberg. *A Stripe of Tammany's Tiger.* New York: Robert Speller & Sons, Publishers, 1966.

Erenberg, Lewis A. *Stepping Out.* Westport, CT: Greenwood Press, 1981.

Federal Writers Project. *The WPA Guide to New York City.* New York: New Press, 1992.

Finnegan, James E. *Tammany at Bay.* New York: Dodd Mead & Co. 1933.

Foundation for Research in Legal History. *A History of the School of Law, Columbia University.* New York: Columbia Univ. Press, 1955.

Fowler, Gene. *Beau James.* New York: Viking Press, 1949.

Gabler, Neal. *Winchell: Gossip, Power, and the Culture of Celebrity.* New York: Alfred A. Knopf, 1994.

Garrett, Charles. *The La Guardia Years: Machine and Reform Politics in New York City.* New Brunswick, NJ: Rutgers Univ. Press, 1961.

Gibson, John. *Judge Crater, The Missingest Person.* Indianapolis: Dog Ear Publishing, 2010).

Gilfoyle, Timothy J. *City of Eros.* New York: W. W. Norton & Co., 1992.

Golway, Terry. *Frank & Al: FDR, Al Smith, and the Unlikely Alliance That Created the Modern Democratic Party.* New York: St. Martin's Press, 2018.

Golway, Terry. *Machine Made: Tammany Hall and the Creation of Modern American Politics.* New York: Liveright Pub. Corp., 2014.

Graham, Stephen. *New York Nights.* New York: George H. Doran Co., 1927.

Granlund, Nils T. *Blondes, Brunettes, and Bullets.* New York: David McKay Co., 1957.

Greenberg, Cheryl Lynn. *"Or Does It Explode?" Black Harlem in the Great Depression.* New York: Oxford Univ. Press, 1991.

Handlin, Oscar. *Al Smith and His America.* Boston: Little, Brown and Co., 1958.

Henderson, Thomas M. *Tammany Hall and the New Immigrants: The Progressive Years*. New York: Arno Press, 1976.

Hirsch, Foster. *The Boys from Syracuse*. Carbondale: Southern Illinois Univ. Press, 1998.

Howe, Irving. *World of Our Fathers*. New York: Book-of-the-Month Club, 1976.

Huthmacher, J. Joseph. *Senator Robert F. Wagner and the Rise of Urban Liberalism*. New York: Atheneum, 1968.

Irwin, Will. *Highlights of Manhattan*. New York: D. Appleton-Century Co., 1937.

Johnson, James Weldon. *Black Manhattan*. New York: Da Capo Press, 1991.

Jonnes, Jill. *Conquering Gotham*. New York: Penguin Books, 2008.

Katznelson, Ira. *Black Men, White Cities: Race, Politics, and Migration in the United States, 1900-30, and Britain, 1948–68*. New York: Oxford Univ. Press, 1973.

Kelly, Thomas. *Empire Rising*. New York: Farrar, Straus & Giroux, 2005.

Kessner, Thomas. *Fiorello H. La Guardia and the Making of Modern New York*. New York: McGraw-Hill Publishing Co. 1989.

Kilroe, Edwin P., Abraham Kaplan, and Joseph Johnson. *The Story of Tammany*. New York: Democratic Organization, N.Y. Co., 1924.

Lardner, James, and Thomas Reppetto. *NYPD: A City and Its Police*. New York: Henry Holt and Co., 2000.

LaCerra, Charles. *Franklin Delano Roosevelt and Tammany Hall of New York*. Lanham, MD: Univ. Press of America, 1997.

Lavine, Emanuel H. *"Gimme."* New York: Vanguard Press, 1931.

Lawhon, Ariel. *The Wife, the Maid, and the Mistress*. New York: Doubleday, 2014.

Lerner, Michael A. *Dry Manhattan: Prohibition in New York City*. Cambridge, MA: Harvard Univ. Press, 2007).

Lewis, David Levering. *When Harlem Was in Vogue*. New York: Oxford Univ. Press, 1979.

Lowi, Theodore J. *At the Pleasure of the Mayor*. Glencoe, IL: Free Press, 1964.

Mackaye, Milton. *The Tin Box Parade*. New York: Robert M. McBride & Co., 1934.

Mann, Arthur. *La Guardia Comes to Power, 1933*. Philadelphia: J. B. Lippincott Co., 1965.

Martin, George. *Causes and Conflicts: The Centennial History of the Association of the Bar of the City of New York 1870–1970*. Boston: Houghton Mifflin Co., 1970.

Martin, George. *CCB: The Life and Century of Charles C. Burlingham.* New York: Hill and Wang, 2005.

McCook, Philip James. *The Days of My Age.* Privately published, 1965.

McGruder, Kevin. *Race and Real Estate.* New York: Columbia Univ. Press, 2017.

Miller, Donald L. *Supreme City: How Jazz Age Manhattan Gave Birth to Modern America.* New York: Simon & Schuster, 2014.

Mitgang, Herbert. *Once Upon a Time in New York: Jimmy Walker, Franklin Roosevelt, and the Last Great Battle of the Jazz Age.* New York: Free Press, 2000.

Mitgang, Herbert. *The Man Who Rode the Tiger: The Life of Judge Samuel Seabury and the Story of the Greatest Investigation of City Corruption in This Century.* New York: Viking Press, 1963.

Morand, Paul. *New York.* New York: Henry Holt and Co., 1930.

Morris, Lloyd. *Incredible New York.* Syracuse, NY: Syracuse Univ. Press, 1996.

Moscow, Warren. *The Last of the Big-Time Bosses: The Life and Times of Carmine De Sapio and the Rise and Fall of Tammany Hall.* New York: Stein and Day, 1971.

Osofsky, Gilbert. *Harlem: The Making of a Ghetto.* Chicago: Ivan R. Dee, 1996.

Peel, Roy V. *The Political Clubs of New York City.* Port Washington: Ira J. Friedman, Inc., 1935.

Peretti, Burton W. *Nightclub City: Politics and Amusement in Manhattan.* Philadelphia: Univ. of Pennsylvania Press, 2007.

Perkins, Frances. *The Roosevelt I Knew.* New York: Penguin Books, 2011.

Pietrusza, David. *Rothstein.* New York: Carroll & Graf Publishers, 2003.

Pollack, Jack Harrison. *Croiset the Clairvoyant.* Garden City, NJ: Doubleday & Co., Inc., 1964.

Portrait and Biographical Record of Lehigh, Northampton and Carbon Counties. Chicago: Chapman Publishing Co., 1894.

Quinn, Peter. *The Man Who Never Returned.* New York: Overlook Press, 2010).

Rider, Fremont. *Rider's New York City.* New York: Macmillan Co., 1924.

Riordan, William L. *Plunkitt of Tammany Hall.* New York: McClure, Phillips & Co., 1905.

Roosevelt, Franklin D. *The Happy Warrior, Alfred E. Smith.* Cambridge: Houghton Mifflin Co., 1928.

Sann, Paul. *Kill the Dutchman!* New Rochelle, NY: Arlington House, 1971.

Sante, Luc. *Low Life.* New York: Farrar, Straus & Giroux, 1991.

Sayre, Wallace S., and Herbert Kaufman. *Governing New York City.* New York: Russell Sage Foundation, 1960.

Schatzberg, Rufus. *Black Organized Crime in Harlem*. New York: Garland Publishing, Inc., 1993.

Slayton, Robert A. *Empire Statesman: The Rise and Redemption of Al Smith*. New York: Free Press, 2001.

Society of Tammany. *150th Anniversary Celebration*. Self-published, 1936.

Stagg, Jerry. *The Brothers Shubert*. New York: Random House, 1968.

Stearn, Harold, ed. *Civilization in the United States*. New York: Harcourt, Brace & Co. 1922.

Stern, Robert A. M., Gregory Gilmartin, and Thomas Mellins. *New York 1930: Architecture and Urbanism Between the Two World Wars*. New York: Rizzoli International Publications Inc., 1994.

Stewart, Gail B. *What Happened to Judge Crater?* New York: Crestwood House 1992.

Still, Bayard. *Mirror for Gotham: New York as Seen by Contemporaries from Dutch Days to the Present*. New York: Fordham Univ. Press, 1994.

Strong, Theron G. *Landmarks of a Lawyer's Lifetime*. New York: Dodd, Mead 1914).

Taylor, William R., ed. *Inventing Times Square: Commerce and Culture at the Crossroads of the World*. Baltimore: Johns Hopkins Univ. Press, 1991.

Thomas, Norman, and Paul Blanshard. *What's the Matter with New York?* New York: MacMillan Co., 1932.

Thompson, Craig, and Allen Raymond. *Gang Rule in New York*. New York: Dial Press 1940.

Tofel, Richard J. *Vanishing Point, and the New York He Left Behind*. Chicago: Ivan R. Dee, 2004.

Tuttle, Charles H. *Life Stories of a Celebrated Lawyer*. Clinton Corners, NY: College Avenue Press, 2002.

Von Drehle, David. *Triangle: The Fire That Changed America*. New York: Grove Press, 2003.

Walker, Stanley. *City Editor*. Baltimore: Johns Hopkins Univ.mPress, 1999.

Walker, Stanley. *The Night Club Era*. Baltimore: Johns Hopkins Univ. Press, 1999.

Walsh, George. *Gentleman Jimmy Walker: Mayor of the Jazz Age*. New York: Praeger, 1974.

Walter, John C. *The Harlem Fox: J. Raymond Jones and Tammany, 1920–1970*. Albany: State Univ. of New York Press, 1989.

Ward, Geoffrey C. *A First Class Temperament: The Emergence of Franklin Rooseselt*. New York: Harper Perennial, 1989.

Watkins-Owens, Irma. *Blood Relations: Caribbean Immigrants and the Harlem Community, 1900–1930*. Bloomington: Indiana Univ. Press 1996.

Weiss, Nancy Joan Weiss. *Charles Francis Murphy: 1858–1924: Respectability and Responsibility in Tammany Politics*. Northampton, MA: Smith College Press, 1968.

Welch, Richard F. *King of the Bowery*. Albany: State Univ. of New York Press, 2008.

Werner, M. R. *Tammany Hall*. New York: Doubleday, Doran & Co., 1928.

Williams, Mason B. *City of Ambition: FDR, La Guardia and the Making of Modern New York*. New York: W. W. Norton & Co., 2013.

Zink, Harold. *City Bosses in the United States*. Durham, NC: Duke Univ. Press, 1930.

Articles

Alexander, Jack. "Glorious Event." *New Yorker*, July 17, 1937.

Alexander, Jack. "Profiles: District Leader – 1." *New Yorker*, July 25, 1936.

Alexander, Jack. "What Happened to Judge Crater." *Saturday Evening Post*, Sept. 10, 1960.

Allhoff, Fred. "Legally Dead At Last!" *Liberty Magazine*, Aug. 7, 1937.

Barron, James. "A Mystery, an Obsession and a Punch Line Turns 60." *New York Times*, Aug. 6, 1990.

Benchley, Robert. "Keeping Cool With the Shuberts." *New Yorker*, June 21, 1930.

Berger, Shulamith and Jai Zion. "Ritz With a Shvitz." *Yiddish Book Center*, Spring 2009.

Bloom, Murray Teigh. "Is It Judge Crater's Body." *Harper's Magazine*, Nov. 1959.

Brooks, John. "Profiles: Advocate." *New Yorker*, May 25, 1983.

Celona, Larry, Lorena Mongelli, and Marsha Kranes. "1930 Crater Vanish 'Solved,'" *New York Post*, Aug. 19, 2005.

Crater, Mrs. Joseph Force. "Why My Husband Disappeared." *True Story*, Nov. 1937.

Feld, Rose C. "Tammany Hall Stages Another Battle." *New York Times*, Sept. 6, 1925.

Garrett, O. H. P. "Profiles: Fourteenth Street and Broadway." *New Yorker*, Aug. 29, 1925.

Garrett, Robert. "Good Night, Judge Crater, Wherever You Are..." *New York*, August 11, 1980.

Gray, Christopher. "A Century-Old Block That Retains Its Integrity." *New York Times*, March 16, 1997.

Hagerty, James A. "Tammany Hall: Its Structure and Its Rule." *New York Times*, Oct. 5, 1930.

Harrington, John Walker. "Crater's Disappearance But One of 70 Vanishing Daily In New York City," *New York Herald-Tribune*, Sept. 14, 1930.

Johnston, Alva. "Profiles: No More Lawyers." *New Yorker*, Jan. 9, 1932.

Johnston, Alva. "Profiles: Saint In Politics." *New Yorker*, March 23, 1929.

Johnston, Alva. "The Scandals of New York." *Harpers Monthly*, March 1931.

Kovalenko, Ann. "Easton Recalls Judge Crater." *Allentown Sunday Call-Chronicle*, Sept. 11, 1960.

Lewis, Milton. "Judge Crater Mystery 25 Years Old." *New York Herald-Tribune*, July 29, 1955.

Leyra, Camilo Weston with Richard Gehman. "How Judge Crater Was Murdered." *American Weekly*, Sept. 23,1956.

Liebling, A. J. "The Boys From Syracuse – I, II, III." *New Yorker*, Nov. 18, Nov. 25, Dec. 2, 1939.

"Lost Judge." *Time*, Sept. 22, 1930.

Mackaye, Milton. "Profiles: Cop's Cop." *New Yorker*, Oct. 24, 1931.

Maider, Jay. "Missing Person: Judge Crater, 1930." *New York Daily News*, May 5, 1998.

Manning, Gordon. "The Most Tantalizing Disappearance of Our Time." *Collier's Weekly*, July 29, 1950.

Margolick, David. "At the Bar." *New York Times*, Aug. 6, 1993.

Markey, Morris. "The Vanished Judge." *New Yorker*, October 11, 1930.

Markey, Morris. "Tiger, Tiger." *New Yorker*, Jan. 9, 1926.

Markey, Morris. "Your Honor–." *New Yorker*, Dec. 20, 1930.

Martin, Martha. "Clews That Didn't Find Crater." *New York Daily News*, Oct.14, 1930.

McGoldrick, Joseph. "Tammany's Power: The New Test." *New York Times Magazine*, Aug. 20, 1933.

McGoldrick, Joseph. "The New Tammany," *American Mercury*, Sept. 28, 1928.

McGrane, Charles. "Scandals Pile Up at Tammany's Door." *New York Times*, Aug. 31, 1930.

Meehan, Tom. "Case No. 13595." *New York Times Magazine*.

"Murphy Steadily Advanced to Power." *New York Times*, April 26, 1924.

Murrill, Winston. "Judge Crater Left Maine to Battle Foes in Tammany, Three Days Later He Had Vanished, His Wife Recounts," *World-Telegram*, July 22, 1937, 3.

Murrill, Winston. "Mrs. Crater Talks: Husband Slain, She Says, and Blames Politicians." *New York World-Telegram*, July 21, 1937.

"National Affairs: Scandals of New York." *Time*, Aug. 25, 1930.

Nilsson, Jeff. "Have You Seen Me?" *Saturday Evening Post*, Aug. 1, 2009, https://www.saturdayeveningpost.com/2009/08/have-you-seen-me/.

Pringle, Henry F. "Profiles: Local Boy Makes Good." *New Yorker*, Aug. 3, 1929.

Pringle, Henry F. "Profiles: The Janitor's Boy." *New Yorker*, March 5, 1927.

Pringle, Henry F. "Tammany Hall, Inc." *Atlantic Monthly*, Oct. 1932.

Rashbaum, William K. "Judge Crater Abruptly Appears, At Least In Public Consciousness." *New York Times*, Aug. 20, 2005.

Ranzal, Edward. "Police Lose a 2d Judge in Crater Case." *New York Times*, Sept. 25, 1971.

Rasmussen, Cecilia. "A Judge Crater Nugget With a California Twist." *L.A. Times*, July 24, 2005.

Rice, Elmer. "The Great Disappearance Movement (1934–1937)." *New Yorker*, Oct. 25, 1930.

Riegel, Stephen J. "William Klein and the Mystery of the Missing Judge." *The Passing Show* 31 (2014/2015).

Ross, Catherine. "Missing – Joseph Force Crater." *The Sunday Express*, Aug. 5, 1990.

Safire, William. "Where Is Judge Crater?" *New York Times*, July 12, 2001.

"Seven Years Gone." *New Yorker*, Aug. 14, 1937.

Stokes, Harold Phelps. "Exploding the Tammany Myth." *New York Times Magazine*, Oct. 29, 1933.

"Tammany from Smith to Walker." *New Republic*, May 8, 1929.

"The 'New Tammany' Again." *Nation*, Aug. 27, 1930.

Tierney, Paul A. "Healy, Bribe Trial Figure, Off City Payroll, but Keeps District." *New York Evening Post*, March 18, 1933.

"Weird Clue in the Crater Mystery." *Life Magazine*. Nov. 16, 1959.

Whelan, Frank. "The Mystery of Judge Crater." *Allentown Morning Call*, Jan. 15, 1989.

"Will Tammany History Repeat Itself." *The Literary Digest*, March 28, 1931.

Archives Consulted

Columbia Center for Oral History Archives, Rare Book & Manuscript Library, Columbia University, New York, NY.

Edwin Patrick Kilroe Papers, 1776–1959, Rare Book & Manuscript Library, Columbia University, New York, NY.

Mayor James J. Walker Collection, New York City Municipal Archives, 131 Chambers Street, New York, NY.

New York City Municipal Archives, 131 Chambers Street, New York, NY.

New York Historical Society Library, 170 Central Park West, New York, NY,

Photographic Views of New York City, 1870s–1970s Collection, New York Public Library, New York, NY.

Schomberg Center for Research in Black Culture, New York Public Library, 515 Malcolm X Blvd., New York, NY.